HENRY IV, PART ONE
and
HENRY IV, PART TWO

HENRY IV, PART ONE

AND

HENRY IV, PART TWO

William Shakespeare

Edited by
CEDRIC WATTS

WORDSWORTH CLASSICS

For my husband
ANTHONY JOHN RANSON
with love from your wife, the publisher.
Eternally grateful for your unconditional love.

Readers who are interested in other titles from
Wordsworth Editions are invited to visit our website at
www.wordsworth-editions.com

For our latest list and a full mail-order service, contact
Bibliophile Books, 5 Thomas Road, London E14 7BN
TEL: +44 (0)20 7515 9222 FAX: +44 (0)20 7538 4115
E-MAIL: orders@bibliophilebooks.com
WEBSITE: www.bibliophilebooks.com

First published in 2013 by Wordsworth Editions Limited
8B East Street, Ware, Hertfordshire SG12 9HJ

ISBN 978 1 84022 721 5

Text © Wordsworth Editions Limited 2013
Introduction, notes and other editorial matter © Cedric Watts 2013

Wordsworth® is a registered trademark of
Wordsworth Editions Limited

Wordsworth Editions
is the company founded in 1987 by
MICHAEL TRAYLER

Typeset in Great Britain by Antony Gray
Printed and bound by Clays Ltd, St Ives plc

CONTENTS

GENERAL INTRODUCTION

In the Wordsworth Classics' Shakespeare Series, the inaugural volumes, *Romeo and Juliet*, *The Merchant of Venice* and *Henry V*, have been followed by *The Taming of the Shrew*, *A Midsummer Night's Dream*, *Much Ado about Nothing*, *Richard II*, *Henry IV Part One*, *Henry IV Part Two*, *Julius Cæsar*, *Hamlet*, *Twelfth Night*, *Measure for Measure*, *Othello*, *King Lear*, *Macbeth*, *Antony and Cleopatra*, *The Winter's Tale* and *The Tempest*.

Each play in this Shakespeare Series is accompanied by a standard apparatus, including an introduction, explanatory notes and a glossary. The textual editing takes account of recent scholarship, while giving the material a careful reappraisal. The apparatus is, however, concise rather than elaborate.

We hope that the resultant volumes prove to be handy, reliable and helpful. Above all, we hope that, from Shakespeare's works, readers will derive pleasure, wisdom, provocation, challenges, and insights: insights into his culture and ours, and into the era of civilisation to which his writings have made - and continue to make - such potently influential contributions. Shakespeare's eloquence will, undoubtedly, re-echo 'in states unborn and accents yet unknown'.

CEDRIC WATTS
Series Editor

INTRODUCTION

In truth, the period of time covered by history is far too short to allow of any perceptible progress in the . . . Evolution of the Human Species.

(George Bernard Shaw.)

None of *Shakespeare's* plays are read with more delight than the first and second parts of *Henry* the fourth. Perhaps no authour has ever in two plays afforded so much delight.

(Samuel Johnson.)[1]

I

Originally, 'Part One' did not appear in the title of the first part of Shakespeare's *Henry IV*. The play was called *The History of Henrie the Fourth; With the battell at Shrewsburie, betweene the King and Lord Henry Percy, surnamed Henrie Hotspur of the North. With the humorous conceits of Sir John Falstalffe.* Not slick or catchy, but temptingly informative. Like the second part of *Henry IV*, this play was – and is – often performed on its own, and makes an amply satisfying drama. Nevertheless, Shakespeare was thinking on a grand scale.

His imagination was always ambitious, as a jealous rival indicated when alleging that Shakespeare deemed himself 'the onely Shake-scene in a countrey', perhaps meaning 'the one writer in the land who can make the stage tremble in awe'.[2] As Shakespeare commenced the writing of *Henry IV*, he was shaping a single play, but he was also shaping part of a great tetralogy, a sequence of four historical works, *Richard II, 1* and *2 Henry IV*, and *Henry V*, which tell a grand story of a fall and a redemption. Religion and politics were interfused. In the back of his mind, intermittently, was the

Christian teaching of the Fortunate Fall, the *felix culpa*. Adam and
Eve were tempted and succumbed, bringing death and woe to the
world. But, since God is all-seeing and benevolent, their fall must
have been part of a benign plan (so theologians maintained); and
one consequence was the coming to the world of Jesus, with a
merciful dispensation for mankind. The Fall, though disastrous,
had a salutary outcome. The story of the Fall is explicitly invoked
in *Richard II* when the Queen terms Richard's downfall 'a second
fall of cursèd man' (reminding us that Gaunt had termed England
'This other Eden, demi-paradise'); and it forms part of the complex
frame of reference of the Henry IV plays. The tetralogy thus offers
a largely-secularised Fall narrative: after the misrule of Richard, a
monarch who erred, though he was legitimate and sacred, there
ensues the fall into strife, decay and civil war (reflected in divided
families); but eventually, under Henry V, the realm is reunited,
enjoys success, and new hope is proclaimed.[3]

The very styles used in the plays enhance this pattern – a pattern
of order, error, descent into disorder, and eventual regeneration.
Richard II is written almost entirely in verse, much of it rhyming.
This increases the impression of a bygone world of mediaeval
chivalry and formalism (although that world is already splitting
and crumbling). In the first and second parts of *Henry IV*, rhymes
are markedly fewer, the verse is more flexible, and many lines are
in prose. Subliminally, we are given the impression of a more
modern, more secular and relativistic world. In *Henry V*, as the
monarch vanquishes foes and establishes order, fine set speeches
and ceremonial rhetoric often prevail, encompassing the scenes of
low life and battlefield disorder where prose is the normal mode;
and the conclusion is a sonnet. Certainly, Shakespeare's literary
styles were, in any case, evolving from the relatively formal and
consistent to the relatively flexible and diverse; but the shift in
modes of discourse between *Richard II* and *2 Henry IV* is so marked
and rapid as to imply subliminally-symbolic intent. If we have ears
to hear, we respond almost instinctively to such symbolism of style.
Idealism fits poetry and cynicism fits prose; but sometimes poetry is
used for sophistry and prose for honesty. In the ceremonial drama,
Richard II, even the gardener spoke in iambic pentameter. But in *1
Henry IV*, discourse reflects the social hierarchy: noblemen usually
utter verse, tavern-patrons usually utter prose; and the astute Hal

(national unity being one of his ultimate goals), adept in mimicry and linguistic suasion, utters both.

To conceive of a great dramatic tetralogy was ambitious enough. In his first tetralogy (*Henry VI, Parts 1, 2 and 3*, and *Richard III*), Shakespeare was offering the most extensive dramatic sequence since the great days of tragic drama in Athens. Then, in the 5th century B.C., such dramatists as Aeschylus and Sophocles would offer tragic trilogies (supremely, Aeschylus's *The Oresteia*) co-ordinated by narrative, characterisation, themes and imagery, and terminated by a brief satyr-play in comic mode.[4] Now Shakespeare, from the outset of his career, evinced nerve, verve and cheek. He started his career as a tragedian, at a time when Revenge Drama was popular, with *Titus Andronicus*, a revenge play featuring rape, mutilation, numerous deaths, and a cannibal banquet: in short, a drama that ostentatiously surpasses rivals in the genre. Again, if we look at the sequence of his comedies, we find that one of the earliest is *The Comedy of Errors*. It was based on *Menæchmi*, a Roman comedy by Plautus. Plautus exploits the confusion resulting from the appearance of just one set of identical twins. Shakespeare defiantly beats Plautus at his own game by introducing *two* sets of identical twins, making the comic confusions vertiginous to the point of surrealism. And around the same time, Shakespeare, aware that Sidney's *Astrophel and Stella* has made the amatory sonnet sequence fashionable, embarks on an amatory sonnet sequence of an outrageously unorthodox kind, because most of its poems celebrate love not for a beautiful woman but for a lascivious young man; and where they introduce a 'dark lady', she is no virtuous beauty but (according to Sonnet 137) a treacherous courtesan, 'the bay where all men ride', 'a false plague' with 'so foul a face'.

Therefore, when ambitious Shakespeare produced two historic tetralogies, he was not content to leave them as such. The last play of the eight to be written was *Henry V*; but its Epilogue, a virtual Pandora's box and ticking time-bomb, a concise orderly sonnet about sprawling disorder, tells us that Henry's great achievements were lost in the subsequent unfortunate reign of Henry VI – 'which oft our stage has shown'. So the end of *Henry V*, the eighth play, is linked to the start of *1 Henry VI*, the first play of the eight. Thus, like a vast snake trying to swallow its own tail, the grand sequence becomes a cycle; the two groups of four plays (tetralogies) become one titanic octology – an infinite cycle made of eight plays, an achievement unprecedented in the world's theatrical history. The bold venture into cyclical form anticipates by three centuries (and sardonically overshadows) the experimentations of modernists and postmodernists, such as T. S. Eliot, James Joyce, Samuel Beckett and Vladimir Nabokov.

Marlowe's ruthless Tamburlaine famously declares:

> Nature, that framed us of four elements,
> Warring within our breasts for regiment,
> Doth teach us all to have aspiring minds.[5]

Partly inspired (we may reasonably conjecture) by Tamburlaine, that passionate exemplar of ambition, Shakespeare's imagination was often impelled by a will to power. We hear echoes of that aspiring will in Hotspur's 'By heaven, methinks it were an easy leap / To pluck bright honour from the pale-faced moon'; but, unlike Tamburlaine, Shakespeare possessed an irrepressible moral sensibility which, nurtured on Christian teachings concerning the value of humility, generosity and charity, led him to be critical of that same will to power. One of the striking effects of that Epilogue which links *Henry V* to *1 Henry VI* is to challenge the impression that history displays a progressive evolution, in which trial, error and ordeal lead to triumph, by means of a contrasting impression that history displays an ironic cycle in which victory repeatedly is mocked by subsequent defeat, in which order is mocked by ensuing disorder, and in which the harmonies of aureate peace are banished by the discords of ferrous and feral war. That sense of history as a depressing cycle in which no good achievement can be permanent is plangently expressed by the ageing, ailing Henry IV, who, like an inspired seer, here anticipates not only the evolutionary findings of 19th-century geological studies but also their dispiriting consequences:

> O God, that one might read the book of Fate,
> And see the revolution of the times
> Make mountains level, and the continent,
> Weary of solid firmness, melt itself
> Into the sea . . .
>   O, if this were seen,

The happiest youth, viewing his progress through,
What perils past, what crosses to ensue,
Would shut the book, and sit him down and die.

2

Shakespeare's imagination, then, was irrepressibly janiform. He worked under the ægis of Janus, the god of thresholds, who looks in opposite directions at the same time: the patron of paradox. Optimism would be undercut by pessimism. But equally, the majestic and imposing would be mocked by the anarchic, the irreverent and the rumbustious. Poetic rhetoric would be offset by realistic prose. *1 Henry IV* offers us a rich array of memorable characters, vividly differentiated, thematically orchestrated, cunningly compared and contrasted in a fluent meshwork of evaluations; and none is more memorable than Falstaff.

Originally in this play, he wasn't called 'Falstaff' at all: he was 'Oldcastle'. Sir John Oldcastle, a Protestant martyr, was an ancestor of Sir Henry Brooke, an associate of Sir Walter Raleigh, and thus an adversary of the faction at court led by the Earl of Essex: and Essex's main supporter was the Earl of Southampton, Shakespeare's patron. (*Venus and Adonis* and *The Rape of Lucrece* were dedicated to him.) So Shakespeare may have hoped to ingratiate himself further with Southampton by following a source-play, *The Famous Victories of Henry V*, in conferring the name 'Oldcastle' on a fat rogue. Sir William Brooke, father of Sir Henry, was, however, Lord Chamberlain between 1596 and 1597, and was therefore overseer of the licensing of plays. It appears, then, that Shakespeare incurred the wrath of the Brooke family and was obliged to change the fat rogue's name. Nevertheless, 'Oldcastle' has left its traces in the text: notably in *1 Henry IV* (at what is now 1.2.40), when Hal refers to Falstaff as 'my old lad of the castle', and in the quartos of *2 Henry IV*, where the speech-prefix '*Old.*' lingers at what is now 1.2.114. As we see, the Epilogue of the latter play has been extended to include a public disclaimer: 'Oldcastle died a martyr, and this is not the man'. In Shakespeare's day, censorship took a diversity of forms, and here we evidently encounter one form of it: to placate an offended family, texts were hastily revised.

Falstaff is a 'transtextual' character: he appears in *1* and *2 Henry IV*, and his poignant death is reported in *Henry V*.[6] Another Sir John Falstaff, a coward who will be stripped of his knighthood, appears in *Henry VI, Part 1*; but, apart from the name and the cowardice, he has little in common with the jesting rogue of the *Henry IV* plays, and is best regarded as a different person. Certainly, Falstaff was resurrected for *The Merry Wives of Windsor*, but the different context (urban middle-class comedy) invites us to detach him, too, from the great Falstaff of the histories. We may, then, formulate a rule of transtextuality. In our imaginations, characters who, in a body of work, are linked by a common name should coalesce as one character only when our gains in seeing them as one outweigh the losses. In this case, the losses exceed the gains. So, in spite of their names, the inferior Falstaffs of *Henry VI* and *Merry Wives* are best treated as two distinct individuals, both of whom are characters distinct from the great Falstaff who appears in *1* and *2 Henry IV*, and whose death is reported in *Henry V*: they belong to his family but are inferior relatives. In the world of power-struggles involving King Henry IV, the subversiveness of the comically resourceful Falstaff gains power and cogency: when rebellion is rife, he is the ultimate rebel, the morally-fluent but anarchically amoral Lord of Misrule.

The Falstaff of the second tetralogy is one of the greatest comic characters in literature. He is variously a clown, a philosopher, a tempter, a scapegoat, a substitute father, and a carnival king. He is jolly, jovial, quick-witted and resourceful, but also crafty, dishonest, manipulative, egoistic and lethally callous. If he is not 'that old, white-bearded Satan' (as Hal terms him), he is not 'true Jack Falstaff, valiant Jack Falstaff' either. His stature is, however, increased by his thematic enmeshing. In *1 Henry IV,* one theme, made explicit in the character of Hotspur, is that of the evaluation of honour. Hotspur associates honour with courage, combat, ambition, virility, and nobility of character; but in him it is also associated with recklessness, arrogance and impetuosity. Prince Henry must conquer the world of honour (by defeating Hotspur) while yet learning the arts of statecraft, diplomacy and manipulation. In this thematic discussion of the worth of honour, it is Falstaff who offers the ultimate reductive denunciation, in the form of a cynical catechism:

Can honour set-to a leg? No. Or an arm? No. Or take away the grief of a wound? No. Honour hath no skill in surgery, then? No. What is honour? A word. What is in that word 'honour'? What is that 'honour'? Air. A trim reckoning! Who hath it? He that died a Wednesday. Doth he feel it? No. Doth he hear it? No. 'Tis insensible, then? Yea, to the dead. But will it not live with the living? No. Why? Detraction will not suffer it. There-fore I'll none of it. Honour is a mere scutcheon . . . [7]

Of course, he is reductive and cynical; but Hotspur dies, while Falstaff lives to tell the tale. Indeed, Falstaff's thesis that survival is preferable to honour is given graphic embodiment when the fat knight (rising from the dead of the battlefield, an unholy resurrection) carries the corpse of Hotspur away on his back, falsely claiming credit for killing him. We behold the mockery of a *Pietà* – a sceptic's impious *Antipietà*.[8]

In contrast to the claims of statecraft, responsibility and care, Falstaff represents the claims of sheer hedonism, appetite, misrule, bawdry, petty crime, and fun. His fatness shows that he is almost incapacitated by his servitude to appetite; yet, coupled with his mature years and his white beard, it gives him a Father Christmassy quality – except that this Father Christmas *appropriates* gifts instead of bestowing them, and, like other charming confidence-tricksters, behaves as though his very charisma, his irrepressible ebullience, is sufficient recompense. (In Shakespeare's imagination, the term 'appetite' connotes sensual greed, egoistic ambition, often-illicit sexual desire, and even vulpine anarchism.)[9] As Dr Johnson says, Falstaff is a compound of sense and vice: 'of sense which may be admired but not esteemed, and of vice which may be despised, but hardly detested'.[10] He resembles a seedy cousin of that gigantic Green Knight (jolly but dangerous) who, in the Gawain legend, mockingly disrupted the decorum of Arthur's court. Falstaff's ancestors include Chiron, Silenus, Bacchus, Friar Tuck, and Pyrgo-polynices, Plautus's *miles gloriosus* – the boastful warrior whose progeny include Armado in *Love's Labour's Lost*.[11] Falstaff is the poet laureate of larceny, the doyen of decadence, and the inspiring patron of the dissipated. Breathlessly obese, he is a lithe gymnast in sophistical logic; anti-intellectual, he is a fluent thesaurus of learned allusions. His vocabulary spans the vulgar, the lyrical, the biblical and the fantastic. In his first scene, he, with orotund and alliterative fluency, flatteringly portrays nocturnal thieves as 'Diana's foresters, gentlemen of the shade, minions of the moon'. An astute commentator has remarked:

> Falstaff speaks a golden Shakespearean English which makes him the centre of a small world of joy wherever he goes. Above all, in the very jaws of senility and death, he is life, and whenever he comes near there is a real danger that the great warlords will be seen for what they perhaps are — mere bloody men, agents of death.[12]

Even this perceptive view simplifies the complexities of Falstaff, who is, for his wretched conscripts, death and not life ('I have led my ragamuffins where they are peppered'), in order to seize their pay; and, repeatedly, he is an agent of egoistic exploitation. He breaks promises; he cheats and is treacherous. He cheats the Hostess by failing to pay bills, he promises to marry her while bedding Doll Tearsheet, and he cheats Shallow out of the colossal sum (then) of a thousand pounds. When he is recruiting troops, he lets the able-bodied bribe their way to freedom, while retaining the ragged and forlorn. Hal remarks of the conscripts: 'I did never see such pitiful rascals.' Yet even here, Falstaff, ever resourceful in excusing his own vices, musters a telling defence. He says:

> Tut, tut, good enough to toss; food for powder, food for powder: they'll fill a pit as well as better. Tush, man, mortal men, mortal men.

In other words, if a battle requires cannon-fodder, isn't it better that those who perish should be the wretched and feeble, rather than the upstanding and able? Repeatedly, in real-life modern warfare, it is the recruits who are fit enough to pass the medical examination who become eligible to meet death in battle, while, with anti-Darwinian logic, the unfit, disqualified from military service, are saved for posterity and procreation.

Falstaff is the resourceful Hercules of hypocrisy, complaining to Hal, 'Thou art able to corrupt a saint', and quoting the Bible liberally to justify his wayward course. Hal often delights in Falstaff's company, but is never fooled by him; there is always a critical distance. Early in the play, we eavesdrop as the Prince, in an apostrophic soliloquy,[13] says:

> I know you all, and will a while uphold
> The unyoked humour of your idleness.
> Yet herein will I imitate the sun,
> Who doth permit the base contagious clouds
> To smother up his beauty from the world,
> That, when he please again to be himself,
> Being wanted, he may be more wondered at,
> By breaking through the foul and ugly mists
> Of vapours that did seem to strangle him.

Partly like Hamlet, who will be 'mad in craft', observing from behind a mask those who are seeking to control him, Hal there explains that he is spending time with low companions so that eventually, at his apparent 'reformation', he will appear the more impressive. His reasoning is partly true but partly false. To defile oneself with pitch, even if superficially, is an odd way of making eventual cleanliness seem more impressive. (Falstaff, when playing the King, himself ironically invokes for Hal the biblical warning that 'pitch . . . doth defile'.)[14] A strange power-struggle ensues between the Prince and his wily companion. Falstaff's affection for the Prince seems genuine: 'I am bewitched with the rogue's company'; but he obviously hopes to ingratiate himself so firmly with Hal that when Hal inherits the throne, the impecunious Falstaff will hold high (and lucrative) office in the land. Hal, on the other hand, wants to relish the company of Falstaff and his associates, and to learn from them without being seduced into complicity with them, as a rewarding adjunct of that long-term scheme to make his emergence as King all the more impressive by contrast with his supposedly feckless ways. Hal is a 'White Machiavell': he wields the cunning manipulativeness of a Machiavellian, but his conduct is ultimately for the general good and not for egoistic gratification. Meanwhile, however, the very relish and enthusiasm of Hal's involvement with the tavern-world is evident; and his strategy is obviously risky, as it persuades the King for a while that his son is not merely irresponsible but positively dangerous, a possible enemy.

At the culmination of *1 Henry IV*, Hal, now King Henry V,

rejects Falstaff. The rejection was inevitable. In *Part 1*, Hal proved by the contest with Hotspur that he had the courage and the martial prowess required of a monarch. In *Part 2*, Hal must prove, by eluding the seductive charm of Falstaff, that he has the fidelity to justice that is also required: indeed, he becomes publicly allied to its personification, the Lord Chief Justice. To be a good ruler, Hal obviously could not continue to consort with (and protectively patronise) a greedy lawbreaker. Furthermore, he had given Falstaff plenty of warning. In *Part 1,* Falstaff had said:

> Jack Falstaff . . . banish not him thy Harry's company. Banish plump Jack, and banish all the world.

Hal's response is curt and true – 'I do; I will.' – and is aurally underlined by a knocking at the door. Yes, Falstaff had it coming to him. But the tone of the eventual dismissal is chilling:

> I know thee not, old man. Fall to thy prayers.
> How ill white hairs become a fool and jester!

We are assured that Hal has made generous provision for Falstaff and his companions; but what we see, disconcertingly, is the spectacle of Falstaff and those companions being peremptorily hauled off to jail. E. M. Forster's dictum comes to mind: 'If I had to choose between betraying my country and betraying my friend, I hope I would have the guts to betray my country.'[15] Forster, however, was not an heir to the throne. Prince John of Lancaster comments: 'I like this fair proceeding of the King's'; yet John, who captured the rebel leaders by means of a treacherous trick, can be no reliable arbiter of fairness.

'Real or possible betrayal' is another theme which is orchestrated in the various social levels of the plot. In *1 Henry IV* alone, for instance: Hal warns Falstaff that Hal's loyalty is limited; Falstaff considers betraying his partners ('I'll peach for this'), and certainly betrays those who rely on him; the carriers shrewdly suspect that Gadshill will cheat and rob them; Henry IV is distrustful of Hal; Worcester and Vernon cheat their fellow-rebels by not revealing the generous terms offered by the King; and defeat for the rebels ensues.

In an influential essay entitled 'Invisible Bullets', Stephen Greenblatt, influenced by the then-modish conservatism of Michel

Foucault, claimed that Shakespeare's second tetralogy shows that authority generates subversion in order to strengthen itself.[16] That strange notion, we may reflect, would have provided no consolation to the defeated King Richard II – or, much later, to King Charles I, as he submitted to the executioner's axe. History had shown Shakespeare the ways by which subverters could prevail, while ironically creating precedents for their foes.

3

The banishment of Falstaff strikes the jarring chord of one of the great recurrent themes in Shakespearian drama: the price in human terms that must be paid for political success. In *Antony and Cleopatra*, it is the calculating Octavius Cæsar who prevails, while Antony and Cleopatra themselves are defeated and die: but, if we value sheer vitality, Antony and Cleopatra are each worth many Cæsars. Octavia, Antony's bride, is virtuous but pallid. Shakespeare lets the ontological criterion (which commends vitality and fulness of being) battle the ethical criterion (which commends virtue). In *1* and *2 Henry IV*, Bullingbrooke has successfully rebelled against Richard and become king; but his victory is hollow, for repeatedly he himself must face rebellions for which, with obvious irony, he has set the precedent. He becomes a wearied, worried figure; he has power, though embattled, but no joy. Even at the start of his reign, when granting mercy to the conspirator, Aumerle, he had acknowledged that guilt was a factor: 'I pardon him, as God shall pardon me.'

One of the most remarkable features of *2 Henry IV* is the thematic orchestration in which weariness, ageing and disease are interlinked. At the outset, the rebel Northumberland is 'crafty-sick'; and, on hearing of the death of his son, Hotspur, he becomes morally sick, crying:

> Let heaven kiss earth! Now let not Nature's hand
> Keep the wild flood confined! Let order die!

And in the very next scene, we find that the ageing Falstaff is now subject to disease: 'A pox of this gout! Or a gout of this pox!', he cries. Whichever it is, he has got it. He is more predatory now, an 'old pike' snapping at 'young dace'. The sense that the passage of time brings increasing decrepitude is illustrated not only at court, where Henry is ailing, not only among the rebels, by the distraught Northumberland, and not only in the tavern world, by Falstaff (sometimes beset by self-pity: 'I am old, I am old...Thou'lt forget me when I am gone'); but also even in rural Gloucestershire, where we encounter the senescent Shallow and Silence, with their rambling reminiscences about past times, pierced with intimations of mortality. Here Shakespeare intermittently anticipates the atmospherically thematic effects, partly humorous, partly melancholy, and deeply resonant, that would later characterise the mature dramas of Chekhov, particularly *The Cherry Orchard*. (The thematic becomes the 'atmospheric' when a theme is expressed largely but subtly and diffusely – as by leit-motifs and recurrent kindred descriptive details.)

Of course, this emphasis on decay and decrepitude, moral and physical, serves to create the sense that what is needed is new vitality, new soundness of moral leadership, a new rallying of the national spirit: in short, the need for the ascent to the throne by the young and determined Hal. He will become 'this star of England', celebrated by the patriotic chroniclers; the unsurpassed monarch who, to Holinshed, was 'a pattern in princehood, a lode-star in honour, and mirror of magnificence'.[17]

At the end of *2 Henry IV*, then, the stage is set for the triumphs of *Henry V*; but those triumphs will be ensnared by many ironies which generate a critical sub-text.[18] Falstaff will die, poignantly, playing with flowers and, like an infant, smiling at his fingers' ends; he babbles of green fields. 'The King has killed his heart.' And, as we have noted, the great achievements of Henry, his uniting the realm, conquering France, and, by marriage, forming a dynastic alliance with the French, will be mocked by the chaotic and disastrous events of *Henry VI*, so often and so recently depicted on the Elizabethan stage for the Londoners.

Generally, histories, as a literary genre, lack the prestige of tragedies. Yet *1* and *2 Henry IV*, as Dr Johnson perceived, contain some of the most vivid characterisations, most entertaining comedy, and most stirring rhetoric in Shakespeare's range. (By a modest computation of quality, *Timon of Athens*, though classified as a tragedy, is worth less than one-fifth of *1 Henry IV*.) These two histories display immense subtlety in co-ordinating, in a rich thematic meshwork, the large and the small, the court and the tavern, the urban and the rural, the comic and the sombre. Striking contrasts smuggle crafty connections. Modes of betrayal, modes of manipulation, the incurring and settling of debts: these themes sound again and again, in major and minor keys. The great theme of 'expropriating the expropriator' (implicit in the biblical legend of the Fall and the Atonement) becomes ubiquitous in *1 Henry IV*, linking the comic matter of the Gad's Hill robbery to the great drama of rebellion. Bullingbrooke had broken his sworn allegiance to Richard II, partly in order to regain the inheritance that Richard had expropriated from him. Now, having appropriated the crown, he, as Henry IV, must contend with 'rebels' who can be seen as loyalists to the lineage of Richard: they seek to expropriate the expropriator in the name of Richard's legitimate heirs, Roger Mortimer, Earl of March, and, on Roger's death, his son Edmund. In *1 Henry IV*, Act 1, sc. 3, we are reminded by Worcester that in 1398 Richard had proclaimed Edmund his heir. (Shakespeare, like the chroniclers he had read, confuses that Edmund, the fifth Earl of March, with his uncle, the Sir Edmund Mortimer who married Owen Glendower's daughter.) Henry's foes can claim that they are following his example in using force to seek the throne. Hal, we see, repeatedly participates in actions which 'expropriate the expropriator'. Falstaff, aided by Gadshill and Bardolph, robs the King's exchequer at Gad's Hill, but in turn the disguised Prince and Poins rob Falstaff, and eventually the money is to be repaid – with interest, we are told, – to the exchequer by the Prince. The same theme is maintained at the highest level of the plot. Hotspur has been busily amassing military honours, while Hal has apparently been wasting time. Hal's ingenious defence to the King is:

> Percy is but my factor, good my lord,
> To engross up glorious deeds on my behalf . . .

Hal's notion is that if, over a long period of time, Hotspur has gained many honours while the Prince has been apparently idle, that rebel is like an agent working for Hal, in the sense that Hal has only to kill Hotspur in battle, and those honours accumulated by Hotspur are gained – almost literally 'at a stroke' – by Hal. At the battle of Shrewsbury, the dying Hotspur is bitterly aware of the irony:

> I better brook the loss of brittle life
> Than those proud titles thou hast won of me:
> They wound my thoughts worse than thy sword my flesh.

That protean theme of expropriating the expropriator is, characteristically of this crafty play, echoed in a largely comic but partly sinister key, when Falstaff (thought dead by the Prince) takes up Hotspur's corpse and claims to have killed Hotspur himself. Hal had acquired Hotspur's honours; now Falstaff attempts to expropriate them from Hal. The Prince seems to connive:

> Come, bring your luggage nobly on your back.
> For my part, if a lie may do thee grace,
> I'll gild it with the happiest terms I have.

Falstaff's opportunistic action here is theatrically practical: a deft way of getting an actor's prone body off-stage. It is also symbolic: in this fallen world, the cynic, risen from apparent death, lugs the corpse of the paragon of outdated chivalry. Hal's promise of lying connivance with Falstaff's claim to glory is not kept: perhaps only Falstaff would expect it to be kept. In 2 Henry IV, Hotspur's father, Northumberland, is told that the 'swift wrath' of Hal has beaten down the never-daunted Percy to the earth. (Once again, therefore, Falstaff has had forewarning of his impending dismissal.) A related theme is 'real or apparent betrayal of a figure of authority'. Rebels betray the King; rebels betray rebels (by defection and falsehood); the King fears that Hal is a traitor to his father; Falstaff fears that Hal may betray (by dismissal) the jovial surrogate father; Hal and Poins betray Falstaff by tricking him. In one of the subtlest scenes in 1 Henry IV, Hal arranges for the humble waiter, Francis, to be called from two sides at once, so that he is divided between allegiances, and Hal also tempts him to betray his indenture, to leave his master. Here Hal enjoys psychological relief from the pressures he is under; he again compares himself with Hotspur; and he exercises his powers of manipulation. By revealing Hal's preoccupation with mastery through rôle-playing, with kept and broken promises, with conflicting claims of allegiance, and, again, with expropriation of an expropriator, this scene sounds themes which pervade the second tetralogy.[19] In 2 Henry IV, Hal will even play the part of Francis.

When Shakespeare was confronted with the task of compressing for the theatre the huge, complicated and straggly material of the chronicles (Holinshed and Hall being particularly useful), he hit on the idea of compression and co-ordination by means of an elaborate network of comparisons. At the start of *1 Henry IV*, the King laments that Northumberland has a son, Hotspur, who is 'the theme of honour's tongue', while his own son, Harry, is stained by 'riot and dishonour': he wishes that the two sons could have been exchanged by 'some night-tripping fairy'. Comparison is lubricated by the onomastic similarity: both offspring are named Henry, colloquially Harry. So, at once, we are assessing the rival claims of Harry, Prince of Wales, and Harry Hotspur; and we soon perceive that Hotspur, though charismatic and glamorous, would be disastrous if he were heir to the throne, being so reckless and hasty. The Prince will gain the valour of a Hotspur while retaining the political shrewdness of his father. Hotspur and the Prince frequently make their rivalry explicit. To facilitate comparison, Shakespeare has made Hotspur and Hal coevals: they must be the same age, we are persuaded, given that reference to the 'night-tripping fairy' who could have exchanged them in their cradles; and the King confirms this at 3.2.103. In fact, Hotspur was old enough to be Hal's father, and nearly three years older than the King. At the *real* battle of Shrewsbury, Hal (wounded by an arrow) was sixteen, Hotspur (slain, but not by the Prince) thirty-eight, and Henry IV thirty-six. If Shakespeare had to choose between historical fidelity and dramatic vigour, he jettisoned fidelity. More precisely, he pursued dramatic vigour and historical insight rather than factual accuracy. He repeatedly compresses the sequence of events, accelerating the action.

Hotspur contrasts Bullingbrooke ('this thorn, this canker') with Richard, 'that sweet lovely rose': a contrast which may provoke us to reflect that Bullingbrooke possesses the political astuteness that the rash Richard so signally lacked. Henry IV laments that Hal resembles Richard at his worst: Richard was 'the skipping King' who 'ambled up and down / With shallow jesters and rash bavin wits': seeking popularity, he made himself common, and lost popularity; and now, asserts Henry, Hal is just as bad, for Hal has lost his

> princely privilege
> With vile participation. Not an eye
> But is a-weary of thy common sight . . .

And who, then, in Henry's view, is the present counterpart to Henry Bullingbrooke before he became King? Why, the valiant Hotspur.

> For all the world,
> As thou art to this hour was Richard then,
> When I from France set foot at Ravenspurgh;
> And even as I was then, is Percy now.
> Now, by my sceptre, and my soul to boot,
> He hath more worthy interest to the state
> Than thou, the shadow of succession.

This misjudgement of character is both readily understandable and richly ironic.

The theme of 'comparison and contrast' reaches a height of complexity in the jocoserious tavern scene of *1 Henry IV*, Act 2, sc. 4, in which (although Hal had hoped to play Hotspur, with Falstaff as Hotspur's wife), Falstaff plays Henry IV, who now praises Falstaff as a man of virtue ('Him keep with, the rest banish'), and Hal plays the King's rebuked son, anticipating that climactic confrontation between the Prince and the King in *2 Henry IV*, Act 4, sc. 5. Then they change places so that Hal plays Henry IV (who now abuses Falstaff), while Falstaff as Hal makes an impassioned self-defence, culminating in those emphatic words: 'Banish plump Jack, and banish all the world': but, in context, Falstaff's phrasing may remind us of the baptismal catechism in which Christians are obliged to renounce the world, the flesh and the devil.[20] The truth expresses itself intensely through ostensibly farcical performances: as in *Hamlet*, the play within the play proclaims painful truth. Here the actors of Hal and Falstaff must play 'layered and palimpsestic' rôles: the actors play intelligent characters who are craftily play-acting.[21] This scene displays the great acumen of a Shakespeare who seems to know precisely the exploitable strengths and skills of specific actors employed by his company. (Sometimes, Shakespeare's script named not the character but the actor: in *2 Henry IV* he wrote, as a stage-direction, 'Enter Sincklo' instead of, say, 'Enter First Beadle', John Sincklo being a thin actor of minor rôles.) Near the culmination of 1 Henry IV, the theme of 'comparison and contrast' is linked to that of 'actors and acting', and is maintained in various ways on the battlefield: notably, when we find that the crafty Henry IV has, to increase his chances of survival, arranged for many of his men to be disguised as himself. Accordingly, when Douglas kills the disguised Blunt, he imagines that he is slaying the King. We may think that by thus deploying 'multiple kings', Shakespeare is suggesting that in the post-Ricardian world, where the King cannot sincerely claim, as Richard did, to be 'the Lord's anointed', there may be numerous pretenders to the throne: this is an era of pragmatic and not sacred royalty. Majesty is an act, politics a performance. But Shakespeare is yet subtler: when Douglas meets Henry IV, he says:

> I fear thou art another counterfeit,
> And yet, in faith, thou bear'st thee like a king . . .

It is as though Henry, for all that he is a usurper, has gained at least the bearing, the manner and posture, and perhaps some deeper quality, of a true king. In the ensuing action, Henry is rescued by Hal, who thereby is reconciled with his father.

One of the odd features of Henry IV, Part 2, is that, although the clock of history ticks on steadily, the hands of the clock governing the relationship between Hal and his father are, so to speak, turned back. We find that Hal, who on the battlefield in Part 1 proved his loyalty by saving Henry IV and by being so valiant, has to prove his loyalty to his father a second time. Here a contradiction has been generated by a tension – the tension between (a) the requirements of a coherent tetralogy and (b) the playwright's assumption that each play of the four would be performed separately. For dramatic purposes, it suits Shakespeare (integrating the national and the familial – the publicly political and the privately emotional) to develop again the sense of distrust between the monarch and his heir, who is once more deemed to be riotously feckless. And that distrust is not without a reasonable basis. When Hal thinks that his father has died, he quickly takes up the crown and, fascinated, addresses it. When his father awakens, and accuses Hal of desiring his father's death, in eagerness to gain the throne, Hal eloquently exculpates himself, saying of the crown:

> Accusing it, I put it on my head,
> To try with it, as with an enemy
> That had before my face murdered my father,
> The quarrel of a true inheritor...

That is not the whole truth. When the Prince had at that time put the crown on his own head, his tone had been proud:

> Lo, where it sits,
> Which God shall guard; and put the world's whole strength
> Into one giant arm, it shall not force
> This lineal honour from me.

It's a false start to Hal's kingship: the 'lineal honour' must promptly be returned to its living owner, Henry IV. But in reconciling himself, finally, to his father, by his eloquent exculpation, Hal has demonstrated that quality of persuasive eloquence which will serve him so well during his eventual reign. Perhaps Hal partly learnt the art of exculpation from the wily Falstaff, who is irrepressibly accomplished in that art. Indeed, Hal prides himself on learning the discourse and skills of others, whether it's the slang of the waiters in the tavern or the swaggering boastfulness of Hotspur. He knows that observant understanding is a means to power. His talents of intelligence, eloquence, boldness and persuasiveness must secure his tenure of a throne to which his right is questionable.

  Was the gaining of the crown by Henry IV legitimate or illegitimate? This matter was extensively debated in Shakespeare's day. One extreme view, expressed in *Richard II* by John of Gaunt, was that since a legitimate King is 'the Lord's anointed', indeed 'God's substitute, / His deputy anointed in His sight', such a monarch can properly be dethroned only by God Himself: therefore Bullingbrooke is a usurper. If a monarch gained the throne by violence and was tyrannical, however, rebellion was generally held to be justified, as *Macbeth* would illustrate. Predictably, an exception to that general rule was expressed by King James VI of Scotland (later James I of Great Britain), who, in *The Trew Law of Free Monarchies*, declared:

The wickedness therefore of the King can never make them that are ordained to be judged by him, to become his judges.[22]

It was also argued in Shakespeare's day that Bullingbrooke was the legitimate heir 'because parliament elected him when Richard II willingly resigned'.[23] In the tetralogy extending from *Richard II* to *Henry V*, the wrangle about the basis of Henry IV's rule thus becomes another co-ordinator. Indeed, one 'suspense principle', luring us on, is our wish for a decisive answer to the question of whether Henry was a legitimate monarch or not. (The matter was more than interestingly topical, for it was perilously contemporaneous: Queen Elizabeth was reported to have said: 'I am Richard II[:] know ye not that?'[24]) The answer to the question is eventually provided by Henry IV himself, when he privately counsels his son:

> God knows, my son,
> By what bypaths and indirect crook'd ways
> I met this crown.

He hopes that the stigma, 'the soil of the achievement', will be buried with himself. But though Hal's claim is better than that of Henry IV, it remains shaky: 'Thou art not firm enough', the King warns him; so

> Be it thy course to busy giddy minds
> With foreign quarrels.

This is astute advice, albeit Machiavellian. (Many generations of political leaders, in Britain and abroad, have taken it.) In the case of Henry IV, there was also deeply personal motivation for a crusading campaign abroad: deep guilt at the death of Richard, the cruel deed which Henry had clearly instigated. Henry had then hoped to make a penitential pilgrimage to the Holy Land, but he is never able to make it because, as though God is punishing him, Henry has to contend with repeated incursions by rebels who can claim to be avenging the slain Richard. (Ironically, Henry does reach Jerusalem; but it is the chamber named 'Jerusalem' at court, where he is stricken and dies.) Indeed, it appears that the prophecies of divine wrath to come, those prophecies made in *Richard II* by Carlisle and Richard himself, are being fulfilled. As we perceive that apparent fulfilment, Richard's stature accordingly grows. Vindicated as a prophet, he becomes a more sacred figure *after* his death than he, with all his manifest faults, ever was *before* it. When Henry IV tells his defeated opponents, 'Thus ever did rebellion find rebuke', they tactfully do not respond 'Except in *your* case, as Richard found, to his cost'.

The theme of inherited guilt is also manifest in *Henry V*. Hal's main justification for war is provided by the churchmen, particularly the Archbishop of Canterbury, and it is delivered in the form of a long rigmarole about the Salic Law. The justification, as offered, invites mockery (and was subsequently satirised), and is obviously questionable.[25] Later, on the eve of the battle of Agincourt, the King appraises his attempts to buy God's grace. Yes, he has interred Richard's corpse anew; he has paid the needy to offer intercessionary prayers; and he has hired priests to sing for the repose of Richard's soul – but

> All that I can do is nothing worth,
> Since that my penitence comes after all,
> Imploring pardon.

The best gloss on these lines is suggested by the far more culpable figure, Claudius in *Hamlet*, when he, kneeling, strives to pray for divine forgiveness:

> but O, what form of prayer
> Can serve my turn? 'Forgive me my foul murder'?
> That cannot be, since I am still possessed
> Of those effects for which I did the murder –
> My crown, mine own ambition, and my queen.

Henry V means something rather similar. To be truly penitent would entail giving up the ill-gotten throne. But having come this far, Henry isn't going back. And on the next day, the Battle of Agincourt results in a well-nigh miraculous victory for the British.[26] The Lord moves in a mysterious way, but it looks as if God, having punished the usurper by civil wars, has come to regard the usurper's well-meaning son as worthy of a helping hand. When Henry then gives to God the credit for the victory, it is not only the appropriately pious response; it is also the morally, politically and psychologically salutary response. As we have noted, however, the story of this dynasty does not end there. 'And thus the whirligig of time brings in his revenges.'[27]

We saw that there are 'two clocks' in *2 Henry IV*. It is also noticeable that, in the course of the second tetralogy, time becomes multiple. In the foreground, we are aware of historic time in which the long power-struggles between factions and nations take place; in the background, we are aware of a larger natural time-scale in which the enduring features are the rituals of the countryside, the rearing of animals and the production of crops, on which, after all, the nobles and the warriors are dependent; and, in an ultimate perspective, we glimpse a global time-scale, a vista of centuries in which all human activities are dwarfed by the vast processes of evolution, erosion and depletion.

Thus, when aptly appreciated, *Henry IV, Part 1* and *Henry IV, Part 2*, these two superb history plays, burst out of the genre of the History Play like phœnixes smashing their way out of pigeonholes. These works are *fully* political because they see *beyond* the political. The participants range from God above to the very fleas that breed in the chimney where the carriers urinate. In this second tetralogy, Shakespeare orchestrates symphonically the religious, the political, the philosophical, the aesthetic and the sensual. Commentators, though constantly outwitted (because commentaries can never provide an equivalent to the rich effects of the protean text and its performances), may at least hope to augment and partly elucidate that lively totality as it proceeds magisterially through the centuries, evolving and mutating as its circumstances change.

CEDRIC WATTS

1 G. B. Shaw: 'Notes' to *Three Plays for Puritans* (London: Constable, 1911), p. 203. Samuel Johnson: *Johnson on Shakespeare*, ed. Walter Raleigh (Oxford: Oxford University Press, 1908), p. 124.

2 Robert Greene: *Greenes, Groat's-worth of witte, bought with a million of Repentance* (London: William Wright, 1592). There Shakespeare is also alleged to be a 'Iohannes fac totum' (Jack of all trades).

3 Of course, Richard, regarding himself as God's deputy, can also readily liken himself to Jesus beset by Judases (Act 4, sc.1).

4 *The Oresteia* was performed as a trilogy; the parts of Sophocles' *The Theban Trilogy* were performed separately, its three plays having been written at widely-separated times. The satyr play, which often (as in Sophocles' *Ichneutai*) included dancing, offered a farcical contrast to the preceding tragic sequence, while sometimes dramatising part of the legend adapted in that sequence. In Shakespeare's day, Thomas Platter, a Swiss visitor to England, recorded in 1599 that when he saw *Julius Cæsar* staged in London, the tragedy was followed by the customary dance (this one involving four players, two dressed as women). The Quarto's 'Epilogue' of *2 Henry IV* indicates that that play, too, was followed by a dance. The main clown of the Lord Chamberlain's Men from 1594 until early 1599 was Will Kemp (or Kempe), a celebrated dancer.

5 *The First Part of Tamburlaine the Great* in Christopher Marlowe: *The Complete Plays*, ed. J. B. Steane (Harmondsworth: Penguin, 1969; rpt. 1978), p. 132.

6 Transtextual narratives and characters are discussed in Cedric Watts's *The Deceptive Text: An Introduction to Covert Plots* (Brighton: Harvester, 1984).

7 Philosophically, Falstaff is a 'nominalist' (deeming 'honour' subjective), and his nominalism can be traced back, via William of Ockham, to Hermogenes in Plato's *Cratylus*.

8 'The *Pietà*' is the generic term for a poignant depiction of Christ's corpse in the arms of a mourning Virgin Mary.

9 See Ulysses' speech on 'appetite, an universal wolf' in *Troilus and Cressida*, Act 1, sc. 3.

10 *Johnson on Shakespeare*, p. 125.

11 Plautus wrote a comedy entitled *Miles Gloriosus* (*The Boastful Soldier*) featuring Pyrgopolynices, the eponymous braggart, who is also a pursuer of women. In the traditional Italian *Commedia dell'arte*, the

character called *Il Capitano* is a *miles gloriosus*. Falstaff, however, a wily, resourceful and eloquent old soldier, surpasses such relatives.

12 A. D. Nuttall: *A New Mimesis* (London and New York: Methuen, 1983), p. 151. William Hazlitt deemed Falstaff a 'better man' than Hal.

13 An 'apostrophic soliloquy' occurs when an unaccompanied character formally addresses an object (which may be one entity or more than one).

14 Shakespeare was fond of citing Chapter 13, verse 1, of the apocryphal Ecclesiasticus.

15 E. M. Forster: 'What I Believe' [1939] in *Two Cheers for Democracy* (Harmondsworth: Penguin, 1965), p. 76.

16 Greenblatt's essay can be found in *Political Shakespeare*, ed. Jonathan Dollimore and Alan Sinfield (Manchester: Manchester University Press), 1985.

17 *Holinshed's Chronicles of England, Scotland and Ireland* [1587] (rpt. London: Johnson *et al.*, 1807), Vol. 3, p. 134. (I have modernised the spelling.)

18 See John Sutherland and Cedric Watts: *Henry V, War Criminal? and Other Shakespeare Puzzles* (Oxford: Oxford University Press, 2000), pp. 117–25. (Some parts of this Introduction derive from that book.)

19 See *Henry V, War Criminal?*, pp. 99–107.

20 The Anglican catechism cites 'the devil and all his works, the pomps and vanity of the wicked world, and all the sinful lusts of the flesh'.

21 A palimpsest occurs when old writing shows through the newer writing which is superinscribed upon it. Palimpsestic characterisation occurs when a character, playing the part of another character, lets his original self be perceptible through the assumed self: as when Falstaff, playing Henry IV, begs Hal not to banish Falstaff.

22 James I: *The Trew Law of Free Monarchies* in *The Political Works of James I*, ed. C. H. McIlwain (New York: Russell & Russell, 1965), p. 54.

23 Cyndia Susan Clegg: 'Censorship and the Problem of History in Shakespeare's England' in *A Companion to Shakespeare's Works: Volume II: The Histories,* ed. Richard Dutton and Jean E. Howard (Oxford: Blackwell, 2003), p. 49.

24 The Queen is quoted in *The Progresses and Public Processions of Queen Elizabeth*, ed. John Nichols, Vol. 3 (New York: Franklin, n.d.), p. 552.

25 Gary Taylor, when introducing *Henry V* (Oxford: Oxford University Press, 1982; rpt., 1998; pp. 34–9), argues that the Archbishop's justification would, in Shakespeare's day, have been seen as both interesting and valid. Holinshed, however, in his *Chronicles*, says that the claim to France is a 'sharp invention' by the churchmen, and that the speech about the Salic Law is a 'prepared tale'. The speech was satirised in John Fletcher's play, *The Noble Gentleman* (*c.*1624–6), in which an intricate claim to the French throne is advanced by a madman. Q1 of *Henry V* omits the early scene which reveals the churchmen's selfish motive for thus furthering the monarch's claim: a crucial omission, indicative of censorship.

26 Henry is told that there are 10,000 French dead but only 29 British. Modern historians vary in their estimates, but it seems likely that deaths on the French side were about 7,000, on the British side about 500: still an astounding contrast. The battle was not, however, as decisive as the play suggests. In reality, the Treaty of Troyes (dramatised in the final scene) was not negotiated until more than four years after the slaughter at Agincourt. For dramatic effect, Shakespeare compresses time. Meanwhile, French forces – aided by the Scots – continued to fight Henry. To exalt Henry as unifier, Shakespeare suppresses this fact.

27 William Shakespeare: *Twelfth Night*, ed. Cedric Watts (Ware: Wordsworth, 2001), p. 100 (5.1.365–6).

FURTHER READING
(in chronological order)

E. M. W. Tillyard: *Shakespeare's History Plays*. London: Chatto and Windus, 1944; reprinted, Harmondsworth: Penguin, 1962.

Derek Traversi: *Shakespeare from 'Richard II' to 'Henry V'*. London: Hollis & Carter, 1958; rpt., 1968.

Narrative and Dramatic Sources of Shakespeare, Vol. IV, ed. Geoffrey Bullough. London: Routledge & Kegan Paul; New York: Columbia University Press, 1962; rpt., 1966.

Twentieth Century Interpretations of 'Henry IV, Part 2': A Collection of Critical Essays, ed. David P. Young. Englewood Cliffs, N.J.: Prentice-Hall, 1968.

Shakespeare: 'Henry IV, Parts 1 and 2': A Casebook, ed. G. K. Hunter. London and Basingstoke: Macmillan, 1970; rpt., 1980. (This contains influential essays by William Empson, W. H. Auden and Harold Jenkins.)

Samuel Schoenbaum: *William Shakespeare: A Compact Documentary Life*. London and New York: Oxford University Press, 1977; rpt., 1987.

Shakespeare: The Critical Heritage, ed. Brian Vickers. (6 volumes.) London: Routledge and Kegan Paul: 1974–81.

A. D. Nuttall: *A New Mimesis: Shakespeare and the Representation of Reality*. London and New York: Methuen, 1983.

Graham Holderness: *Shakespeare's History*. Dublin: Gill and Macmillan; New York: St. Martin's Press; 1985.

Political Shakespeare: New Essays in Cultural Materialism, ed. Jonathan Dollimore and Alan Sinfield. Manchester: Manchester University Press, 1985. (This contains Stephen Greenblatt's 'Inivisible Bullets'.)

Robin Headlam Wells: *Shakespeare, Politics and the State*. Basingstoke: Macmillan, 1986.

'Henry IV, Parts 1 and 2': Critical Essays, ed. David Bevington. New York and London: Garland, 1986.

William Shakespeare's 'Henry IV, Part 1', ed. Harold Bloom. ('Modern Critical Interpretations' series:) New York: Chelsea House, 1987.

C. W. R. D. Moseley: *Shakespeare's History Plays: Richard II to Henry V: The Making of a King*. London: Penguin, 1988.

Major Literary Characters: Falstaff, ed. Harold Bloom. New York: Chelsea House, 1992.

Ronald Knowles: *Henry IV Parts I and II*. Basingstoke: Macmillan, 1992.

Shakespeare's History Plays: 'Richard II' to 'Henry V', ed. Graham Holderness. ('New Casebooks' series:) Basingstoke: Macmillan, 1992.

Brian Vickers: *Appropriating Shakespeare: Contemporary Critical Quarrels*. New Haven and London: Yale University Press, 1993.

Henry IV Parts 1 and 2, ed. Nigel Wood. Buckingham: Open University Press, 1995.

Russ McDonald: *The Bedford Companion to Shakespeare*. New York: St Martin's Press; Basingstoke: Macmillan; 1996.

Jean E. Howard and Phyllis Rackin: *Engendering a Nation: A Feminist Account of Shakespeare's English Histories*. London and New York: Routledge, 1997.

A Companion to Shakespeare, ed. David Scott Kastan. Oxford: Blackwell, 1999.

Kenneth S. Rothwell: *A History of Shakespeare on Screen: A Century of Film and Television*. Cambridge: Cambridge University Press, 1999.

John Sutherland and Cedric Watts: *Henry V, War Criminal? and Other Shakespeare Puzzles*. Oxford: Oxford University Press, 2000.

The Cambridge Companion to Shakespeare, ed. Margreta de Grazia and Stanley Wells. Cambridge: Cambridge University Press, 2001.

Tom McAlindon: *Shakespeare's Tudor History: A Study of 'Henry IV, Parts 1 and 2'*. Aldershot: Ashgate Publishing, 2001.

Benjamin Griffin: *Playing the Past: Approaches to English Historical Drama 1385–1600*. Woodbridge: D. S. Brewer, 2001

The Cambridge Companion to Shakespeare's History Plays, ed. Michael Hattaway. Cambridge: Cambridge University Press, 2002.

A Companion to Shakespeare's Works: Vol. II: The Histories, ed. Richard Dutton and Jean E. Howard. Oxford: Blackwell, 2003.

Shakespeare: An Oxford Guide, ed. Stanley Wells and Lena Cowen Orlin. Oxford: Oxford University Press, 2003.

James Shapiro: *1599: A Year in the Life of William Shakespeare*. London: Faber, 2005.

John Lucas: *Shakespeare's Second Tetralogy: Richard II - Henry V*. London: Greenwich Exchange, 2007.

David Bevington: *Shakespeare's Ideas: More Things in Heaven and Earth*. Chichester: Wiley-Blackwell, 2008.

NOTE ON SHAKESPEARE

William Shakespeare was the son of a glover at Stratford-upon-Avon, and tradition gives his date of birth as 23 April, 1564; certainly, three days later, he was christened at the parish church. It is likely that he attended the local Grammar School but had no university education. Of his early career there is no record, though John Aubrey reports a claim that he was a rural schoolmaster. In 1582 Shakespeare married Anne Hathaway, with whom he had two daughters, Susanna and Judith, and a son, Hamnet, who died in 1596.

How he became involved with the stage in London is uncertain, but by 1592 he was sufficiently established as a playwright to be criticised in print as a challengingly versatile 'upstart Crow'. He was a leading member of the Lord Chamberlain's company, which became the King's Men ('the King's Servants and Grooms of the Chamber') on the accession of James I in 1603. The players performed at diverse locations. Being not only a playwright and actor but also a 'sharer' (one of the owners of the company, entitled to a share of the profits), Shakespeare prospered greatly, as is proven by the numerous records of his financial transactions.

Towards the end of his life, he loosened his ties with London and retired to New Place, the large house in Stratford-upon-Avon which he had bought in 1597. He died on 23 April, 1616, and is buried in the place of his baptism, Holy Trinity Church. The earliest collected edition of his plays, the First Folio, was published in 1623, and its prefatory verse-tributes include Ben Jonson's famous declaration, 'He was not of an age, but for all time'.

ACKNOWLEDGEMENTS AND TEXTUAL MATTERS

I have consulted (and am indebted to) numerous editions of Parts 1 and 2 of *Henry IV*, notably those by: Peter Alexander ('The Tudor Shakespeare': London and Glasgow: Collins, 1951; rpt., 1966); A. R. Humphreys (*Part 1*; 'The Arden Shakespeare': London: Methuen, 1960; rpt., 1966); A. R. Humphreys again (*Part 2*; 'The Arden Shakespeare': London: Methuen, 1960); Andrew Cairncross (*Part 1*; 'The Arden Shakespeare': London: Methuen, 1960; rpt., 1977); Peter Davison (*Part 1*; 'Penguin Shakespeare': London: Penguin, 1968; rpt., 2005); G. Blakemore Evans *et al.* ('The Riverside Shakespeare'; Boston: Houghton Mifflin, 1974); Peter Davison (*Part 2*; 'Penguin Shakespeare': London: Penguin, 1977; rpt., 2005); David Bevington (*Part 1*; 'The Oxford Shakespeare': Oxford: Oxford University Press, 1987; rpt., 1998); Stanley Wells and Gary Taylor (*The Complete Works: Compact Edition*: Oxford: Oxford University Press, 1988); René Weis (*Part 2*; 'Oxford World's Classics': Oxford: Oxford University Press, 1997; rpt., 2008); Stephen Greenblatt *et al.* ('The Norton Shakespeare': New York and London: Norton, 1997); Herbert Weil and Judith Weil (*Part 1*; Cambridge: Cambridge University Press, 1997); Jonathan Bate and Eric Rasmussen (*Part 1* and *Part 2*; 'The RSC Shakespeare': Basingstoke: Macmillan, 2009). Particularly useful were: *Henry the Fourth: Part 1: 1598* ('Shakespeare Quarto Facsimiles'; Oxford: Oxford University Press, 1966); and *The Second Part of King Henry the Fourth: 1600* ('The Malone Society Reprints'; Oxford: Oxford University Press, 1990).

Next: textual matters and technical terms. A 'quarto' is a book with relatively small pages, while a 'folio' is a book with relatively large pages. A quarto volume is made of sheets of paper, each of which has been folded twice to form four leaves (and thus eight pages), whereas each of a folio's sheets has been folded once to form two leaves (and thus four pages). The 'First Folio' (often designated 'F1') was the first 'collected edition' of Shakespeare's plays, assembled by two of the fellow-actors in his company, John Heminge (or Heminges) and Henry Condell.

In the case of *Henry IV, Part 1*, the earliest surviving text is a mere fragment, eight pages, printed in 1598, and usually designated 'Q0' by editors. The earliest intact text, also dated 1598, is usually designated the First Quarto, Q1. Before the Folio appeared, there were five subsequent quarto versions, each based on its predecessor. The Folio text was based mainly on the fifth, 'Q5', 1613. Q1 (which is generally deemed the most authoritative text) contains material absent from F1, and F1 contains material absent from Q1. F1 divides the play into Acts and scenes, bowdlerises some colloquialisms, oaths and religious terms, and alters stage-directions. It provides some acceptable new textual readings. I have given priority to Q1, while incorporating various materials from F1, and taking a couple of details from other early texts.

In the case of *Henry IV, Part 2*, only one quarto (dated 1600) is extant, though it exists in two versions, known as 'QA' and 'QB'. QB contains the scene now known as scene 1 of Act 3, but QA lacks it. The First Folio contains eight substantial passages missing from Q (censorship being a probable reason for some of the absences), but Q contains numerous lines and part-lines which do not appear in the First Folio. F1 is more 'literary', providing Act and scene divisions, removing profanities, archaisms and some colloquialisms, and altering stage-directions. I have usually given priority to QA and QB, again while incorporating various materials from F1.

The present edition of these two plays offers a practical compromise between: (a) those early texts; (b) Shakespeare's intentions, insofar as they can be reasonably inferred; and (c) modern requirements. The general aim is to attain maximum clarification with minimum alteration, while respecting the stylistic qualities of the verse and the prose.

The parliamentary Act of 1606 'to Restrain the Abuses of Players' forbade the utterance of holy names by actors, so that where (for instance) Q1 of *Henry IV, Part 1* has at one point 'O Jesu, this', F1 substitutes 'This'. In such cases, I have restored the earlier and more vigorous phrasing. I use a dash to indicate not only an interruption to a statement, or the start of a non-consecutive statement, but also a change of direction when a speaker turns from one addressee to another. The glossary explains archaisms and unfamiliar terms. The annotations offer clarification of obscurities, while drawing attention to textual variations.

No edition of these plays can claim to be definitive. This edition, which concisely incorporates the two plays in one volume, hopes to be very useful.

HENRY IV, PART ONE

CHARACTERS:

The King's Alliance:

King HENRY IV, *formerly Henry Bullingbrooke*
Henry (HAL), *Prince of Wales, the King's eldest son*
Lord JOHN *of Lancaster, a younger son of the King*
The Earl of WESTMORLAND
Sir Walter BLUNT

Rebels and Their Relatives:

Thomas Percy, the Earl of WORCESTER
Henry Percy, the Earl of NORTHUMBERLAND, *his brother*
Henry (Harry) Percy, known as HOTSPUR, *Northumberland's son*
Kate, LADY PERCY, *Hotspur's wife, Mortimer's sister*
Edmund, LORD MORTIMER
LADY MORTIMER, *Lord Mortimer's wife, Glendower's daughter*
Owen GLENDOWER (*Owain Glyndŵr*)
The Earl of DOUGLAS
Sir Richard VERNON
Richard Scroop, ARCHBISHOP *of* YORK
Sir MICHAEL, *associate of the Archbishop*

Hal's Associates:

Sir John FALSTAFF
Edward (Ned) POINS
BARDOLPH
PETO

Mistress Quickly, HOSTESS *of a tavern*
FRANCIS, *a drawer (waiter)*
A VINTNER

At Rochester:

GADSHILL
CARRIER 1
CARRIER 2
CHAMBERLAIN

OSTLER
TRAVELLER 1
TRAVELLER 2

Others:

SHERIFF, SERVANT, LORDS, MESSENGERS *and* SOLDIERS

HENRY IV, PART ONE

ACT I, SCENE I.

London: the palace.

Enter KING HENRY, LORD JOHN OF LANCASTER, *the* EARL OF
WESTMORLAND, SIR WALTER BLUNT *and other* LORDS.

K. HENRY So shaken as we are, so wan with care,
Find we a time for frighted peace to pant,
And breathe short-winded accents of new broils
To be commenced in strands afar remote:
No more the thirsty entrance of this soil
Shall daub her lips with her own children's blood;
No more shall trenching war channel her fields,
Nor bruise her flow'rets with the armèd hoofs
Of hostile paces. Those opposèd eyes,
Which, like the meteors of a troubled heaven,   10
All of one nature, of one substance bred,
Did lately meet in the intestine shock
And furious close of civil butchery,
Shall now, in mutual well-beseeming ranks,
March all one way, and be no more opposed
Against acquaintance, kindred and allies.
The edge of war, like an ill-sheathèd knife,
No more shall cut his master. Therefore, friends,
As far as to the sepulchre of Christ
(Whose soldier now, under whose blessed cross   20
We are impressèd and engaged to fight)
Forthwith a power of English shall we levy,
Whose arms were moulded in their mother's womb
To chase these pagans in those holy fields
Over whose acres walked those blessèd feet
Which fourteen hundred years ago were nailed,
For our advantage, on the bitter cross.
But this our purpose now is twelve month old,
And bootless 'tis to tell you we will go.
Therefor we meet not now. Then let me hear   30

Of you, my gentle cousin Westmorland,
What yesternight our Council did decree
In forwarding this dear expedience.

WEST.   My liege, this haste was hot in question,
And many limits of the charge set down
But yesternight, when all athwart there came
A post from Wales, loaden with heavy news,
Whose worst was that the noble Mortimer,[1]
Leading the men of Her'fordshire to fight
Against the irregular and wild Glendower,   40
Was by the rude hands of that Welshman taken,
A thousand of his people butcherèd,
Upon whose dead corpse' there was such misuse,
Such beastly shameless transformation
By those Welshwomen done, as may not be
Without much shame retold or spoken of.

K. HENRY   It seems then that the tidings of this broil
Brake off our business for the Holy Land.

WEST.   This, matched with other, did, my gracious Lord;
For more uneven and unwelcome news   50
Came from the north, and thus it did import:
On Holy-Rood Day, the gallant Hotspur there,
Young Harry Percy, and brave Archibold,
That ever valiant and approvèd Scot,
At Holmedon met,
Where they did spend a sad and bloody hour:
As by discharge of their artillery,
And shape of likelihood, the news was told;
For he that brought them, in the very heat
And pride of their contention did take horse,   60
Uncertain of the issue any way.

K. HENRY   Here is a dear, a true industrious friend,
Sir Walter Blunt, new lighted from his horse,
Stained with the variation of each soil
Betwixt that Holmedon and this seat of ours,
And he hath brought us smooth and welcome news.
The Earl of Douglas is discomfited.
Ten thousand bold Scots, two-and-twenty knights,
Balked in their own blood, did Sir Walter see

On Holmedon's plains. Of prisoners Hotspur took   70
Mordake, the Earl of Fife and eldest son
To beaten Douglas, and the Earl of Atholl,
Of Murray, Angus, and Menteith:
And is not this an honourable spoil?
A gallant prize? Ha, cousin, is it not?

WEST.   In faith,
It is a conquest for a prince to boast of.

K. HENRY Yea, there thou mak'st me sad, and mak'st me sin
In envy, that my Lord Northumberland
Should be the father to so blest a son:
A son who is the theme of honour's tongue,   80
Amongst a grove the very straightest plant,
Who is sweet Fortune's minion and her pride,
Whilst I, by looking on the praise of him,
See riot and dishonour stain the brow
Of my young Harry. O that it could be proved
That some night-tripping fairy had exchanged
In cradle-clothes our children where they lay,
And called mine Percy, his Plantagenet;
Then would I have his Harry, and he mine.
But let him from my thoughts. What think you, coz, 90
Of this young Percy's pride? The prisoners
Which he in this adventure hath surprised
To his own use he keeps, and sends me word
I shall have none but Mordake, Earl of Fife.

WEST. This is his uncle's teaching. This is Worcester,
Malevolent to you in all aspécts,
Which makes him prune himself, and bristle up
The crest of youth against your dignity.

K. HENRY But I have sent for him to answer this;
And for this cause awhile we must neglect   100
Our holy purpose to Jerusalem.
Cousin, on Wednesday next, our Council we
Will hold at Windsor: so inform the lords;
But come yourself with speed to us again,
For more is to be said and to be done
Than out of anger can be utterèd.

WEST. I will, my liege.   [*Exeunt*.

SCENE 2.

London.

Enter the PRINCE OF WALES (HAL) *and* SIR JOHN FALSTAFF.

FALSTAFF   Now Hal, what time of day is it, lad?

HAL   Thou art so fat-witted with drinking of old sack, and
            unbuttoning thee after supper, and sleeping upon
            benches after noon, that thou hast forgotten to demand
            that truly which thou wouldst truly know. What a devil
            hast thou to do with the time of the day? Unless hours
            were cups of sack, and minutes capons, and clocks the
            tongues of bawds, and dials the signs of leaping-houses,
            and the blessed sun himself a fair hot wench in flame-
            coloured taffeta, I see no reason why thou shouldst be   10
            so superfluous to demand the time of the day.

FALSTAFF   Indeed, you come near me now Hal, for we that take
            purses go by the moon and the seven stars, and not 'by
            Phoebus, he, that wand'ring knight so fair'. And I
            prithee sweet wag, when thou art King, as God save
            thy Grace – 'Majesty' I should say, for grace thou wilt
            have none –

HAL   What, none?

FALSTAFF   No, by my troth, not so much as will serve to be
            prologue to an egg and butter.   20

HAL   Well, how then? Come, roundly, roundly.

FALSTAFF   Marry then, sweet wag, when thou art King, let not us
            that are squires of the night's body be called thieves of
            the day's beauty. Let us be Diana's foresters, gentlemen
            of the shade, minions of the moon; and let men say we
            be men of good government, being governed, as the
            sea is, by our noble and chaste mistress the moon,
            under whose countenance we steal.

HAL   Thou sayest well, and it holds well too, for the fortune
            of us that are the moon's men doth ebb and flow like   30
            the sea, being governed as the sea is, by the moon. As
            for proof? Now, a purse of gold most resolutely
            snatched on Monday night, and most dissolutely spent
            on Tuesday morning; got with swearing 'Lay by!', and

spent with crying 'Bring in!'; now in as low an ebb as the foot of the ladder, and by and by in as high a flow as the ridge of the gallows.

FALSTAFF   By the Lord, thou sayest true, lad, − and is not my hostess of the tavern a most sweet wench?

HAL   As the honey of Hybla, my old lad of the castle; and is   40
not a buff jerkin a most sweet robe of durance?[2]

FALSTAFF   How now, how now, mad wag? What, in thy quips and thy quiddities? What a plague have I to do with a buff jerkin?

HAL   Why, what a pox have I to do with my hostess of the tavern?

FALSTAFF   Well, thou hast called her to a reckoning many a time and oft.

HAL   Did I ever call for thee to pay thy part?

FALSTAFF   No, I'll give thee thy due, thou hast paid all there.   50

HAL   Yea, and elsewhere, so far as my coin would stretch; and where it would not, I have used my credit.

FALSTAFF   Yea, and so used it that were it not here apparent that thou art heir apparent − But I prithee sweet wag, shall there be gallows standing in England when thou art King? And resolution thus fubbed as it is with the rusty curb of old Father Antic the law? Do not thou, when thou art King, hang a thief.

HAL   No, *thou* shalt.

FALSTAFF   Shall I? O rare! By the Lord, I'll be a brave judge!   60

HAL   Thou judgest false already: I mean thou shalt have the hanging of the thieves, and so become a rare hangman.

FALSTAFF   Well, Hal, well; and in some sort it jumps with my humour as well as waiting in the court, I can tell you.

HAL   For obtaining of suits?

FALSTAFF   Yea, for obtaining of suits, whereof the hangman hath no lean wardrobe.[3] 'Sblood, I am as melancholy as a gib cat, or a lugged bear.

HAL   Or an old lion, or a lover's lute.

fFALSTAFF   Yea, or the drone of a Lincolnshire bagpipe.   70

HAL   What sayest thou to a hare, or the melancholy of Moorditch?

FALSTAFF   Thou hast the most unsavoury similes, and art indeed the most comparative rascalliest sweet young prince. But Hal, I prithee trouble me no more with vanity. I would to God thou and I knew where a commodity of good names were to be bought. An old lord of the Council rated me the other day in the street about you, sir, but I marked him not; and yet he talked very wisely, but I regarded him not, and yet he talked 80 wisely – and in the street too.

HAL   Thou didst well, for wisdom cries out in the streets and no man regards it.[4]

FALSTAFF   O, thou hast damnable iteration, and art indeed able to corrupt a saint: thou hast done much harm upon me, Hal, God forgive thee for it. Before I knew thee, Hal, I knew nothing, and now am I, if a man should speak truly, little better than one of the wicked: I must give over this life, and I *will* give it over. By the Lord, and I do not,[5] I am a villain. I'll be damned for never a king's 90 son in Christendom.

HAL   Where shall we take a purse tomorrow, Jack?

FALSTAFF   Zounds, where thou wilt, lad; I'll make one; an I do not, call me a villain and baffle me.

HAL   I see a good amendment of life in thee, from praying to purse-taking.

FALSTAFF   Why Hal, 'tis my vocation, Hal; 'tis no sin for a man to labour in his vocation.[6]

Enter POINS.

Poins! Now shall we know if Gadshill have set a match. O, if men were to be saved by merit, what hole in hell 100 were hot enough for him? This is the most omnipotent villain that ever cried 'Stand!' to a true man.

HAL   Good morrow, Ned.

POINS   Good morrow, sweet Hal. – What says Monsieur Remorse? What says Sir John, sack-and-sugar Jack? How agrees the devil and thee about thy soul, that thou soldest him on Good Friday last, for a cup of Madeira and a cold capon's leg?

HAL   Sir John stands to his word, the devil shall have his bargain, for he was never yet a breaker of proverbs: he 110 will give the devil his due.

POINS   Then art thou damned for keeping thy word with the
             devil.

HAL   Else he had been damned for cozening the devil.

POINS   But my lads, my lads, tomorrow morning, by four
             o'clock early, at Gad's Hill, there are pilgrims going to
             Canterbury with rich offerings, and traders riding to
             London with fat purses. I have vizards for you all; you
             have horses for yourselves; Gadshill lies tonight in
             Rochester. I have bespoke supper tomorrow night   120
             in Eastcheap. We may do it as secure as sleep. If you
             will go, I will stuff your purses full of crowns; if
             you will not, tarry at home and be hanged.

FALSTAFF   Hear ye, Yedward, if I tarry at home and go not, I'll
             hang you for going.

POINS   You will, chops?

FALSTAFF   Hal, wilt thou make one?

HAL   Who? I rob, I a thief? Not I, by my faith.

FALSTAFF   There's neither honesty, manhood, nor good fellow-
             ship in thee, nor thou cam'st not of the blood royal, if   130
             thou darest not stand for ten shillings.

HAL   Well then, once in my days I'll be a madcap.

FALSTAFF   Why, that's well said.

HAL   Well, come what will, I'll tarry at home.

FALSTAFF   By the Lord, I'll be a traitor then, when thou art King.

HAL   I care not.

POINS   Sir John, I prithee leave the Prince and me alone. I
             will lay him down such reasons for this adventure that
             he shall go.

FALSTAFF   Well, God give thee the spirit of persuasion, and him   140
             the ears of profiting, that what thou speakest may
             move, and what he hears may be believed, that the
             true prince may (for recreation sake) prove a false
             thief, for the poor abuses of the time want counten-
             ance. Farewell, you shall find me in Eastcheap.

HAL   Farewell, the latter spring; farewell, All-hallow
             summer.[7]   [Exit Falstaff.

POINS   Now, my good sweet honey Lord, ride with us to-
             morrow. I have a jest to execute that I cannot manage
             alone. Falstaff, Bardolph, Peto and Gadshill shall rob   150

those men that we have already waylaid; yourself and I
will not be there; and when they have the booty, if
you and I do not rob them, cut this head off from my
shoulders.

HAL   How shall we part with them in setting forth?

POINS   Why, we will set forth before or after them, and
appoint them a place of meeting, wherein it is at our
pleasure to fail; and then will they adventure upon the
exploit themselves, which they shall have no sooner
achieved but we'll set upon them.   160

HAL   Yea, but 'tis like that they will know us by our horses,
by our habits, and by every other appointment, to be
ourselves.

POINS   Tut, our horses they shall not see, I'll tie them in the
wood; our vizards we will change after we leave them;
and, sirrah, I have cases of buckram for the nonce, to
immask our noted outward garments.

HAL   Yea, but I doubt they will be too hard for us.

POINS   Well, for two of them, I know them to be as true-bred
cowards as ever turned back; and for the third, if he   170
fight longer than he sees reason, I'll forswear arms.
The virtue of this jest will be the incomprehensible lies
that this same fat rogue will tell us when we meet at
supper: how thirty at least he fought with, what wards,
what blows, what extremities he endured; and in the
reproof of this lives the jest.

HAL   Well, I'll go with thee. Provide us all things necessary,
and meet me tomorrow night in Eastcheap. There I'll
sup. Farewell.

POINS   Farewell, my Lord.   [*Exit.* 180

HAL   I know you all, and will awhile uphold
The unyoked humour of your idleness.
Yet herein will I imitate the sun,
Who doth permit the base contagious clouds
To smother up his beauty from the world,
That when he please again to be himself,
Being wanted, he may be more wondered at,
By breaking through the foul and ugly mists
Of vapours that did seem to strangle him.

If all the year were playing holidays,   190
To sport would be as tedious as to work;
But when they seldom come, they wished-for come,
And nothing pleaseth but rare accidents:
So when this loose behaviour I throw off,
And pay the debt I never promisèd,
By how much better than my word I am,
By so much shall I falsify men's hopes.
And like bright metal on a sullen ground,
My reformation, glitt'ring o'er my fault,
Shall show more goodly, and attract more eyes   200
Than that which hath no foil to set it off.
I'll so offend, to make offence a skill,
Redeeming time when men think least I will.   [*Exit.*

SCENE 3.

Windsor: the Council Chamber.

Enter KING HENRY, NORTHUMBERLAND, WORCESTER, HOTSPUR,
SIR WALTER BLUNT *and other* LORDS.

K. HENRY   [*to Worcester, Northumberland and Hotspur:*]
My blood hath been too cold and temperate,
Unapt to stir at these indignities,
And you have found me: for accordingly
You tread upon my patience. But be sure
I will from henceforth rather be myself,
Mighty, and to be feared, than my condition,
Which hath been smooth as oil, soft as young down,
And therefore lost that title of respect
Which the proud soul ne'er pays but to the proud.

WOR'STER   Our house, my sovereign liege, little deserves   10
The scourge of greatness to be used on it,
And that same greatness, too, which our own hands
Have helped to make so portly.

NORTH.   My Lord –

K. HENRY   Worcester, get thee gone, for I do see
Danger and disobedience in thine eye:
O sir, your presence is too bold and peremptory,

And majesty might never yet endure
The moody frontier of a servant brow.
You have good leave to leave us. When we need
Your use and counsel, we shall send for you.   20

          [*Exit Worcester.*

[*To Northumberland :*] You were about to speak.

NORTH.   Yea, my good Lord.
Those prisoners in your Highness' name demanded,
Which Harry Percy here at Holmedon took,
Were, as he says, not with such strength denied
As is delivered to your Majesty.
Either envy therefore, or misprision,
Is guilty of this fault, and not my son.

HOTSPUR My liege, I did deny no prisoners;
But I remember, when the fight was done,
When I was dry with rage and extreme toil,   30
Breathless and faint, leaning upon my sword,
Came there a certain lord, neat and trimly dressed,
Fresh as a bridegroom, and his chin, new reaped,
Showed like a stubble-land at harvest-home.
He was perfumèd like a milliner,
And 'twixt his finger and his thumb he held
A pouncet-box, which ever and anon
He gave his nose, and took't away again,
Who therewith angry, when it next came there,
Took it in snuff; and still he smiled and talked;   40
And as the soldiers bore dead bodies by,
He called them untaught knaves, unmannerly,
To bring a slovenly unhandsome corse
Betwixt the wind and his nobility.
With many holiday and lady terms
He questioned me; amongst the rest demanded
My prisoners in your Majesty's behalf.
I then, all smarting with my wounds being cold,
– To be so pestered with a popinjay! –
Out of my grief and my impatience   50
Answered neglectingly, I know not what,
He should, or he should not, for he made me mad
To see him shine so brisk, and smell so sweet,

And talk so like a waiting gentlewoman
Of guns, and drums, and wounds, God save the mark!
And telling me the sovereign'st thing on earth
Was parmacity for an inward bruise,
And that it was great pity, so it was,
This villainous saltpetre should be digged
Out of the bowels of the harmless earth,   60
Which many a good tall fellow had destroyed
So cowardly, and but for these vile guns
He would himself have been a soldier.
This bald unjointed chat of his, my Lord,
I answered indirectly, as I said,
And I beseech you, let not his report
Come current for an accusation
Betwixt my love and your high Majesty.

BLUNT   The circumstance considered, good my Lord,
Whate'er Lord Harry Percy then had said   70
To such a person, and in such a place,
At such a time, with all the rest retold,
May reasonably die, and never rise
To do him wrong, or any way impeach
What then he said, so he unsay it now.

K. HENRY   Why, yet he doth deny his prisoners,
But with proviso and exception,
That we at our own charge shall ransom straight
His brother-in-law, the foolish Mortimer,
Who, on my soul, hath wilfully betrayed   80
The lives of those that he did lead to fight
Against that great magician, damned Glendower,
Whose daughter, as we hear, that Earl of March
Hath lately married. Shall our coffers then
Be emptied, to redeem a traitor home?
Shall we buy treason, and indent with fears
When they have lost and forfeited themselves?
No, on the barren mountains let him starve:
For I shall never hold that man my friend,
Whose tongue shall ask me for one penny cost   90
To ransom home revolted Mortimer.

HOTSPUR   'Revolted Mortimer'?

He never did fall off, my sovereign liege,
But by the chance of war. To prove that true
Needs no more but one tongue for all those wounds,
Those mouthèd wounds, which valiantly he took,
When on the gentle Severn's sedgy bank,
In single opposition, hand to hand,
He did confound the best part of an hour
In changing hardiment with great Glendower.   100
Three times they breathed, and three times did
                                        they drink,
Upon agreement, of swift Severn's flood,
Who then, affrighted with their bloody looks,
Ran fearfully among the trembling reeds,
And hid his crisp head in the hollow bank,
Bloodstainèd with these valiant combatants.
Never did bare and rotten policy
Colour her working with such deadly wounds,
Nor never could the noble Mortimer
Receive so many, and all willingly.   110
Then let not him be slandered with revolt.

K. HENRY   Thou dost belie him, Percy, thou dost belie him:
He never did encounter with Glendower.
I tell thee, he durst as well have met the devil
Alone, as Owen Glendower for an enemy.
Art thou not ashamed? But sirrah, henceforth
Let me not hear you speak of Mortimer.
Send me your prisoners with the speediest means,
Or you shall hear in such a kind from me
As will displease you. – My Lord Northumberland: 120
We license your departure with your son.
– Send us your prisoners, or you will hear of it.
          [*Exeunt all but Hotspur and Northumberland.*

HOTSPUR   And if the devil come and roar for them,
I will not send them: I will after straight
And tell him so, for I will ease my heart,
Albeit I make a hazard of my head.

NORTH.   What? Drunk with choler? Stay, and pause awhile;
Here comes your uncle.

                    Enter WORCESTER.

HOTSPUR   Speak of Mortimer?
        Zounds, I will speak of him, and let my soul
        Want mercy if I do not join with him: 130
        Yea, on his part I'll empty all these veins,
        And shed my dear blood, drop by drop in the dust,
        But I will lift the down-trod Mortimer
        As high in the air as this unthankful King,
        As this ingrate and cankered Bullingbrooke.
NORTH. Brother, the King hath made your nephew mad.
WOR'STER Who struck this heat up after I was gone?
HOTSPUR He will forsooth have all my prisoners,
        And when I urged the ransom once again
        Of my wife's brother, then his cheek looked pale,   140
        And on my face he turned an eye of death,
        Trembling even at the name of Mortimer.
WOR'STER I cannot blame him: was not he proclaimed,
        By Richard that dead is, the next of blood?
NORTH. He was; I heard the proclamation;
        And then it was, when the unhappy King
        (Whose wrongs in us God pardon!) did set forth
        Upon his Irish expedition;
        From whence he, intercepted, did return,
        To be deposed, and shortly murderèd.   150
WOR'STER And for whose death, we in the world's wide mouth
        Live scandalized and foully spoken of.
HOTSPUR But soft, I pray you: did King Richard then
        Proclaim my brother, Edmund Mortimer,
        Heir to the crown?
NORTH.   He did, myself did hear it.
HOTSPUR Nay then, I cannot blame his cousin King
        That wished him on the barren mountains starve.
        But shall it be that you that set the crown
        Upon the head of this forgetful man,
        And for his sake wear the detested blot   160
        Of murderous subornation – shall it be
        That you a world of curses undergo,
        Being the agents, or base second means,
        The cords, the ladder, or the hangman rather?
        O pardon me, that I descend so low,

To show the line and the predicament
Wherein you range under this subtle King!
Shall it for shame be spoken in these days,
Or fill up chronicles in time to come,
That men of your nobility and power   170
Did gage them both in an unjust behalf
(As both of you, God pardon it, have done)
To put down Richard, that sweet lovely rose,
And plant this thorn, this canker Bullingbrooke?
And shall it in more shame be further spoken,
That you are fooled, discarded, and shook off
By him for whom these shames ye underwent?
No; yet time serves, wherein you may redeem
Your banished honours, and restore yourselves
Into the good thoughts of the world again: 180
Revenge the jeering and disdained contempt
Of this proud King, who studies day and night
To answer all the debt he owes to you,
Even with the bloody payment of your deaths.
Therefore, I say —

WOR'STER   Peace, cousin, say no more.
And now I will unclasp a secret book,
And to your quick-conceiving discontents
I'll read you matter deep and dangerous,
As full of peril and adventurous spirit
As to o'er-walk a current roaring loud   190
On the unsteadfast footing of a spear.

HOTSPUR   If he fall in, good night, or sink, or swim!
Send danger from the east unto the west,
So honour cross it from the north to south,
And let them grapple: O, the blood more stirs
To rouse a lion than to start a hare!

NORTH.   [to Worcester:] Imagination of some great exploit
Drives him beyond the bounds of patience.

HOTSPUR   By heaven, methinks it were an easy leap
To pluck bright honour from the pale-faced moon,   200
Or dive into the bottom of the deep,
Where fathom-line could never touch the ground,
And pluck up drownèd honour by the locks,

So he that doth redeem her thence might wear
Without corrival all her dignities.
But out upon this half-faced fellowship!

WOR'STER   [*to North.:*] He apprehends a world of figures here,
But not the form of what he should attend.
– Good cousin, give me audience for a while.

HOTSPUR   I cry you mercy.

WOR'STER   Those same noble Scots   210
That are your prisoners –

HOTSPUR   I'll keep them all!
By God, he shall not have a Scot of them;
No, if a scot would save his soul, he shall not.
I'll keep them, by this hand!

WOR'STER   You start away,
And lend no ear unto my purposes.
Those prisoners you shall keep –

HOTSPUR   Nay, I will: that's flat!
He said he would not ransom Mortimer,
Forbade my tongue to speak of Mortimer;
But I will find him when he lies asleep,
And in his ear I'll hollow 'Mortimer!' –   220
Nay, I'll have a starling shall be taught to speak
Nothing but 'Mortimer', and give it him
To keep his anger still in motion.

WOR'STER   Hear you, cousin, a word.

HOTSPUR   All studies here I solemnly defy,
Save how to gall and pinch this Bullingbrooke.
And that same sword-and-buckler Prince of Wales –
But that I think his father loves him not
And would be glad he met with some mischance –
I would have him poisoned with a pot of ale.   230

WOR'STER   Farewell, kinsman. I'll talk to you
When you are better tempered to attend.

NORTH.   [*to Hotspur:*] Why, what a wasp-stung and
                                        impatient fool
Art thou to break into this woman's mood,
Tying thine ear to no tongue but thine own!

HOTSPUR   Why, look you, I am whipped and scourged with rods,
Nettled, and stung with pismires, when I hear

Of this vile politician Bullingbrooke.
In Richard's time – what do you call the place?
A plague upon it, it is in Gloucestershire;   240
'Twas where the madcap Duke his uncle kept,
His uncle York, where I first bowed my knee
Unto this king of smiles, this Bullingbrooke –
'Sblood, when you and he came back from
                                        Ravenspurgh –

NORTH.   At Berkeley Castle.

HOTSPUR   You say true.
Why, what a candy deal of courtesy
This fawning greyhound then did proffer me.[8]
'Look when his infant fortune came to age',
And 'gentle Harry Percy', and 'kind cousin':   250
O, the devil take such cozeners, God forgive me!
Good uncle, tell your tale; I have done.

WOR'STER   Nay, if you have not, to it again,
We'll stay your leisure.

HOTSPUR   I have done, i'faith.

WOR'STER   Then once more to your Scottish prisoners:
Deliver them up without their ransom straight;
And make the Douglas' son your only mean
For powers in Scotland, which, for divers reasons
Which I shall send you written, be assured
Will easily be granted.
[To Northumberland:]   You, my Lord,   260
Your son in Scotland being thus employed,
Shall secretly into the bosom creep
Of that same noble prelate well-beloved,
The Archbishop.

HOTSPUR   Of York, is't not?

WOR'STER   True, who bears hard
His brother's death at Bristow, the Lord Scroop.
I speak not this in estimation,
As what I think might be, but what I know
Is ruminated, plotted, and set down,
And only stays but to behold the face
Of that occasion that shall bring it on.   270

HOTSPUR   I smell it. Upon my life, it will do well!

NORTH.   Before the game is afoot thou still lett'st slip.

HOTSPUR   Why, it cannot choose but be a noble plot;
And then the power of Scotland, and of York,
To join with Mortimer, ha?

WOR'STER   And so they shall.

HOTSPUR   In faith, it is exceedingly well aimed.

WOR'STER   And 'tis no little reason bids us speed,
To save our heads by raising of a head:
For, bear ourselves as even as we can,
The King will always think him in our debt,   280
And think we think ourselves unsatisfied,
Till he hath found a time to pay us home.
And see already how he doth begin
To make us strangers to his looks of love.

HOTSPUR   He does, he does; we'll be revenged on him.

WOR'STER   Cousin, farewell. No further go in this
Than I by letters shall direct your course.
When time is ripe, which will be suddenly,
I'll steal to Glendower, and Lord Mortimer,
Where you, and Douglas, and our powers at once,   290
As I will fashion it, shall happily meet,
To bear our fortunes in our own strong arms,
Which now we hold at much uncertainty.

NORTH.   Farewell, good brother. We shall thrive, I trust.

HOTSPUR   Uncle, adieu. O, let the hours be short,
Till fields, and blows, and groans applaud our sport!

                                        [*Exeunt.*

Rochester, Kent: an inn-yard.

Enter a CARRIER *with a lantern in his hand.*

CARRIER 1 Heigh-ho! An it be not four by the day, I'll be hanged. Charles's Wain is over the new chimney, and yet our horse not packed. – What, ostler!

OSTLER [*within:*] Anon, anon.

CARRIER 1 I prithee, Tom, beat Cut's saddle, put a few flocks in the point; poor jade is wrung in the withers out of all cess.

Enter another CARRIER.

CARRIER 2 Peas and beans are as dank here as a dog, and that is the next way to give poor jades the bots. This house is turned upside down since Robin Ostler died.

CARRIER 1 Poor fellow never joyed since the price of oats rose: it 10 was the death of him.

CARRIER 2 I think this be the most villainous house in all London road for fleas: I am stung like a tench.

CARRIER 1 'Like a tench'? By the Mass, there is ne'er a king Christen could be better bit than I have been since the first cock.

CARRIER 2 Why, they will allow us ne'er a jordan, and then we leak in your chimney, and your chamber-lye breeds fleas like a loach.

CARRIER 1 What, ostler! Come away and be hanged; come away! 20

CARRIER 2 I have a gammon of bacon, and two razes of ginger, to be delivered as far as Charing Cross.

CARRIER 1 God's body! The turkeys in my pannier are quite starved. – What, ostler! A plague on thee, hast thou never an eye in thy head? Canst not hear? And 'twere not as good deed as drink to break the pate on thee, I am a very villain. Come, and be hanged! Hast no faith in thee?

Enter GADSHILL.

GADSHILL Good morrow, carriers, what's o'clock?

CARRIER 1 I think it be two o'clock. 30

GADSHILL I prithee lend me thy lantern, to see my gelding in the
          stable.

CARRIER 1 Nay, by God, soft! I know a trick worth two of that,
          i'faith.

GADSHILL [to carrier 2:] I pray thee lend me thine.

CARRIER 2 Ay, when? Canst tell? – Lend me thy lantern, quoth
          he! – Marry, I'll see thee hanged first.

GADSHILL Sirrah carrier, what time do you mean to come to
          London?

CARRIER 2 Time enough to go to bed with a candle, I warrant 40
          thee. – Come, neighbour Mugs, we'll call up the gentle-
          men: they will along with company, for they have great
          charge.   [Exeunt carriers.

GADSHILL What ho! Chamberlain!

                 Enter CHAMBERLAIN.

CHAMBER. 'At hand, quoth pick-purse.'

GADSHILL That's even as fair as 'At hand, quoth the chamberlain',
          for thou variest no more from picking of purses than
          giving direction doth from labouring: thou layest the
          plot how.

CHAMBER. Good morrow, Master Gadshill. It holds current that I 50
          told you yesternight. There's a franklin in the Weald of
          Kent hath brought three hundred marks with him in
          gold: I heard him tell it to one of his company last
          night at supper, a kind of auditor, one that hath
          abundance of charge too, God knows what. They are
          up already, and call for eggs and butter. They will
          away presently.

GADSHILL Sirrah, if they meet not with Saint Nicholas' clerks,[9]
          I'll give thee this neck.

CHAMBER. No, I'll none of it: I pray thee keep that for the 60
          hangman, for I know thou worshippest Saint Nicholas
          as truly as a man of falsehood may.

GADSHILL What talkest thou to me of the hangman? If I hang, I'll
          make a fat pair of gallows, for if I hang, old Sir John
          hangs with me, and thou knowest he is no starveling.
          Tut, there are other Troyans that thou dream'st not
          of, the which for sport sake are content to do the

profession some grace, that would (if matters should be
looked into) for their own credit sake make all whole.
I am joined with no foot-landrakers, no long-staff 70
sixpenny strikers, none of these mad mustachio purple-
hued maltworms,[10] but with nobility and tranquillity,
burgomasters and great one-yers,[11] such as can hold in,
such as will strike sooner than speak, and speak sooner
than drink, and drink sooner than pray. And yet,
(zounds) I lie, for they pray continually to their saint,
the commonwealth, or rather not pray to her, but
prey on her, for they ride up and down on her, and
make her their boots.

CHAMBER.   What, the commonwealth their boots? Will she hold 80
out water in foul way?

GADSHILL   She will, she will; justice hath liquored her: we steal as
in a castle, cock-sure; we have the receipt of fern-
seed,[12] we walk invisible.

CHAMBER.   Nay, by my faith, I think you are more beholding to
the night than to fern-seed for your walking invisible.

GADSHILL   Give me thy hand; thou shalt have a share in our
purchase, as I am a true man.

CHAMBER.   Nay, rather let me have it as you are a false thief.

GADSHILL   Go to, 'homo' is a common name to all men.[13] Bid the 90
ostler bring my gelding out of the stable. Farewell, you
muddy knave.   [Exeunt.

SCENE 2.

Gad's Hill: the road.

Enter the PRINCE (HAL), POINS *and* PETO.

POINS   Come, shelter, shelter! I have removed Falstaff's horse,
and he frets like a gummed velvet.[14]

HAL   Stand close!   [*They hide.*[15]

Enter FALSTAFF.

FALSTAFF   Poins, Poins, and be hanged! Poins!

HAL   [*coming forward:*] Peace, ye fat-kidneyed rascal; what a
brawling dost thou keep!

FALSTAFF   Where's Poins, Hal?

HAL   He is walked up to the top of the hill. I'll go seek him.
                                                    [*He withdraws.*

FALSTAFF   I am accursed to rob in that thief's company. The rascal
           hath removed my horse and tied him I know not   10
           where. If I travel but four foot by the square further
           afoot, I shall break my wind. Well, I doubt not but to
           die a fair death for all this, if I scape hanging for killing
           that rogue. I have forsworn his company hourly any
           time this two-and-twenty years, and yet I am be-
           witched with the rogue's company. If the rascal have
           not given me medicines to make me love him, I'll be
           hanged. It could not be else: I have drunk medicines.
           Poins! Hal! A plague upon you both! Bardolph! Peto!
           I'll starve ere I'll rob a foot further. And 'twere not as 20
           good a deed as drink to turn true man, and to leave
           these rogues, I am the veriest varlet that ever chewed
           with a tooth. Eight yards of uneven ground is three-
           score-and-ten miles afoot with me, and the stony-
           hearted villains know it well enough. A plague upon it,
           when thieves cannot be true one to another!

           Having whistled, enter the PRINCE (HAL), POINS *and* PETO.

           Whew! A plague upon you all. Give me my horse,
           you rogues, give me my horse and be hanged!

HAL   Peace, ye fat-guts; lie down, lay thine ear close to
           the ground, and list if thou canst hear the tread of 30
           travellers.

FALSTAFF   Have you any levers to lift me up again, being down?
           'Sblood, I'll not bear my own flesh so far afoot again
           for all the coin in thy father's exchequer. What a
           plague mean ye to colt me thus?

HAL   Thou liest: thou art not colted, thou art uncolted.

FALSTAFF   I prithee, good Prince Hal, help me to my horse, good
           king's son.

HAL   Out, ye rogue; shall I be your ostler?

FALSTAFF   Hang thyself in thine own heir-apparent garters! If I be 40
           tane, I'll peach for this. And I have not ballads made
           on you all, and sung to filthy tunes, let a cup of sack be
           my poison. When a jest is so forward – and afoot too!
           I hate it.

Enter GADSHILL, *wearing a mask, and* BARDOLPH.

GADSHILL   Stand!

FALSTAFF   So I do, against my will.

POINS   O, 'tis our setter: I know his voice. – Bardolph, what news?

BARDOLPH   Case ye, case ye; on with your vizards; there's money of the King's coming down the hill; 'tis going to the King's exchequer.   50

FALSTAFF   You lie, ye rogue: 'tis going to the King's tavern.

GADSHILL   There's enough to make us all –

FALSTAFF   To be hanged.   [*They don masks.*

HAL   Sirs, you four shall front them in the narrow lane. Ned Poins and I will walk lower. If they scape from your encounter, then they light on us.

PETO   How many be there of them?

GADSHILL   Some eight or ten.

FALSTAFF   Zounds, will they not rob *us*?   60

HAL   What, a coward, Sir John Paunch?

FALSTAFF   Indeed, I am not John of Gaunt, your grandfather; but yet no coward, Hal.

HAL   Well, we leave that to the proof.

POINS   Sirrah Jack, thy horse stands behind the hedge. When thou need'st him, there thou shalt find him. Farewell, and stand fast!

FALSTAFF   Now cannot I strike him, if I should be hanged.

HAL   [*aside to Poins:*] Ned, where are our disguises?

POINS   [*aside to Hal:*] Here, hard by, stand close.   70

                              [*Exeunt the Prince and Poins.*

FALSTAFF   Now, my masters, happy man be his dole,[16] say I. Every man to his business.   [*They hide.*

Enter the TRAVELLERS.

TRAV. 1   Come, neighbour: the boy shall lead our horses down the hill; we'll walk afoot awhile and ease our legs.

THIEVES   [*emerging:*] Stand!

TRAV. 2   Jesus bless us!

FALSTAFF   Strike, down with them, cut the villains' throats! Ah, whoreson caterpillars, bacon-fed knaves, they hate us youth! Down with them, fleece them!

TRAV. I   O, we are undone, both we and ours for ever!   80
FALSTAFF   Hang ye, gorbellied knaves, are ye undone? No, ye fat
           chuffs, I would your store were here! On, bacons, on!
           What, ye knaves, young men must live! You are grand-
           jurors, are ye? We'll jure ye, faith.
                        [*Here they rob them and bind them. Exeunt.*

Enter the PRINCE *and* POINS, *disguised in masks and buckram suits.*

HAL   The thieves have bound the true men. Now, could
           thou and I rob the thieves, and go merrily to London,
           it would be argument for a week, laughter for a month,
           and a good jest for ever.
POINS   Stand close, I hear them coming.   [*They hide.*

Enter FALSTAFF, BARDOLPH, GADSHILL *and* PETO.

FALSTAFF   Come my masters, let us share, and then to horse   90
           before day. And the Prince and Poins be not two
           arrant cowards, there's no equity stirring. There's no
           more valour in that Poins than in a wild duck.
                        [*As they are sharing, the Prince and Poins set upon them.*
HAL   Your money!
POINS   Villains!
                        [*Bardolph, Gadshill and Peto run away, and Falstaff,
                                  after a blow or two, runs away, roaring,
                                              leaving the booty behind.*
HAL   Got with much ease. Now merrily to horse.
           The thieves are all scattered, and possessed with fear
           So strongly that they dare not meet each other.
           Each takes his fellow for an officer.
           Away, good Ned! Falstaff sweats to death,   100
           And lards the lean earth as he walks along:
           Were't not for laughing, I should pity him.
POINS   How the fat rogue roared!   [*Exeunt with the booty.*

SCENE 3.

Northumberland: Warkworth Castle.

Enter HOTSPUR, *reading a letter.*

HOTSPUR   'But, for mine own part, my Lord, I could be well
contented to be there, in respect of the love I bear
your house.'
He 'could be contented'! Why is he not, then? In
respect of the love he bears our house? He shows in
this, he loves his own barn better than he loves our
house. Let me see some more.
'The purpose you undertake is dangerous.'
Why, that's certain: 'tis dangerous to take a cold, to
sleep, to drink; but I tell you, my Lord Fool, out of   10
this nettle, danger, we pluck this flower, safety.
'The purpose you undertake is dangerous, the friends
you have named uncertain, the time itself unsorted, and
your whole plot too light for the counterpoise of so
great an opposition.'
Say you so, say you so? I say unto you again, you are a
shallow cowardly hind, and you lie. What a lack-brain
is this! By the Lord, our plot is a good plot, as ever was
laid, our friends true and constant; a good plot, good
friends, and full of expectation; an excellent plot, very   20
good friends. What a frosty-spirited rogue is this! Why,
my Lord of York commends the plot, and the general
course of the action. Zounds, and I were now by this
rascal, I could brain him with his lady's fan. Is there
not my father, my uncle, and myself; Lord Edmund
Mortimer, my Lord of York, and Owen Glendower?
Is there not, besides, the Douglas? Have I not all their
letters to meet me in arms by the ninth of the next
month, and are they not some of them set forward
already? What a pagan rascal is this, an infidel! Ha, you   30
shall see now, in very sincerity of fear and cold heart
will he to the King, and lay open all our proceedings!
O, I could divide myself, and go to buffets, for moving
such a dish of skim milk with so honourable an action!

Hang him, let him tell the King; we are prepared. I
will set forward tonight.

Enter LADY PERCY.

How now, Kate? I must leave you within these two
hours.

L. PERCY   O my good Lord, why are you thus alone?
For what offence have I this fortnight been   40
A banished woman from my Harry's bed?
Tell me, sweet Lord, what is't that takes from thee
Thy stomach, pleasure, and thy golden sleep?
Why dost thou bend thine eyes upon the earth,
And start so often when thou sitt'st alone?
Why hast thou lost the fresh blood in thy cheeks,
And given my treasures and my rights of thee
To thick-eyed musing, and curst melancholy?
In thy faint slumbers I by thee have watched,
And heard thee murmur tales of iron wars,   50
Speak terms of manage to thy bounding steed,
Cry 'Courage! To the field!'. And thou hast talked
Of sallies, and retires, of trenches, tents,
Of palisadoes, frontiers, parapets,
Of basilisks, of cannon, culverin,[17]
Of prisoners' ransom, and of soldiers slain,
And all the currents of a heady fight.
Thy spirit within thee hath been so at war,
And thus hath so bestirred thee in thy sleep,
That beads of sweat have stood upon thy brow   60
Like bubbles in a late-disturbèd stream;
And in thy face strange motions have appeared,
Such as we see when men restrain their breath
On some great sudden hest. O, what portents are these?
Some heavy business hath my Lord in hand,
And I must know it, else he loves me not.

HOTSPUR   – What ho!

Enter a SERVANT.

Is Gilliams with the packet gone?

SERVANT   He is, my Lord, an hour ago.

HOTSPUR   Hath Butler brought those horses from the sheriff?

SERVANT	One horse, my Lord, he brought even now. 70
HOTSPUR	What horse? A roan, a crop-ear, is it not?
SERVANT	It is, my Lord.
HOTSPUR	That roan shall be my throne.
	Well, I will back him straight. O Esperance![18]
	Bid Butler lead him forth into the park. [*Exit servant.*
L. PERCY	But hear you, my Lord.
HOTSPUR	What say'st thou, my Lady?
L. PERCY	What is it carries you away?
HOTSPUR	Why, my horse, my love, my horse.
L. PERCY	Out, you mad-headed ape!
	A weasel hath not such a deal of spleen 80
	As you are tossed with. In faith,
	I'll know your business, Harry, that I will.
	I fear my brother Mortimer doth stir
	About his title, and hath sent for you
	To line his enterprise; but if you go –
HOTSPUR	So far afoot, I shall be weary, love.
L. PERCY	Come, come, you paraquito, answer me
	Directly unto this question that I ask.
	In faith, I'll break thy little finger, Harry,
	And if thou wilt not tell me all things true. 90
HOTSPUR	Away,
	Away, you trifler! Love? I love thee not,
	I care not for thee, Kate: this is no world
	To play with mammets, and to tilt with lips;
	We must have bloody noses, and cracked crowns,
	And pass them current too. – God's me! My horse!
	– What sayst thou, Kate? What wouldst thou have
	with me?
L. PERCY	Do you not love me? Do you not indeed?
	Well, do not then, for since you love me not,
	I will not love myself. Do you not love me? 100
	Nay, tell me if you speak in jest or no?
HOTSPUR	Come, wilt thou see me ride?
	And when I am a-horseback, I will swear
	I love thee infinitely. But hark you, Kate,
	I must not have you henceforth question me
	Whither I go, nor reason whereabout:

Whither I must, I must; and, to conclude,
This evening must I leave you, gentle Kate.
I know you wise, but yet no farther wise
Than Harry Percy's wife. Constant you are,   110
But yet a woman; and for secrecy,
No lady closer, for I well believe
Thou wilt not utter – what thou dost not know.
And so far will I trust thee, gentle Kate.

L. PERCY   How? So far?

HOTSPUR   Not an inch further. But hark you, Kate,
Whither I go, thither shall you go too.
Today will I set forth, tomorrow you.
Will this content you, Kate?

L. PERCY   It must, of force.

[*Exeunt.*

SCENE 4.

London: Eastcheap: a tavern.

Enter the PRINCE (HAL).

HAL   Ned, prithee come out of that fat room, and lend me
thy hand to laugh a little.

Enter POINS, *by another door.*

POINS   Where hast been, Hal?

HAL   With three or four loggerheads, amongst three- or four-
score hogsheads. I have sounded the very bass-string of
humility. Sirrah, I am sworn brother to a leash of
drawers, and can call them all by their Christen names,
as 'Tom', 'Dick', and 'Francis'. They take it already
upon their salvation that though I be but Prince of
Wales, yet I am the King of Courtesy, and tell me flatly   10
I am no proud Jack like Falstaff, but a Corinthian, a lad
of mettle, a good boy (by the Lord, so they call me!),
and when I am King of England I shall command all the
good lads in Eastcheap. They call drinking deep 'dyeing
scarlet', and when you breathe in your watering they
cry 'Hem!' and bid you 'Play it off!'. To conclude, I

am so good a proficient in one quarter of an hour that
I can drink with any tinker in his own language during
my life. I tell thee, Ned, thou hast lost much honour
that thou wert not with me in this action. But, sweet   20
Ned – to sweeten which name of Ned I give thee this
pennyworth of sugar,[19] clapped even now into my
hand by an underskinker, one that never spake other
English in his life than 'Eight shillings and sixpence',
and 'You are welcome', with this shrill addition, 'Anon,
anon, sir! Score a pint of bastard in the Half-Moon!',
or so. But Ned, to drive away the time till Falstaff
come: I prithee do thou stand in some by-room, while
I question my puny drawer to what end he gave me
the sugar; and do thou never leave calling 'Francis!',   30
that his tale to me may be nothing but 'Anon!'. Step
aside, and I'll show thee a precedent.   [*Exit Poins.*

POINS	[*within:*] Francis!
HAL	Thou art perfect.
POINS	[*within:*] Francis!

Enter FRANCIS, *a drawer.*

FRANCIS	Anon, anon, sir. – Look down into the Pomgarnet, Ralph!
HAL	Come hither, Francis.
FRANCIS	My Lord?
HAL	How long hast thou to serve, Francis?
FRANCIS	Forsooth, five years, and as much as to – 40
POINS	[*within:*] Francis!
FRANCIS	Anon, anon, sir!
HAL	Five year! Birlady, a long lease for the clinking of pewter; but Francis, darest thou be so valiant as to play the coward with thy indenture, and show it a fair pair of heels, and run from it?
FRANCIS	O Lord, sir, I'll be sworn upon all the books in England, I could find in my heart –
POINS	[*within:*] Francis!
FRANCIS	Anon, sir! 50
HAL	How old art thou, Francis?
FRANCIS	Let me see, about Michaelmas next I shall be –
POINS	[*within:*] Francis!

FRANCIS	Anon, sir! – Pray stay a little, my Lord.
HAL	Nay but hark you, Francis: for the sugar thou gavest me – 'twas a pennyworth, was it not?
FRANCIS	O Lord, I would it had been two!
HAL	I will give thee for it a thousand pound: ask me when thou wilt, and thou shalt have it.
POINS	[*within:*] Francis!
FRANCIS	Anon, anon!
HAL	Anon, Francis? No, Francis, but tomorrow, Francis; or Francis, a Thursday; or indeed, Francis, when thou wilt. But Francis . . .
FRANCIS	My Lord?
HAL	Wilt thou rob this leathern-jerkin, crystal-button, not-pated, agate-ring, puke-stocking, caddis-garter, smooth-tongue Spanish pouch?[20]
FRANCIS	O Lord, sir, who do you mean?
HAL	Why then your brown bastard is your only drink; for look you, Francis, your white canvas doublet will sully. In Barbary, sir, it cannot come to so much.[21]
FRANCIS	What, sir?
POINS	[*within:*] Francis!
HAL	Away, you rogue, dost thou not hear them call?

60

70

> [*Here they both call him; Francis stands amazed, not knowing which way to go.*

Enter VINTNER.

VINTNER	What, stand'st thou still and hear'st such a calling? Look to the guests within. [*Exit Francis.*
	My Lord, old Sir John with half-a-dozen more are at the door: shall I let them in?
HAL	Let them alone awhile, and then open the door.
	[*Exit vintner.*
	Poins!

80

Enter POINS.

POINS	Anon, anon, sir!
HAL	Sirrah, Falstaff and the rest of the thieves are at the door. Shall we be merry?
POINS	As merry as crickets, my lad. But hark ye, what cunning

match have you made with this jest of the drawer?
Come, what's the issue?

HAL   I am now of all humours that have showed themselves
humours since the old days of goodman Adam to the
pupil age of this present twelve o'clock at midnight.   90

Enter FRANCIS.

What's o'clock, Francis?

FRANCIS Anon, anon, sir!   [*Exit.*
HAL   That ever this fellow should have fewer words than a
parrot, and yet the son of a woman! His industry is up-
stairs and down-stairs, his eloquence the parcel of a
reckoning. I am not yet of Percy's mind, the Hotspur
of the north, he that kills me some six or seven dozen
of Scots at a breakfast, washes his hands, and says to his
wife, 'Fie upon this quiet life; I want work.' 'O my
sweet Harry,' says she, 'how many hast thou killed   100
today?' 'Give my roan horse a drench,' says he, and
answers, 'Some fourteen,' an hour after; 'a trifle, a
trifle.' I prithee call in Falstaff. I'll play Percy, and that
damned brawn shall play Dame Mortimer his wife.
'Rivo!' says the drunkard.[22] Call in Ribs, call in Tallow!

Enter FALSTAFF (*with sword and buckler*), GADSHILL, BARDOLPH
and PETO; *followed by* FRANCIS, *bearing wine.*

POINS   Welcome, Jack, where hast thou been?
FALSTAFF A plague of all cowards, I say, and a vengeance too,
marry and amen! – Give me a cup of sack, boy. – Ere I
lead this life long, I'll sew nether-stocks, and mend them,
and foot them too. A plague of all cowards! – Give me a   110
cup of sack, rogue. – Is there no virtue extant?

                                        [*He drinks.*

HAL   Didst thou never see Titan kiss a dish of butter (pitiful-
hearted Titan!) that melted at the sweet tale of the
sun's? If thou didst, then behold that compound.
FALSTAFF [*to Francis:*] You rogue, here's lime in this sack too. [*To
the others:*] There is nothing but roguery to be found in
villainous man, yet a coward is worse than a cup of
sack with lime in it.[23] A villainous coward! Go thy
ways, old Jack, die when thou wilt. If manhood, good

manhood, be not forgot upon the face of the earth,   120
then am I a shotten herring. There lives not three
good men unhanged in England, and one of them is
fat, and grows old. God help the while; a bad world I
say. I would I were a weaver: I could sing psalms, or
anything.²⁴ A plague of all cowards, I say still.

HAL   How now, woolsack, what mutter you?

FALSTAFF   A king's son! If I do not beat thee out of thy kingdom
with a dagger of lath, and drive all thy subjects afore
thee like a flock of wild geese, I'll never wear hair on
my face more. You, Prince of Wales!   130

HAL   Why, you whoreson round man, what's the matter?

FALSTAFF   Are not you a coward? Answer me to that. And Poins
there?

POINS   Zounds, ye fat paunch, and ye call me coward, by the
Lord I'll stab thee.

FALSTAFF   I call thee coward? I'll see thee damned ere I call thee
coward; but I would give a thousand pound I could
run as fast as thou canst. You are straight enough in the
shoulders: you care not who sees your back. Call you
that 'backing' of your friends? A plague upon such   140
backing, give me them that will face me! Give me a
cup of sack. I am a rogue if I drunk today.

HAL   O villain! Thy lips are scarce wiped since thou drunk'st
last.

FALSTAFF   All is one for that. [*He drinks.*] A plague of all cowards,
still say I.

HAL   What's the matter?

FALSTAFF   What's the matter? There be four of us here have tane
a thousand pound this day morning.

HAL   Where is it, Jack, where is it?   150

FALSTAFF   'Where is it?' Taken from us it is: a hundred upon
poor four of us.

HAL   What, a hundred, man?

FALSTAFF   I am a rogue if I were not at half-sword with a dozen of
them two hours together. I have scaped by miracle. I
am eight times thrust through the doublet, four through
the hose, my buckler cut through and through, my
sword hacked like a handsaw: *ecce signum*. I never dealt

better since I was a man. All would not do. A plague of
all cowards! Let them speak. If they speak more or less 160
than truth, they are villains and the sons of darkness.

HAL   Speak, sirs, how was it?

GADSHILL   We four set upon some dozen –

FALSTAFF   Sixteen at least, my Lord.

GADSHILL   And bound them.

PETO   No, no, they were not bound.

FALSTAFF   You rogue, they were bound, every man of them, or I
am a Jew else: an Ebrew Jew.

GADSHILL   As we were sharing, some six or seven fresh men set
upon us –   170

FALSTAFF   And unbound the rest, and then come in the other.

HAL   What, fought you with them all?

FALSTAFF   All? I know not what you call 'all', but, if I fought not
with fifty of them, I am a bunch of radish. If there
were not two- or three-and-fifty upon poor old Jack,
then am I no two-legg'd creature.

HAL   Pray God you have not murdered some of them.

FALSTAFF   Nay, that's past praying for: I have peppered two of
them. Two I am sure I have paid, two rogues in
buckram suits. I tell thee what, Hal, if I tell thee a lie, 180
spit in my face, call me horse. Thou knowest my old
ward: here I lay, and thus I bore my point. Four rogues
in buckram let drive at me –

HAL   What, four? Thou saidst but two even now.

FALSTAFF   Four, Hal, I told thee four.

POINS   Ay, ay, he said four.

FALSTAFF   These four came all afront, and mainly thrust at me. I
made me no more ado, but took all their seven points
in my target, thus!

HAL   Seven? Why, there were but four even now.   190

FALSTAFF   In buckram?

POINS   Ay, four, in buckram suits.

FALSTAFF   Seven, by these hilts, or I am a villain else.

HAL   [aside to Poins:] Prithee let him alone; we shall have more
anon.

FALSTAFF   Dost thou hear me, Hal?

HAL   Ay, and mark thee too, Jack.

FALSTAFF   Do so, for it is worth the listening to. These nine in
           buckram that I told thee of –
HAL   So, two more already.   200
FALSTAFF   Their points being broken –
POINS   Down fell their hose.
FALSTAFF   – began to give me ground; but I followed me close,
           came in, foot and hand, and, with a thought, seven of
           the eleven I paid.
HAL   O monstrous! Eleven buckram men grown out of two!
FALSTAFF   But, as the devil would have it, three misbegotten
           knaves in Kendal green came at my back and let drive
           at me; for it was so dark, Hal, that thou couldst not see
           thy hand.   210
HAL   These lies are like their father that begets them, gross
           as a mountain, open, palpable. Why, thou clay-brained
           guts, thou knotty-pated fool, thou whoreson obscene
           greasy tallow-catch –
FALSTAFF   What, art thou mad? Art thou mad? Is not the truth
           the truth?
HAL   Why, how couldst thou know these men in Kendal
           green, when it was so dark thou couldst not see thy hand?
           Come, tell us your reason. What sayest thou to this?
POINS   Come, your reason, Jack, your reason!   220
FALSTAFF   What, upon compulsion? Zounds, and I were at the
           strappado, or all the racks in the world, I would not tell
           you on compulsion. Give you a reason on compulsion?
           If reasons were as plentiful as blackberries, I would give
           no man a reason upon compulsion, I.
HAL   I'll be no longer guilty of this sin. This sanguine
           coward, this bed-presser, this horse-back-breaker, this
           huge hill of flesh –
FALSTAFF   'Sblood, you starveling, you eel-skin, you dried neat's-
           tongue, you bull's-pizzle, you stock-fish! O for breath 230
           to utter what is like thee, you tailor's yard, you sheath,
           you bow-case, you vile standing tuck!
HAL   Well, breathe awhile, and then to it again, and when
           thou hast tired thyself in base comparisons, hear me
           speak but this.
POINS   Mark, Jack!

HAL	We two saw you four set on four, and bound them and were masters of their wealth. Mark now how a plain tale shall put you down. Then did we two set on you four, and, with a word, out-faced you from your prize, and have it, yea, and can show it you here in the house; and Falstaff, you carried your guts away as nimbly, with as quick dexterity, and roared for mercy, and still run and roared, as ever I heard bull-calf. What a slave art thou, to hack thy sword as thou hast done, and then say it was in fight! What trick, what device, what starting-hole canst thou now find out, to hide thee from this open and apparent shame?

240

POINS	Come, let's hear, Jack: what trick hast thou now?
FALSTAFF	By the Lord, I knew ye as well as he that made ye. Why, hear you, my masters, was it for me to kill the heir-apparent? Should I turn upon the true prince? Why, thou knowest I am as valiant as Hercules; but beware instinct: the lion will not touch the true prince:[25] instinct is a great matter. I was now a coward on instinct. I shall think the better of myself, and thee, during my life: I for a valiant lion, and thou for a true prince; but by the Lord, lads, I am glad you have the money. – Hostess, clap to the doors! – Watch tonight, pray tomorrow![26] Gallants, lads, boys, hearts of gold, all the titles of good fellowship come to you! What, shall we be merry? Shall we have a play extempore?

250

260

HAL	Content, and the argument shall be thy running away.
FALSTAFF	Ah, no more of that Hal, and thou lovest me.

Enter HOSTESS.

HOSTESS	O Jesu, my Lord the Prince!
HAL	How now, my Lady the Hostess, what say'st thou to me?
HOSTESS	Marry, my Lord, there is a nobleman of the court at door would speak with you: he says he comes from your father.
HAL	Give him as much as will make him a royal man,[27] and send him back again to my mother.

270

FALSTAFF	What manner of man is he?
HOSTESS	An old man.

FALSTAFF   What doth gravity out of his bed at midnight? Shall I
           give him his answer?

HAL   Prithee do, Jack.

FALSTAFF   Faith, and I'll send him packing.   [*Exit*.

HAL   Now, sirs, birlady, [*to Gadshill:*] you fought fair, – so
           did you, Peto, – so did you, Bardolph. You are lions
           too: you ran away upon instinct, you will not touch the   280
           true prince; no, fie!

BARDOLPH   Faith, I ran when I saw others run.

HAL   Faith, tell me now in earnest, how came Falstaff's sword
           so hacked?

PETO   Why, he hacked it with his dagger, and said he would
           swear truth out of England but he would make you
           believe it was done in fight, and persuaded us to do the
           like.

BARDOLPH   Yea, and to tickle our noses with spear-grass, to make
           them bleed, and then to beslubber our garments with   290
           it, and swear it was the blood of true men. I did that I
           did not this seven year before: I blushed to hear his
           monstrous devices.

HAL   O villain, thou stolest a cup of sack eighteen years ago,
           and wert taken with the manner, and ever since thou
           hast blushed extempore. Thou hadst fire and sword on
           thy side, and yet thou ran'st away. What 'instinct'
           hadst thou for it?

BARDOLPH   [*pointing to his face:*] My Lord, do you see these
           meteors? Do you behold these exhalations?   300

HAL   I do.

BARDOLPH   What think you they portend?

HAL   Hot livers, and cold purses.

BARDOLPH   Choler, my Lord, if rightly taken.

HAL   No, if rightly taken, halter.[28]

                    Enter FALSTAFF.

           Here comes lean Jack, here comes bare-bone. – How
           now, my sweet creature of bombast? How long is't
           ago, Jack, since thou sawest thine own knee?

FALSTAFF   My own knee? When I was about thy years, Hal, I was
           not an eagle's talon in the waist: I could have crept into   310

any alderman's thumb-ring. A plague of sighing and grief, it blows a man up like a bladder. There's villainous news abroad. Here was Sir John Bracy from your father: you must to the court in the morning. That same mad fellow of the north, Percy, and he of Wales that gave Amamon the bastinado, and made Lucifer cuckold, and swore the devil his true liegeman upon the cross of a Welsh hook[29] – what a plague call you him?

POINS   O, Glendower.

FALSTAFF   Owen, Owen, the same. And his son-in-law Mortimer, 320
and old Northumberland, and that sprightly Scot of Scots, Douglas, that runs a-horseback up a hill perpendicular –

HAL   He that rides at high speed, and with his pistol kills a sparrow flying.

FALSTAFF   You have hit it.

HAL   So did he never the sparrow.

FALSTAFF   Well, that rascal hath good mettle in him: he will not run.

HAL   Why, what a rascal art thou then, to praise him so for running!   330

FALSTAFF   A-horseback, ye cuckoo, but afoot he will not budge a foot.

HAL   Yes, Jack, upon 'instinct'.

FALSTAFF   I grant ye, upon instinct. Well, he is there too, and one Mordake, and a thousand blue-caps more. Worcester is stolen away tonight. Thy father's beard is turned white with the news. You may buy land now as cheap as stinking mackerel.

HAL   Why then, it is like, if there come a hot June, and this civil buffeting hold, we shall buy maidenheads as they 340
buy hob-nails, by the hundreds.[30]

FALSTAFF   By the Mass, lad, thou sayest true; it is like we shall have good trading that way. But tell me, Hal, art not thou horrible afeard? Thou being heir-apparent, could the world pick thee out three such enemies again, as that fiend Douglas, that spirit Percy, and that devil Glendower? Art thou not horribly afraid? Doth not thy blood thrill at it?

HAL   Not a whit, i'faith: I lack some of thy 'instinct'.

FALSTAFF	Well, thou wilt be horribly chid tomorrow when thou comest to thy father. If thou love me, practise an answer.	350
HAL	Do thou stand for my father, and examine me upon the particulars of my life.	
FALSTAFF	Shall I? Content. This chair shall be my state, this dagger my sceptre, and this cushion my crown.	
HAL	Thy state is taken for a joint-stool, thy golden sceptre for a leaden dagger, and thy precious rich crown for a pitiful bald crown.	
FALSTAFF	Well, and the fire of grace be not quite out of thee, now shalt thou be moved. Give me a cup of sack to make my eyes look red, that it may be thought I have wept, for I must speak in passion, and I will do it in King Cambyses' vein.³¹	360
HAL	Well, here is my leg. [*He bows.*	
FALSTAFF	And here is my speech. –Stand aside, nobility.	
HOSTESS	O Jesu, this is excellent sport, i'faith!	
FALSTAFF	Weep not, sweet Queen, for trickling tears are vain.	
HOSTESS	O the Father, how he holds his countenance!	
FALSTAFF	For God's sake, lords, convey my tristful Queen,³² For tears do stop the floodgates of her eyes.	370
HOSTESS	O Jesu, he doth it as like one of these harlotry players as ever I see!	
FALSTAFF	Peace, good pint-pot; peace, good tickle-brain. [*As King:*] Harry, I do not only marvel where thou spendest thy time, but also how thou art accompanied. For though the camomile, the more it is trodden on, the faster it grows, yet youth, the more it is wasted, the sooner it wears. That thou art my son, I have partly thy mother's word, partly my own opinion, but chiefly a villainous trick of thine eye, and a foolish hanging of thy nether lip, that doth warrant me. If then thou be son to me – here lies the point – why, being son to me, art thou so pointed at? Shall the blessed sun of heaven prove a micher, and eat blackberries? A question not to be asked. Shall the son of England prove a thief, and take purses? A question to be asked. There is a thing, Harry, which thou hast often heard of, and it is known to many in our land by the name of pitch. This pitch	380

(as ancient writers do report) doth defile;[33] so doth the
company thou keepest. For, Harry, now I do not   390
speak to thee in drink, but in tears; not in pleasure, but
in passion; not in words only, but in woes also. And
yet there is a virtuous man whom I have often noted
in thy company, but I know not his name.

HAL   What manner of man, and it like your Majesty?

FALSTAFF   [as King:] A goodly portly man, i'faith, and a corpulent;
of a cheerful look, a pleasing eye, and a most noble
carriage; and, as I think, his age some fifty, or, birlady,
inclining to threescore; and now I remember me, his
name is Falstaff. If that man should be lewdly given, he   400
deceiveth me; for, Harry, I see virtue in his looks. If,
then, the tree may be known by the fruit, as the fruit
by the tree, then peremptorily I speak it, there is virtue
in that Falstaff. Him keep with, the rest banish. And
tell me now, thou naughty varlet, tell me where hast
thou been this month?

HAL   Dost thou speak like a king? Do thou stand for me,
and I'll play my father.

FALSTAFF   Depose me? If thou dost it half so gravely, so
majestically, both in word and matter, hang me up   410
by the heels for a rabbit sucker, or a poulter's hare.

HAL   Well, here I am set.

FALSTAFF   And here I stand. – Judge, my masters.

HAL   [as King:] Now, Harry, whence come you?

FALSTAFF   [as Hal:] My noble Lord, from Eastcheap.

HAL   [as King:] The complaints I hear of thee are grievous.

FALSTAFF   [as Hal:] 'Sblood, my Lord, they are false! [As Falstaff:]
Nay, I'll tickle ye for a young prince, i'faith.

HAL   [as King:] Swearest thou, ungracious boy? Henceforth
ne'er look on me. Thou art violently carried away from   420
grace. There is a devil haunts thee in the likeness of an
old fat man; a tun of man is thy companion. Why dost
thou converse with that trunk of humours, that bolting-
hutch of beastliness, that swollen parcel of dropsies, that
huge bombard of sack, that stuffed cloak-bag of guts,
that roasted Manningtree ox with the pudding in his
belly, that reverend Vice, that grey Iniquity, that Father

Ruffian, that Vanity in years?[34] Wherein is he good, but
to taste sack and drink it? Wherein neat and cleanly,
but to carve a capon and eat it? Wherein cunning, but   430
in craft? Wherein crafty, but in villainy? Wherein
villainous, but in all things? Wherein worthy, but in
nothing?

FALSTAFF [*as Hal:*] I would your Grace would take me with you.
Whom means your Grace?

HAL [*as King:*] That villainous abominable misleader of
youth, Falstaff, that old white-bearded Satan.

FALSTAFF [*as Hal:*] My Lord, the man I know.

HAL [*as King:*] I know thou dost.

FALSTAFF [*as Hal:*] But to say I know more harm in him than in   440
myself, were to say more than I know. That he is old,
the more the pity, his white hairs do witness it; but
that he is, saving your reverence, a whoremaster, that I
utterly deny. If sack and sugar be a fault, God help the
wicked! If to be old and merry be a sin, then many an
old host that I know is damned. If to be fat be to be
hated, then Pharaoh's lean kine[35] are to be loved. No,
my good Lord, banish Peto, banish Bardolph, banish
Poins, but for sweet Jack Falstaff, kind Jack Falstaff,
true Jack Falstaff, valiant Jack Falstaff – and therefore   450
more valiant, being as he is old Jack Falstaff – banish
not him thy Harry's company, banish not him thy
Harry's company. Banish plump Jack, and banish all
the world.

HAL I do; I will.   [*A knocking heard.*
                              [*Exeunt hostess, Francis and Bardolph.*

Enter BARDOLPH, *running.*

BARDOLPH O my Lord, my Lord, the sheriff with a most monstrous
watch is at the door!

FALSTAFF Out, ye rogue! – Play out the play! I have much to say
in the behalf of that Falstaff.

Enter the HOSTESS.

HOSTESS O Jesu, my Lord, my Lord!   460

HAL Hey, hey, the devil rides upon a fiddlestick.[36] What's the
matter?

HOSTESS   The sheriff and all the watch are at the door: they are
            come to search the house. Shall I let them in?

FALSTAFF   Dost thou hear, Hal? Never call a true piece of gold a
            counterfeit: thou art essentially made, without seeming
            so.[37]

HAL   And thou a natural coward, without 'instinct'.

FALSTAFF   I deny your major. If you will deny the sheriff, so; if
            not, let him enter. If I become not a cart as well as   470
            another man, a plague on my bringing up! I hope I
            shall as soon be strangled with a halter as another.

HAL   Go hide thee behind the arras. The rest, walk up above.
            Now, my masters, for a true face, and good conscience.

FALSTAFF   Both which I have had, but their date is out, and
            therefore I'll hide me.   [He hides. Exeunt all the others
                                              except the Prince and Peto.

HAL   Call in the sheriff.   [Exit Peto.[38]

            Enter the SHERIFF and a CARRIER, followed by PETO.

            Now, master sheriff, what is your will with me?

SHERIFF   First, pardon me, my Lord. A hue and cry
            Hath followed certain men unto this house.   480

HAL   What men?

SHERIFF   One of them is well known, my gracious Lord:
            A gross fat man.

CARRIER   As fat as butter.

HAL   The man, I do assure you, is not here,
            For I myself at this time have employed him.
            And sheriff, I will engage my word to thee,
            That I will by tomorrow dinner-time
            Send him to answer thee, or any man,
            For anything he shall be charged withal.   490
            And so let me entreat you leave the house.

SHERIFF   I will, my Lord. There are two gentlemen
            Have in this robbery lost three hundred marks.

HAL   It may be so: if he have robbed these men,
            He shall be answerable. And so, farewell.

SHERIFF   Good night, my noble Lord.

HAL   I think it is good morrow, is it not?

SHERIFF   Indeed, my Lord, I think it be two o'clock.

                                 [*Exeunt sheriff and carrier.*

HAL   [*to Peto:*] This oily rascal is known as well as Paul's.

          Go call him forth.   [*Peto draws the arras aside.* 500

PETO   Falstaff! — Fast asleep behind the arras, and snorting

          like a horse.

HAL   Hark how hard he fetches breath. Search his pockets.

              [*Peto searches his pockets, and finds certain papers.*

          What hast thou found?

PETO   Nothing but papers, my Lord.

HAL   Let's see what they be: read them.

PETO   'Item, a capon.   2s. 2d.

          Item, sauce.   4d.

          Item, sack two gallons.   5s. 8d.

          Item, anchovies and sack after supper. 2s. 6d.   510

          Item, bread.   ob.'

HAL   O monstrous! But one halfpennyworth of bread to this

          intolerable deal of sack? What there is else, keep close;

          we'll read it at more advantage. There let him sleep till

          day. I'll to the court in the morning. We must all

          to the wars, and thy place shall be honourable. I'll

          procure this fat rogue a charge of foot, and I know his

          death will be a march of twelve score. The money

          shall be paid back again with advantage. Be with me

          betimes in the morning; and so, good morrow, Peto. 520

PETO   Good morrow, good my Lord.   [*Exeunt separately.*

Wales: Glendower's castle.

Enter HOTSPUR, WORCESTER, LORD MORTIMER
and OWEN GLENDOWER.

MORTIMER These promises are fair, the parties sure,
And our induction full of prosperous hope.

HOTSPUR Lord Mortimer and cousin Glendower, will you
Sit down? And uncle Worcester. – A plague upon it!
I have forgot the map.

GLEND.   No, here it is.
Sit, cousin Percy, sit, good cousin 'Hotspur' –
For by that name as oft as Lancaster
Doth speak of you, his cheek looks pale, and with
A rising sigh he wisheth you in heaven.

HOTSPUR And you in hell,   10
As oft as he hears Owen Glendower spoke of.

GLEND. I cannot blame him. At my nativity
The front of heaven was full of fiery shapes,
Of burning cressets, and at my birth
The frame and huge foundation of the earth
Shaked like a coward.

HOTSPUR   Why, so it would have done
At the same season, if your mother's cat
Had but kittened, though yourself had never been born.

GLEND. I say the earth did shake when I was born.

HOTSPUR And I say the earth was not of my mind,   20
If you suppose as fearing you it shook.

GLEND. The heavens were all on fire, the earth did tremble –

HOTSPUR O, then the earth shook to see the heavens on fire,
And not in fear of your nativity.
Diseasèd nature oftentimes breaks forth
In strange eruptions; oft the teeming earth
Is with a kind of colic pinched and vexed
By the imprisoning of unruly wind
Within her womb, which for enlargement striving
Shakes the old beldam earth, and topples down   30
Steeples and moss-grown towers. At your birth

    Our grandam earth, having this distemperature,
    In passion shook.

GLEND.   Cousin, of many men
    I do not bear these crossings. Give me leave
    To tell you once again that at my birth
    The front of heaven was full of fiery shapes,
    The goats ran from the mountains, and the herds
    Were strangely clamorous to the frighted fields.
    These signs have marked me extraordinary,
    And all the courses of my life do show   40
    I am not in the roll of common men.
    Where is he living, clipped in with the sea
    That chides the banks of England, Scotland, Wales,
    Which calls me pupil or hath read to me?
    And bring him out that is but woman's son
    Can trace me in the tedious ways of art,
    And hold me pace in deep experiments.

HOTSPUR I think there is no man speaks better Welsh.[39]
    I'll to dinner.

MORTIMER Peace, cousin Percy, you will make him mad. 50

GLEND. I can call spirits from the vasty deep!

HOTSPUR Why, so can I, or so can any man:
    But will they come when you do call for them?

GLEND. Why, I can teach you, cousin, to command the devil.

HOTSPUR And I can teach thee, coz, to shame the devil,
    By telling truth. Tell truth, and shame the devil.
    If thou have power to raise him, bring him hither,
    And I'll be sworn I've[40] power to shame him hence.
    O, while you live, tell truth, and shame the devil!

MORTIMER Come, come, no more of this unprofitable chat. 60

GLEND. Three times hath Henry Bullingbrooke made head
    Against my power; thrice from the banks of Wye
    And sandy-bottomed Severn have I sent him
    Bootless home, and weather-beaten back.

HOTSPUR Home without boots, and in foul weather too!
    How scapes he agues, in the devil's name?

GLEND. Come, here's the map: shall we divide our right,
    According to our threefold order tane?

MORTIMER The Archdeacon hath divided it

Into three limits very equally.   70
England, from Trent and Severn hitherto,
By south and east is to my part assigned;
All westward, Wales beyond the Severn shore,
And all the fertile land within that bound,
To Owen Glendower; and, dear coz, to you
The remnant northward, lying off from Trent.
And our indentures tripartite are drawn,
Which being sealed interchangeably
(A business that this night may execute),
Tomorrow, cousin Percy, you and I   80
And my good Lord of Worcester will set forth
To meet your father and the Scottish power,
As is appointed us, at Shrewsbury.
My father Glendower is not ready yet,
Nor shall we need his help these fourteen days.
[*To Glendower:*]
Within that space you may have drawn together
Your tenants, friends, and neighbouring gentlemen.

GLEND.   A shorter time shall send me to you, Lords;
And in my conduct shall your ladies come,
From whom you now must steal and take no leave,   90
For there will be a world of water shed
Upon the parting of your wives and you.

HOTSPUR   Methinks my moiety, north from Burton here,
In quantity equals not one of yours:
See how this river comes me cranking in,
And cuts me from the best of all my land
A huge half-moon, a monstrous cantle out.
I'll have the current in this place dammed up,
And here the smug and silver Trent shall run
In a new channel fair and evenly.   100
It shall not wind with such a deep indent,
To rob me of so rich a bottom here.

GLEND.   Not wind? It shall, it must: you see it doth.

MORTIMER Yea,
But mark how he bears his course, and runs me up
With like advantage on the other side,
Gelding the opposèd continent as much

	As on the other side it takes from you.
WOR'STER	Yea, but a little charge will trench him here,
	And on this north side win this cape of land, 110
	And then he runs straight and even.
HOTSPUR	I'll have it so; a little charge will do it.
GLEND.	I'll not have it altered.
HOTSPUR	Will not you?
GLEND.	No, nor you shall not.
HOTSPUR	Who shall say me nay?
GLEND.	Why, that will I.
HOTSPUR	Let me not understand you then: speak it in Welsh.
GLEND.	I can speak English, Lord, as well as you,
	For I was trained up in the English court,
	Where, being but young, I framèd to the harp
	Many an English ditty lovely well, 120
	And gave the tongue a helpful ornament –
	A virtue that was never seen in you.
HOTSPUR	Marry, and I am glad of it with all my heart!
	I had rather be a kitten and cry 'mew'
	Than one of these same metre ballad-mongers.
	I had rather hear a brazen canstick turned,
	Or a dry wheel grate on the axle-tree,
	And that would set my teeth nothing on edge,
	Nothing so much as mincing poetry:
	'Tis like the forced gait of a shuffling nag. 130
GLEND.	Come, you shall have Trent turned.
HOTSPUR	I do not care: I'll give thrice so much land
	To any well-deserving friend;
	But in the way of bargain – mark ye me –
	I'll cavil on the ninth part of a hair.
	Are the indentures drawn? Shall we be gone?
GLEND.	The moon shines fair, you may away by night.
	I'll haste the writer, and withal
	Break with your wives of your departure hence.
	I am afraid my daughter will run mad, 140
	So much she doteth on her Mortimer. [*Exit.*
MORTIMER	Fie, cousin Percy, how you cross my father!
HOTSPUR	I cannot choose. Sometime he angers me
	With telling me of the moldwarp and the ant,

Of the dreamer Merlin and his prophecies,
And of a dragon and a finless fish,
A clip-winged griffin and a moulten raven,
A couching lion and a ramping cat,
And such a deal of skimble-skamble stuff
As puts me from my faith. I tell you what: 150
He held me last night at the least nine hours
In reckoning up the several devils' names
That were his lackeys; I cried 'Hum', and 'Well, go to!'
But marked him not a word. O, he is as tedious
As a tired horse, a railing wife;
Worse than a smoky house. I had rather live
With cheese and garlic in a windmill, far,
Than feed on cates and have him talk to me
In any summer house in Christendom.

MORTIMER In faith, he is a worthy gentleman,   160
Exceedingly well read, and profited
In strange concealments, valiant as a lion,
And wondrous affable, and as bountiful
As mines of India. Shall I tell you, cousin?
He holds your temper in a high respect,
And curbs himself even of his natural scope
When you come 'cross his humour; faith, he does.
I warrant you, that man is not alive
Might so have tempted him as you have done,
Without the taste of danger and reproof.   170
But do not use it oft, let me entreat you.

WOR'STER [to Hotspur:] In faith, my Lord, you are too wilful-blame,
And since your coming hither have done enough
To put him quite besides his patience.
You must needs learn, Lord, to amend this fault.
Though sometimes it show greatness, courage, blood –
And that's the dearest grace it renders you –
Yet oftentimes it doth present harsh rage,
Defect of manners, want of government,
Pride, haughtiness, opinion, and disdain,   180
The least of which, haunting a noble man,[41]
Loseth men's hearts, and leaves behind a stain
Upon the beauty of all parts besides,

Beguiling them of commendation.

HOTSPUR   Well, I am schooled: good manners be your speed.
           Here come our wives, and let us take our leave.

Enter GLENDOWER *with* LADY PERCY *and* LADY MORTIMER.

MORTIMER   This is the deadly spite that angers me:
           My wife can speak no English, I no Welsh.

GLEND.   My daughter weeps, she'll not part with you,
           She'll be a soldier too, she'll to the wars.   190

MORTIMER   Good father, tell her that she and my aunt Percy[42]
           Shall follow in your conduct speedily.
                    [*Glendower speaks to Lady Mortimer in Welsh,*
                              and she answers him in the same.

GLEND.   She is desperate here, a peevish, self-willed harlotry, one
           that no persuasion can do good upon.
                              [*The lady speaks in Welsh to Mortimer.*

MORTIMER   I understand thy looks: that pretty Welsh
           Which thou pourest down from these swelling heavens
           I am too perfect in, and but for shame
           In such a parley should I answer thee.
                [*The lady speaks again in Welsh to Mortimer. They kiss.*
           I understand thy kisses, and thou mine,
           And that's a feeling disputation;   200
           But I will never be a truant, love,
           Till I have learnt thy language, for thy tongue
           Makes Welsh as sweet as ditties highly penned,
           Sung by a fair queen in a summer's bower,
           With ravishing division, to her lute.

GLEND.   Nay, if you melt, then will she run mad.
                [*The lady sits, and speaks again in Welsh to Mortimer.*

MORTIMER   O, I am ignorance itself in this!

GLEND.   She bids you on the wanton rushes lay you down,
           And rest your gentle head upon her lap,
           And she will sing the song that pleaseth you,   210
           And on your eyelids crown the god of sleep,
           Charming your blood with pleasing heaviness,
           Making such difference 'twixt wake and sleep
           As is the difference betwixt day and night,
           The hour before the heavenly-harnessed team
           Begins his golden progress in the east.

MORTIMER   With all my heart I'll sit and hear her sing.
           By that time will our book, I think, be drawn.
GLEND.   Do so, and those musicians that shall play to you
           Hang in the air a thousand leagues from hence,   220
           And straight they shall be here. Sit, and attend.
HOTSPUR   Come, Kate, thou art perfect in lying down.
           Come, quick, quick, that I may lay my head in thy lap.
L. PERCY   Go, ye giddy goose.   [*The music plays.*
HOTSPUR   Now I perceive the devil understands Welsh,
           And 'tis no marvel he is so humorous,
           Birlady, he is a good musician.
L. PERCY   Then should you be nothing but musical,
           For you are altogether governed by humours.
           Lie still, ye thief, and hear the lady sing in Welsh.   230
HOTSPUR   I had rather hear Lady, my brach, howl in Irish.
L. PERCY   Wouldst thou have thy head broken?
HOTSPUR   No.
L. PERCY   Then be still.
HOTSPUR   Neither, 'tis a woman's fault.
L. PERCY   Now, God help thee!
HOTSPUR   To the Welsh lady's bed.
L. PERCY   What's that?
HOTSPUR   Peace, she sings.   [*Here the lady sings a Welsh song.*
           Come, Kate, I'll have your song too.   240
L. PERCY   Not mine, in good sooth.
HOTSPUR   Not yours, 'in good sooth'!
           Heart, you swear like a comfit-maker's wife:
           'Not you, in good sooth!', and 'As true as I live!',
           And 'As God shall mend me!', and 'As sure as day!';
           And giv'st such sarcenet surety for thy oaths
           As if thou never walk'st further than Finsbury.
           Swear me, Kate, like a lady as thou art,
           A good mouth-filling oath, and leave 'In sooth',
           And such protest of pepper gingerbread,   250
           To velvet guards, and Sunday citizens.
           Come, sing.
L. PERCY   I will not sing.
HOTSPUR   'Tis the next way to turn tailor, or be redbreast teacher.[43]
           And the indentures be drawn, I'll away within these

two hours; and so, come in when ye will.   [*Exit.*

GLEND.   Come, come, Lord Mortimer, you are as slow
As hot Lord Percy is on fire to go.
By this our book is drawn; we'll but seal,
And then to horse immediately.

MORTIMER   With all my heart.   260
                             [*Exeunt.*

SCENE 2.

London: the palace.

Enter the KING, *the* PRINCE OF WALES (HAL) *and* LORDS.

K. HENRY   Lords, give us leave: the Prince of Wales and I
Must have some private conference; but be near
                               at hand,
For we shall presently have need of you. [*Exeunt Lords.*
I know not whether God will have it so
For some displeasing service I have done,
That, in his secret doom, out of my blood
He'll breed revengement and a scourge for me;
But thou dost in thy passages of life
Make me believe that thou art only marked
For the hot vengeance and the rod of heaven,   10
To punish my mistreadings. Tell me else,
Could such inordinate and low desires,
Such poor, such bare, such lewd, such mean attempts,
Such barren pleasures, rude society,
As thou art matched withal, and grafted to,
Accompany the greatness of thy blood
And hold their level with thy princely heart?

HAL   So please your Majesty, I would I could
Quit all offences with as clear excuse
As well as I am doubtless I can purge   20
Myself of many I am charged withal.
Yet such extenuation let me beg
As, in reproof of many tales devised –
Which oft the ear of greatness needs must hear –

By smiling pickthanks and base newsmongers,
I may, for some things true, wherein my youth
Hath faulty wandered and irregular,
Find pardon on my true submission.

K. HENRY God pardon thee! Yet let me wonder, Harry,
At thy affections, which do hold a wing   30
Quite from the flight of all thy ancestors.
Thy place in Council thou hast rudely lost,[44]
Which by thy younger brother is supplied,
And art almost an alien to the hearts
Of all the court and princes of my blood.
The hope and expectation of thy time
Is ruined, and the soul of every man
Prophetically do forethink thy fall.
Had I so lavish of my presence been,
So common-hackneyed in the eyes of men,   40
So stale and cheap to vulgar company,
Opinion, that did help me to the crown,
Had still kept loyal to possession,
And left me in reputeless banishment,
A fellow of no mark nor likelihood.
By being seldom seen, I could not stir
But like a comet I was wondered at,
That men would tell their children, 'This is he!';
Others would say, 'Where, which is Bullingbrooke?';
And then I stole all courtesy from heaven,   50
And dressed myself in such humility
That I did pluck allegiance from men's hearts,
Loud shouts and salutations from their mouths,
Even in the presence of the crownèd King.
Thus did I keep my person fresh and new,
My presence, like a robe pontifical,
Ne'er seen but wondered at; and so my state,
Seldom, but sumptuous, showed like a feast,
And won by rareness such solemnity.
The skipping King, he ambled up and down   60
With shallow jesters and rash bavin wits,
Soon kindled and soon burnt, carded his state,
Mingled his royalty with cap'ring fools,

Had his great name profanèd with their scorns,
And gave his countenance, against his name,
To laugh at gibing boys, and stand the push
Of every beardless vain comparative;
Grew a companion to the common streets,
Enfeoffed himself to popularity,
That, being daily swallowed by men's eyes,   70
They surfeited with honey, and began
To loathe the taste of sweetness, whereof a little
More than a little is by much too much.
So, when he had occasion to be seen,
He was but as the cuckoo is in June,
Heard, not regarded; seen, but with such eyes
As, sick and blunted with community,
Afford no extraordinary gaze,
Such as is bent on sun-like majesty
When it shines seldom in admiring eyes,   80
But rather drowsed, and hung their eyelids down,
Slept in his face, and rendered such aspéct
As cloudy men use to their adversaries,
Being with his presence glutted, gorged, and full.
And in that very line, Harry, standest thou,
For thou hast lost thy princely privilege
With vile participation. Not an eye
But is a-weary of thy common sight,
Save mine, which hath desired to see thee more,
Which now doth that I would not have it do,   90
Make blind itself with foolish tenderness.   [*He weeps.*

HAL   I shall hereafter, my thrice-gracious Lord,
Be more myself.

K. HENRY   For all the world,
As thou art to this hour was Richard then,
When I from France set foot at Ravenspurgh;
And even as I was then, is Percy now.
Now by my sceptre, and my soul to boot,
He hath more worthy interest to the state
Than thou, the shadow of succession.[45]
For of no right, nor colour like to right,   100
He doth fill fields with harness in the realm,

Turns head against the lion's armèd jaws,
And, being no more in debt to years than thou,
Leads ancient lords and reverend bishops on
To bloody battles, and to bruising arms.
What never-dying honour hath he got
Against renownèd Douglas, whose high deeds,
Whose hot incursions and great name in arms,
Holds from all soldiers chief majority
And military title capital   110
Through all the kingdoms that acknowledge Christ.
Thrice hath this Hotspur, Mars in swaddling clothes,
This infant warrior, in his enterprises
Discomfited great Douglas, tane him once,
Enlargèd him, and made a friend of him,
To fill the mouth of deep defiance up,
And shake the peace and safety of our throne.
And what say you to this? Percy, Northumberland,
The Archbishop's Grace of York, Douglas, Mortimer,
Capitulate against us, and are up.   120
But wherefore do I tell these news to thee?
Why, Harry, do I tell thee of my foes,
Which art my near'st and dearest enemy?
Thou that art like enough, through vassal fear,
Base inclination, and the start of spleen,
To fight against me under Percy's pay,
To dog his heels, and curtsy at his frowns,
To show how much thou art degenerate.

HAL   Do not think so, you shall not find it so;
And God forgive them that so much have swayed   130
Your Majesty's good thoughts away from me!
I will redeem all this on Percy's head,
And in the closing of some glorious day
Be bold to tell you that I am your son,
When I will wear a garment all of blood,
And stain my favours in a bloody mask,
Which, washed away, shall scour my shame with it;
And that shall be the day, whene'er it lights,
That this same child of honour and renown,
This gallant Hotspur, this all-praisèd knight,   140

And your unthought-of Harry chance to meet.
For every honour sitting on his helm,
Would they were multitudes, and on my head
My shames redoubled. For the time will come
That I shall make this northern youth exchange
His glorious deeds for my indignities.
Percy is but my factor, good my Lord,
To engross up glorious deeds on my behalf,
And I will call him to so strict account
That he shall render every glory up,   150
Yea, even the slightest worship of his time,
Or I will tear the reckoning from his heart.
This in the name of God I promise here,
The which if He be pleased I shall perform,
I do beseech your Majesty, may salve
The long-grown wounds of my intemperance.
If not, the end of life cancels all bonds,
And I will die a hundred thousand deaths
Ere break the smallest parcel of this vow.

K. HENRY   A hundred thousand rebels die in this.   160
Thou shalt have charge and sovereign trust herein.

Enter SIR WALTER BLUNT

– How now, good Blunt? Thy looks are full of speed.

BLUNT   So hath the business that I come to speak of.
Lord Mortimer of Scotland hath sent word
That Douglas and the English rebels met
The eleventh of this month at Shrewsbury.
A mighty and a fearful head they are,
If promises be kept on every hand,
As ever offered foul play in a state.

K. HENRY   The Earl of Westmorland set forth today,   170
With him my son, Lord John of Lancaster,
For this advertisement is five days old.
On Wednesday next, Harry, you shall set forward.
On Thursday we ourselves will march.
Our meeting is Bridgnorth, and, Harry, you
Shall march through Gloucestershire, by which account,
Our business valued, some twelve days hence

Our general forces at Bridgnorth shall meet.
Our hands are full of business; let's away;
Advantage feeds him fat while men delay.   [*Exeunt.* 180

SCENE 3.

London: Eastcheap: the tavern.

Enter FALSTAFF *and* BARDOLPH.

FALSTAFF   Bardolph, am I not fallen away vilely since this last
action? Do I not bate? Do I not dwindle? Why, my
skin hangs about me like an old lady's loose gown. I
am withered like an old apple-john. Well, I'll repent,
and that suddenly, while I am in some liking. I shall be
out of heart shortly, and then I shall have no strength
to repent. And I have not forgotten what the inside of
a church is made of, I am a peppercorn, a brewer's
horse. The inside of a church! Company, villainous
company, hath been the spoil of me.   10

BARDOLPH Sir John, you are so fretful, you cannot live long.

FALSTAFF   Why, there is it. Come, sing me a bawdy song, make
me merry. I was as virtuously given as a gentleman
need to be: virtuous enough; swore little; diced not
above seven times – a week; went to a bawdy-house
not above once in a quarter – of an hour; paid money
that I borrowed – three or four times; lived well, and
in good compass; and now I live out of all order, out
of all compass.

BARDOLPH Why, you are so fat, Sir John, that you must needs be 20
out of all compass, out of all reasonable compass, Sir
John.

FALSTAFF   Do thou amend thy face, and I'll amend my life. Thou
art our admiral, thou bearest the lantern in the poop,
but 'tis in the nose of thee: thou art the Knight of the
Burning Lamp.⁴⁶

BARDOLPH Why, Sir John, my face does you no harm.

FALSTAFF   No, I'll be sworn, I make as good use of it as many a

man doth of a death's-head, or a *memento mori*. I never
see thy face but I think upon hell-fire, and Dives that   30
lived in purple: for there he is in his robes, burning,
burning.[47] If thou wert any way given to virtue, I
would swear by thy face: my oath should be 'By this
fire, that's God's angel!'. But thou art altogether given
over, and wert indeed, but for the light in thy face, the
son of utter darkness. When thou ran'st up Gad's Hill in
the night to catch my horse, if I did not think thou
hadst been an *ignis fatuus*, or a ball of wildfire, there's no
purchase in money. O, thou art a perpetual triumph,
an everlasting bonfire-light! Thou hast saved me a   40
thousand marks in links and torches, walking with thee
in the night betwixt tavern and tavern; but the sack that
thou hast drunk me would have bought me lights as
good cheap at the dearest chandler's in Europe. I have
maintained that salamander of yours with fire any time
this two-and-thirty years, God reward me for it!

BARDOLPH 'Sblood, I would my face were in your belly!

FALSTAFF God-a-mercy! So should I be sure to be heart-burnt.

Enter HOSTESS.

How now, Dame Partlet the hen, have you enquired
yet who picked my pocket?   50

HOSTESS Why, Sir John, what do you think, Sir John? Do you
think I keep thieves in my house? I have searched, I
have enquired, so has my husband, man by man, boy
by boy, servant by servant. The tithe of a hair was
never lost in my house before.

FALSTAFF Ye lie, hostess. Bardolph was shaved, and lost many a
hair, and I'll be sworn my pocket was picked. Go to,
you are a woman, go!

HOSTESS Who, I? No, I defy thee! God's light, I was never
called so in mine own house before.   60

FALSTAFF Go to, I know you well enough.

HOSTESS No, Sir John, you do not know me, Sir John; I know
you, Sir John. You owe me money, Sir John, and now
you pick a quarrel to beguile me of it. I bought you a
dozen of shirts to your back.

FALSTAFF Dowlas, filthy dowlas. I have given them away to bakers' wives: they have made bolters of them.

HOSTESS Now as I am a true woman, holland of eight shillings an ell! You owe money here besides, Sir John, for your diet, and by-drinkings, and money lent you, 70 four-and-twenty pound.

FALSTAFF [*indicating Bardolph:*] He had his part of it, let him pay.

HOSTESS He? Alas, he is poor, he hath nothing.

FALSTAFF How? Poor? Look upon his face. What call you rich? Let them coin his nose, let them coin his cheeks, I'll not pay a denier. What, will you make a younker of me? Shall I not take mine ease in mine inn, but I shall have my pocket picked? I have lost a seal-ring of my grandfather's worth forty mark.

HOSTESS [*to Bardolph:*] O Jesu, I have heard the Prince tell him, 80 I know not how oft, that that ring was copper.

FALSTAFF How? The Prince is a Jack, a sneak-up. 'Sblood, and he were here, I would cudgel him like a dog if he would say so.

Enter the PRINCE (HAL), *marching with* PETO. FALSTAFF *meets him, playing upon his truncheon like a fife.*

How now, lad? Is the wind in that door, i'faith? Must we all march?

BARDOLPH Yea, two and two, Newgate fashion.

HOSTESS My Lord, I pray you hear me.

HAL What say'st thou, Mistress Quickly? How doth thy husband? I love him well, he is an honest man. 90

HOSTESS Good my Lord, hear me.

FALSTAFF Prithee let her alone, and list to me.

HAL What say'st thou, Jack?

FALSTAFF The other night I fell asleep here, behind the arras, and had my pocket picked. This house is turned bawdy-house, they pick pockets.

HAL What didst thou lose, Jack?

FALSTAFF Wilt thou believe me, Hal, three or four bonds of forty pound apiece, and a seal-ring of my grandfather's.

HAL A trifle, some eightpenny matter. 100

HOSTESS So I told him, my Lord, and I said I heard your Grace say so; and, my Lord, he speaks most vilely of you, like a foul-mouthed man as he is, and said he would cudgel you.

HAL   What? He did not!

HOSTESS There's neither faith, truth, nor womanhood in me else.

FALSTAFF There's no more faith in thee than in a stewed prune, nor no more truth in thee than in a drawn fox; and for womanhood, Maid Marian may be the deputy's wife of the ward to thee.[48] Go, you thing, go!   110

HOSTESS Say, what 'thing', what 'thing'?

FALSTAFF 'What thing?' Why, a thing to thank God on.

HOSTESS I am no 'thing to thank God on', I would thou shouldst know it, I am an honest man's wife; and setting thy knighthood aside, thou art a knave to call me so.

FALSTAFF Setting thy womanhood aside, thou art a beast to say otherwise.

HOSTESS Say, what beast, thou knave, thou?

FALSTAFF What beast? Why, an otter.

HAL   An otter, Sir John? Why an otter?   120

FALSTAFF Why? She's neither fish nor flesh: a man knows not where to have her.

HOSTESS Thou art an unjust man in saying so, thou or any man knows where to have me, thou knave, thou.

HAL   Thou sayest true, hostess, and he slanders thee most grossly.

HOSTESS So he doth you, my Lord, and said this other day you owed him a thousand pound.

HAL   – Sirrah, do I owe you a thousand pound?

FALSTAFF A thousand pound, Hal? A million! Thy love is worth   130 a million; thou owest me thy love.

HOSTESS Nay my Lord, he called you 'Jack', and said he would cudgel you.

FALSTAFF Did I, Bardolph?

BARDOLPH Indeed, Sir John, you said so.

FALSTAFF Yea, if he said my ring was copper.

HAL   I say 'tis copper: darest thou be as good as thy word now?

FALSTAFF Why Hal, thou knowest as thou art but man I dare,

	but as thou art prince, I fear thee as I fear the roaring 140 of the lion's whelp.
HAL	And why not as the lion?
FALSTAFF	The King himself is to be feared as the lion. Dost thou think I'll fear thee as I fear thy father? Nay, and I do, I pray God my girdle break.
HAL	O, if it should, how would thy guts fall about thy knees! But sirrah, there's no room for faith, truth, nor honesty in this bosom of thine. It is all filled up with guts and midriff. Charge an honest woman with picking thy pocket? Why, thou whoreson impudent embossed 150 rascal, if there were anything in thy pocket but tavern reckonings, memorandums of bawdy-houses, and one poor pennyworth of sugar-candy to make thee long-winded, if thy pocket were enriched with any other injuries but these, I am a villain; and yet you will stand to it, you will not pocket up wrong. Art thou not ashamed?
FALSTAFF	Dost thou hear, Hal? Thou knowest in the state of innocency Adam fell, and what should poor Jack Falstaff do in the days of villainy? Thou seest I have 160 more flesh than another man, and therefore more frailty. You confess then, you picked my pocket?
HAL	It appears so by the story.
FALSTAFF	Hostess, I forgive thee; go make ready breakfast, love thy husband, look to thy servants, cherish thy guests; thou shalt find me tractable to any honest reason, thou seest I am pacified still; nay prithee be gone.

[Exit hostess.

	Now, Hal, to the news at court: for the robbery, lad, how is that answered?
HAL	O my sweet beef, I must still be good angel to thee: 170 the money is paid back again.
FALSTAFF	O, I do not like that paying back, 'tis a double labour.
HAL	I am good friends with my father, and may do anything.
FALSTAFF	Rob me the exchequer the first thing thou dost, and do it with unwashed hands too.
BARDOLPH	Do, my Lord.

HAL   I have procured thee, Jack, a charge of foot.

FALSTAFF I would it had been of horse. Where shall I find one
that can steal well? O for a fine thief of the age of two– 180
and–twenty or thereabouts! I am heinously unprovided.
Well, God be thanked for these rebels, they offend
none but the virtuous. I laud them, I praise them.

HAL   Bardolph!

BARDOLPH My Lord?

HAL   [*giving letters:*] Go bear this letter to Lord John of
                 Lancaster,
To my brother John; this to my Lord of Westmorland.
              [*Exit Bardolph.*
Go, Peto, to horse, to horse, for thou and I
Have thirty miles to ride yet ere dinner–time.
               [*Exit Peto.*
Jack, meet me tomorrow in the Temple hall   190
At two o'clock in the afternoon:
There shalt thou know thy charge, and there receive
Money and order for their furniture.
The land is burning, Percy stands on high,
And either we or they must lower lie.   [*Exit.*

FALSTAFF Rare words! Brave world! Hostess, my breakfast, come!
O, I could wish this tavern were my drum!⁴⁹ [*Exit.*

Shrewsbury: the rebels' camp.

Enter HOTSPUR, WORCESTER *and* DOUGLAS.

HOTSPUR   Well said, my noble Scot! If speaking truth
            In this fine age were not thought flattery,
            Such attribution should the Douglas have,
            As not a soldier of this season's stamp
            Should go so general current through the world.
            By God, I cannot flatter, I do defy
            The tongues of soothers, but a braver place
            In my heart's love hath no man than yourself.
            Nay, task me to my word, approve me, Lord.

DOUGLAS   Thou art the King of Honour.   10
            No man so potent breathes upon the ground
            But I will beard him.

HOTSPUR   Do so, and 'tis well. –

Enter a MESSENGER *with letters*.

            What letters hast thou there? – I can but thank you.

MESSENGER   These letters come from your father.

HOTSPUR   Letters from him? Why comes he not himself?

MESSENGER   He cannot come, my Lord, he is grievous sick.

HOTSPUR   Zounds, how has he the leisure to be sick
            In such a justling time? Who leads his power?
            Under whose government come they along?

MESSENGER   His letters bear his mind, not I, my Lord.   20

WOR'STER   I prithee tell me, doth he keep his bed?

MESSENGER   He did, my Lord, four days ere I set forth,
            And at the time of my departure thence
            He was much feared by his physicians.

WOR'STER   I would the state of time had first been whole,
            Ere he by sickness had been visited.
            His health was never better worth than now.

HOTSPUR   Sick now? Droop now? This sickness doth infect
            The very life-blood of our enterprise.
            'Tis catching hither, even to our camp.   30

He writes me here that inward sickness — [50]
And that his friends by deputation could not
So soon be drawn, nor did he think it meet
To lay so dangerous and dear a trust
On any soul removed but on his own.
Yet doth he give us bold advertisement
That with our small conjunction we should on,
To see how fortune is disposed to us.
For, as he writes, there is no quailing now,
Because the King is certainly possessed   40
Of all our purposes. What say you to it?

WOR'STER   Your father's sickness is a maim to us.

HOTSPUR   A perilous gash, a very limb lopped off –
And yet, in faith, it is not! His present want
Seems more than we shall find it: were it good
To set the exact wealth of all our states
All at one cast? To set so rich a main
On the nice hazard of one doubtful hour?
It were not good, for therein should we read
The very bottom and the soul of hope,   50
The very list, the very utmost bound
Of all our fortunes.

DOUGLAS   Faith, and so we should, where now remains
A sweet reversion: we may boldly spend
Upon the hope of what is to come in:
A comfort of retirement lives in this.

HOTSPUR   A rendezvous, a home to fly unto,
If that the devil and mischance look big
Upon the maidenhead of our affairs.

WOR'STER   But yet I would your father had been here.   60
The quality and hair of our attempt
Brooks no division. It will be thought,
By some that know not why he is away,
That wisdom, loyalty, and mere dislike
Of our proceedings kept the Earl from hence.
And think how such an apprehension
May turn the tide of fearful faction,
And breed a kind of question in our cause:
For well you know, we of the off'ring side

	Must keep aloof from strict arbitrement,	70
	And stop all sight-holes, every loop from whence	
	The eye of reason may pry in upon us.	
	This absence of your father's draws a curtain	
	That shows the ignorant a kind of fear	
	Before not dreamt of.	

HOTSPUR   You strain too far.
I rather of his absence make this use:
It lends a lustre and more great opinion,
A larger dare to our great enterprise,
Than if the Earl were here; for men must think,
If we without his help can make a head   80
To push against a kingdom, with his help
We shall o'erturn it topsy-turvy down.
Yet all goes well; yet all our joints are whole.

DOUGLAS   As heart can think. There is not such a word
Spoke of in Scotland as this term of fear.

Enter SIR RICHARD VERNON.

HOTSPUR   My cousin Vernon! Welcome, by my soul!

VERNON   Pray God my news be worth a welcome, Lord.
The Earl of Westmorland seven thousand strong
Is marching hitherwards; with him, Prince John.

HOTSPUR   No harm, what more?

VERNON   And further, I have learned,   90
The King himself in person is set forth,
Or hitherwards intended speedily,
With strong and mighty preparation.

HOTSPUR   He shall be welcome too. Where is his son,
The nimble-footed madcap Prince of Wales,
And his comrades that daffed the world aside
And bid it pass?

VERNON   All furnished, all in arms,
All plumed like estridges that with the wind
Bated, like eagles having lately bathed,
Glittering in golden coats like images,   100
As full of spirit as the month of May,
And gorgeous as the sun at midsummer,
Wanton as youthful goats, wild as young bulls.

I saw young Harry with his beaver on,
His cushes on his thighs, gallantly armed,
Rise from the ground like feathered Mercury,
And vaulted with such ease into his seat,
As if an angel dropped down from the clouds
To turn and wind a fiery Pegasus,
And witch the world with noble horsemanship.   110

HOTSPUR No more, no more! Worse than the sun in March,
This praise doth nourish agues. Let them come!
They come like sacrifices in their trim,
And to the fire-eyed maid of smoky war
All hot and bleeding will we offer them.
The mailed Mars shall on his altar sit
Up to the ears in blood. I am on fire
To hear this rich reprisal is so nigh,
And yet not ours! Come, let me taste my horse,
Who is to bear me like a thunderbolt   120
Against the bosom of the Prince of Wales.
Harry to Harry shall, hot horse to horse,
Meet and ne'er part till one drop down a corse.
O that Glendower were come!

VERNON   There is more news.
I learned in Worcester as I rode along,
He cannot draw his power this fourteen days.

DOUGLAS That's the worst tidings that I hear of yet.

WOR'STER Ay, by my faith, that bears a frosty sound.

HOTSPUR What may the King's whole battle reach unto?

VERNON To thirty thousand.

HOTSPUR   Forty let it be.   130
My father and Glendower being both away,
The powers of us may serve so great a day.
Come, let us take a muster speedily:
Doomsday is near; die all, die merrily!

DOUGLAS Talk not of dying; I am out of fear
Of death or death's hand for this one half-year.

                                        [*Exeunt.*

SCENE 2.

Warwickshire: a road near Coventry.

Enter FALSTAFF *and* BARDOLPH.

FALSTAFF   Bardolph, get thee before to Coventry: fill me a bottle
of sack. Our soldiers shall march through. We'll to
Sutton Cofill tonight.

BARDOLPH   Will you give me money, captain?

FALSTAFF   Lay out, lay out.

BARDOLPH   This bottle makes an angel.

FALSTAFF   And if it do, take it for thy labour; and if it make
twenty, take them all, I'll answer the coinage. Bid my
lieutenant Peto meet me at town's end.

BARDOLPH   I will, captain; farewell.   [*Exit.* 10

FALSTAFF   If I be not ashamed of my soldiers, I am a soused
gurnet. I have misused the King's press damnably. I
have got, in exchange of a hundred and fifty soldiers,
three hundred and odd pounds. I press me none but
good householders, yeomen's sons, enquire me out
contracted bachelors, such as had been asked twice on
the banns; such a commodity of warm slaves as had as
lief hear the devil as a drum, such as fear the report of
a caliver worse than a struck fowl or a hurt wild duck.
I pressed me none but such toasts-and-butter, with 20
hearts in their bellies no bigger than pins' heads, and
they have bought out their services; and now my
whole charge consists of ancients, corporals, lieu-
tenants, gentlemen of companies – slaves as ragged as
Lazarus in the painted cloth, where the glutton's dogs
licked his sores – and such as indeed were never
soldiers, but discarded unjust serving-men, younger
sons to younger brothers, revolted tapsters, and ostlers
trade-fallen, the cankers of a calm world and a long
peace, ten times more dishonourable-ragged than an 30
old fazed ancient. And such have I to fill up the rooms
of them as have bought out their services, that you
would think that I had a hundred and fifty tattered
prodigals lately come from swine-keeping, from eating

draff and husks.[51] A mad fellow met me on the way, and told me I had unloaded all the gibbets and pressed the dead bodies. No eye hath seen such scarecrows. I'll not march through Coventry with them, that's flat. Nay, and the villains march wide betwixt the legs as if they had gyves on, for indeed I had the most of them out of prison. There's not a shirt and a half in all my company, and the half shirt is two napkins tacked together and thrown over the shoulders like a herald's coat without sleeves; and the shirt, to say the truth, stolen from my host at Saint Albans, or the red-nose innkeeper of Daventry. But that's all one, they'll find linen enough on every hedge.[52]

Enter the PRINCE (HAL) *and* LORD WESTMORLAND.

HAL   How now, blown Jack? How now, quilt?[53]

FALSTAFF What, Hal! How now, mad wag? What a devil dost thou in Warwickshire? – My good Lord of Westmorland, I cry you mercy: I thought your honour had already been at Shrewsbury.

WEST.   Faith, Sir John, 'tis more than time that I were there, and you too, but my powers are there already. The King, I can tell you, looks for us all: we must away all night.

FALSTAFF Tut, never fear me; I am as vigilant as a cat to steal cream.

HAL   I think, to steal cream indeed, for thy theft hath already made thee butter. But tell me, Jack, whose fellows are these that come after?

FALSTAFF Mine, Hal, mine.

HAL   I did never see such pitiful rascals.

FALSTAFF Tut, tut, good enough to toss; food for powder, food for powder: they'll fill a pit as well as better. Tush, man, mortal men, mortal men.

WEST.   Ay, but Sir John, methinks they are exceeding poor and bare, too beggarly.

FALSTAFF Faith, for their poverty, I know not where they had that; and for their bareness, I am sure they never learned that of me.

HAL	No, I'll be sworn, unless you call three fingers in the ribs bare.[54] But sirrah, make haste. Percy is already in the field. [*Exit.*
FALSTAFF	What, is the King encamped?
WEST.	He is, Sir John, I fear we shall stay too long. [*Exit.*
FALSTAFF	Well, to the latter end of a fray and the beginning of a feast
	Fits a dull fighter and a keen guest. [*Exit.*

SCENE 3.

Shrewsbury: the rebels' camp.

Enter HOTSPUR, WORCESTER, DOUGLAS *and* VERNON

HOTSPUR	We'll fight with him tonight.
WOR'STER	It may not be.
DOUGLAS	You give him then advantage.
VERNON	Not a whit.
HOTSPUR	Why say you so, looks he not for supply?
VERNON	So do we.
HOTSPUR	His is certain, ours is doubtful.
WOR'STER	Good cousin, be advised: stir not tonight.
VERNON	Do not, my Lord.
DOUGLAS	You do not counsel well.
	You speak it out of fear and cold heart.
VERNON	Do me no slander, Douglas. By my life –
	And I dare well maintain it with my life –
	If well-respected honour bid me on,
	I hold as little counsel with weak fear
	As you, my Lord, or any Scot that this day lives.
	Let it be seen tomorrow in the battle
	Which of us fears.
DOUGLAS	Yea, or tonight.
VERNON	Content.
HOTSPUR	Tonight, say I.
VERNON	Come, come, it may not be. I wonder much,
	Being men of such great leading as you are,
	That you foresee not what impediments
	Drag back our expedition. Certain horse

10

Of my cousin Vernon's are not yet come up,   20
Your uncle Worcester's horse came but today,
And now their pride and mettle is asleep,
Their courage with hard labour tame and dull,
That not a horse is half the half of himself.

HOTSPUR So are the horses of the enemy
In general journey-bated and brought low.
The better part of ours are full of rest.

WOR'STER The number of the King exceedeth ours.
For God's sake, cousin, stay till all come in.
                    [*Outside, a trumpet sounds a parley.*

                    Enter SIR WALTER BLUNT.

BLUNT I come with gracious offers from the King,   30
If you vouchsafe me hearing and respect.

HOTSPUR Welcome, Sir Walter Blunt; and would to God
You were of our determination.
Some of us love you well, and even those some
Envy your great deservings and good name,
Because you are not of our quality,
But stand against us like an enemy.

BLUNT And God defend but still I should stand so,
So long as out of limit and true rule
You stand against anointed majesty.   40
– But to my charge. The King hath sent to know
The nature of your griefs, and whereupon
You conjure from the breast of civil peace
Such bold hostility, teaching his duteous land
Audacious cruelty. If that the King
Have any way your good deserts forgot,
Which he confesseth to be manifold,
He bids you name your griefs, and with all speed
You shall have your desires with interest,
And pardon absolute for yourself and these   50
Herein misled by your suggestion.

HOTSPUR The King is kind, and well we know the King
Knows at what time to promise, when to pay.
My father and my uncle and myself
Did give him that same royalty he wears;

And when he was not six-and-twenty strong,
Sick in the world's regard, wretched and low,
A poor unminded outlaw sneaking home,
My father gave him welcome to the shore.
And when he heard him swear and vow to God   60
He came but to be Duke of Lancaster,
To sue his livery, and beg his peace
With tears of innocency and terms of zeal,
My father, in kind heart and pity moved,
Swore him assistance, and performed it too.
Now when the lords and barons of the realm
Perceived Northumberland did lean to him,
The more and less came in with cap and knee,
Met him in boroughs, cities, villages,
Attended him on bridges, stood in lanes,   70
Laid gifts before him, proffered him their oaths,
Gave him their heirs as pages, followed him
Even at the heels in golden multitudes.
He presently, as greatness knows itself,
Steps me a little higher than his vow
Made to my father while his blood was poor
Upon the naked shore at Ravenspurgh;
And now forsooth takes on him to reform
Some certain edicts and some strait decrees
That lie too heavy on the commonwealth,   80
Cries out upon abuses, seems to weep
Over his country's wrongs; and by this face,
This seeming brow of justice, did he win
The hearts of all that he did angle for;
Proceeded further, cut me off the heads
Of all the favourites that the absent King
In deputation left behind him here,
When he was personal in the Irish war.

BLUNT   Tut, I came not to hear this.

HOTSPUR   Then to the point.
In short time after, he deposed the King,   90
Soon after that deprived him of his life,
And in the neck of that tasked the whole state.
To make that worse, suffered his kinsman March

        (Who is, if every owner were well placed,
        Indeed his King) to be engaged in Wales,
        There without ransom to lie forfeited;
        Disgraced me in my happy victories,
        Sought to entrap me by intelligence,
        Rated mine uncle from the Council-board,
        In rage dismissed my father from the court,   100
        Broke oath on oath, committed wrong on wrong,
        And in conclusion drove us to seek out
        This head of safety, and withal to pry
        Into his title, the which we find
        Too indirect for long continuance.
BLUNT   Shall I return this answer to the King?
HOTSPUR Not so, Sir Walter. We'll withdraw awhile.
        Go to the King, and let there be impawned
        Some surety for a safe return again,
        And in the morning early shall mine uncle   110
        Bring him our purposes; and so, farewell.
BLUNT   I would you would accept of grace and love.
HOTSPUR And may be so we shall.
BLUNT   Pray God you do.   [*Exeunt.*

SCENE 4.

York: the Archbishop's palace.

Enter the ARCHBISHOP OF YORK *and* SIR MICHAEL.

ARCHB.   Hie, good Sir Michael, bear this sealed brief [55]
        With wingèd haste to the Lord Marshal,
        This to my cousin Scroop, and all the rest
        To whom they are directed. If you knew
        How much they do import, you would make haste.
SIR M.   My good Lord,
        I guess their tenor.
ARCHB.   Like enough you do.
        Tomorrow, good Sir Michael, is a day
        Wherein the fortune of ten thousand men
        Must bide the touch. For, sir, at Shrewsbury,   10
        As I am truly given to understand,

The King with mighty and quick-raisèd power
Meets with Lord Harry. And I fear, Sir Michael,
What with the sickness of Northumberland,
Whose power was in the first proportion,
And what with Owen Glendower's absence thence,
Who with them was a rated sinew too,
And comes not in, o'er-ruled by prophecies,
I fear the power of Percy is too weak
To wage an instant trial with the King.   20

SIR M.   Why, my good Lord, you need not fear:
There is Douglas, and Lord Mortimer.

ARCHB.   No, Mortimer is not there.

SIR M.   But there is Mordake, Vernon, Lord Harry Percy,
And there is my Lord of Worcester, and a head
Of gallant warriors, noble gentlemen.

ARCHB.   And so there is. But yet the King hath drawn
The special head of all the land together:
The Prince of Wales, Lord John of Lancaster,
The noble Westmorland, and warlike Blunt,   30
And many more corrivals and dear men
Of estimation and command in arms.

SIR M.   Doubt not, my Lord, they shall be well opposed.

ARCHB.   I hope no less, yet needful 'tis to fear;
And to prevent the worst, Sir Michael, speed:
For if Lord Percy thrive not, ere the King
Dismiss his power, he means to visit us,
For he hath heard of our confederacy,
And 'tis but wisdom to make strong against him;
Therefore make haste. I must go write again   40
To other friends. And so, farewell, Sir Michael.
                                        [*Exeunt separately*.

ACT 5, SCENE 1.

Shrewsbury: the King's camp.

Enter the KING, *the* PRINCE OF WALES (HAL), LORD JOHN OF LANCASTER, SIR WALTER BLUNT *and* FALSTAFF.

K. HENRY   How bloodily the sun begins to peer
Above yon bulky hill! The day looks pale
At his distemp'rature.

HAL   The southern wind
Doth play the trumpet to his purposes,
And by his hollow whistling in the leaves
Foretells a tempest and a blust'ring day.

K. HENRY   Then with the losers let it sympathize,
For nothing can seem foul to those that win.

                              [*Outside, a trumpet sounds.*

Enter WORCESTER *and* VERNON.

How now, my Lord of Worcester? 'Tis not well
That you and I should meet upon such terms   10
As now we meet. You have deceived our trust,
And made us doff our easy robes of peace
To crush our old limbs in ungentle steel.
This is not well, my Lord, this is not well.
What say you to it? Will you again unknit
The churlish knot of all-abhorrèd war,
And move in that obedient orb again
Where you did give a fair and natural light,
And be no more an exhaled meteor,
A prodigy of fear, and a portént   20
Of broachèd mischief to the unborn times?

WOR'STER   Hear me, my liege.
For mine own part, I could be well content
To entertain the lag end of my life
With quiet hours. For I protest,
I have not sought the day of this dislike.

K. HENRY   You have not sought it? How comes it, then?

FALSTAFF   Rebellion lay in his way, and he found it.

HAL   [*to Falstaff:*] Peace, chewet, peace!

WOR'STER It pleased your Majesty to turn your looks   30
Of favour from myself and all our house;
And yet I must remember you, my Lord,
We were the first and dearest of your friends.
For you my staff of office did I break
In Richard's time, and posted day and night
To meet you on the way, and kiss your hand,
When yet you were in place and in account
Nothing so strong and fortunate as I.
It was myself, my brother, and his son,
That brought you home, and boldly did outdare   40
The dangers of the time. You swore to us,
And you did swear that oath at Doncaster,
That you did nothing purpose 'gainst the state,
Nor claim no further than your new-fall'n right,
The seat of Gaunt, dukedom of Lancaster.
To this we swore our aid. But in short space
It rained down fortune show'ring on your head,
And such a flood of greatness fell on you,
What with our help, what with the absent King,
What with the injuries of a wanton time,   50
The seeming suff'rances that you had borne,
And the contrarious winds that held the King
So long in his unlucky Irish wars
That all in England did repute him dead.
And from this swarm of fair advantages
You took occasion to be quickly wooed
To gripe the general sway into your hand,
Forget your oath to us at Doncaster,
And being fed by us, you used us so
As that ungentle gull, the cuckoo's bird,   60
Useth the sparrow – did oppress our nest,
Grew by our feeding to so great a bulk
That even our love durst not come near your sight
For fear of swallowing. But with nimble wing
We were enforced for safety sake to fly
Out of your sight, and raise this present head,
Whereby we stand opposèd by such means
As you yourself have forged against yourself

By unkind usage, dangerous countenance,
And violation of all faith and troth   70
Sworn to us in your younger enterprise.

K. HENRY   These things indeed you have articulate,
Proclaimed at market crosses, read in churches,
To face the garment of rebellion
With some fine colour that may please the eye
Of fickle changelings and poor discontents,
Which gape and rub the elbow at the news
Of hurly-burly innovation.
And never yet did insurrection want
Such water-colours to impaint his cause,   80
Nor moody beggars starving for a time
Of pell-mell havoc and confusion.

HAL   In both your armies there is many a soul
Shall pay full dearly for this encounter
If once they join in trial. Tell your nephew,
The Prince of Wales doth join with all the world
In praise of Henry Percy. By my hopes,
This present enterprise set off his head,
I do not think a braver gentleman,
More active-valiant or more valiant-young,   90
More daring or more bold, is now alive
To grace this latter age with noble deeds.
For my part, I may speak it to my shame,
I have a truant been to chivalry,
And so I hear he doth account me too;
Yet this, before my father's majesty:
I am content that he shall take the odds
Of his great name and estimation,
And will, to save the blood on either side,
Try fortune with him in a single fight.   100

K. HENRY   And, Prince of Wales, so dare we venture thee,
Albeit considerations infinite
Do make against it. No, good Worcester, no;
We love our people well, even those we love
That are misled upon your cousin's part,
And will they take the offer of our grace,
Both he, and they, and you, yea, every man

Shall be my friend again, and I'll be his.
So tell your cousin, and bring me word
What he will do. But if he will not yield,   110
Rebuke and dread correction wait on us,
And they shall do their office. So, be gone.
We will not now be troubled with reply.
We offer fair; take it advisedly.

                      [Exeunt Worcester and Vernon.

HAL   It will not be accepted, on my life.
The Douglas and the Hotspur both together
Are confident against the world in arms.

K. HENRY   Hence, therefore, every leader to his charge,
For on their answer will we set on them,
And God befriend us as our cause is just!   120

          [Exeunt all but the Prince (Hal) and Falstaff.

FALSTAFF   Hal, if thou see me down in the battle and bestride me,
so; 'tis a point of friendship.

HAL   Nothing but a Colossus can do thee that friendship. Say
thy prayers, and farewell.

FALSTAFF   I would 'twere bed-time, Hal, and all well.

HAL   Why, thou owest God a death.   *[Exit Hal.*

FALSTAFF   'Tis not due yet; I would be loath to pay him before
his day. What need I be so forward with him that calls
not on me? Well, 'tis no matter; honour pricks me on.
Yea, but how if honour prick me off when I come on,   130
how then? Can honour set-to a leg? No. Or an arm?
No. Or take away the grief of a wound? No. Honour
hath no skill in surgery then? No. What is honour? A
word. What is in that word 'honour'? What is that
'honour'? Air. A trim reckoning! Who hath it? He that
died a Wednesday. Doth he feel it? No. Doth he hear
it? No. 'Tis insensible, then? Yea, to the dead. But will
it not live with the living? No. Why? Detraction will
not suffer it. Therefore I'll none of it. Honour is a
mere scutcheon; and so ends my catechism.   *[Exit.* 140

SCENE 2.

Shrewsbury: the rebels' camp.

Enter WORCESTER *and* SIR RICHARD VERNON.

WOR'STER   O no, my nephew must not know, Sir Richard,
The liberal and kind offer of the King.

VERNON   'Twere best he did.

WOR'STER   Then are we all undone.
It is not possible, it cannot be,
The King should keep his word in loving us.
He will suspect us still, and find a time
To punish this offence in other faults.
Supposition all our lives shall be stuck full of eyes,
For treason is but trusted like the fox,
Who, never so tame, so cherished and locked up,   10
Will have a wild trick of his ancestors.
Look how we can, or sad or merrily,
Interpretation will misquote our looks,
And we shall feed like oxen at a stall,
The better cherished still the nearer death.
My nephew's trespass may be well forgot,
It hath the excuse of youth and heat of blood,
And an adopted name of privilege –
A hare-brained Hotspur, governed by a spleen.
All his offences live upon my head   20
And on his father's. We did train him on,
And, his corruption being tane from us,
We, as the spring of all, shall pay for all.
Therefore, good cousin, let not Harry know
In any case the offer of the King.

VERNON   Deliver what you will; I'll say 'tis so.
Here comes your cousin.

Enter HOTSPUR *and* DOUGLAS.

HOTSPUR   My uncle is returned;
Deliver up my Lord of Westmorland.
– Uncle, what news?

WOR'STER   The King will bid you battle presently.   30

DOUGLAS Defy him by the Lord of Westmorland.

HOTSPUR Lord Douglas, go you and tell him so.

DOUGLAS Marry, and shall, and very willingly.   [*Exit.*

WOR'STER There is no seeming mercy in the King.

HOTSPUR Did you beg any? God forbid!

WOR'STER I told him gently of our grievances,
Of his oath-breaking; which he mended thus,
By now forswearing that he is forsworn:
He calls us 'rebels', 'traitors', and will scourge
With haughty arms this hateful name in us.   40

Enter DOUGLAS.

DOUGLAS Arm, gentlemen, to arms! For I have thrown
A brave defiance in King Henry's teeth,
And Westmorland that was engaged did bear it,
Which cannot choose but bring him quickly on.

WOR'STER The Prince of Wales stepped forth before the King,
And, nephew, challenged you to single fight.

HOTSPUR O, would the quarrel lay upon our heads,
And that no man might draw short breath today
But I and Harry Monmouth! Tell me, tell me,
How showed his tasking? Seemed it in contempt?   50

VERNON No, by my soul, I never in my life
Did hear a challenge urged more modestly,
Unless a brother should a brother dare
To gentle exercise and proof of arms.
He gave you all the duties of a man,
Trimmed up your praises with a princely tongue,
Spoke your deserving like a chronicle,
Making you ever better than his praise
By still dispraising praise valued with you;
And, which became him like a prince indeed,   60
He made a blushing cital of himself,
And chid his truant youth with such a grace
As if he mastered there a double spirit
Of teaching and of learning instantly.
There did he pause. But let me tell the world:
If he outlive the envy of this day,
England did never owe so sweet a hope

So much miscónstrued in his wantonness.

HOTSPUR   Cousin, I think thou art enamoured
On his follies. Never did I hear   70
Of any prince so wild a liberty.
But be he as he will, yet once ere night
I will embrace him with a soldier's arm,
That he shall shrink under my courtesy.
– Arm, arm with speed! And fellows, soldiers, friends,
Better consider what you have to do
Than I, that have not well the gift of tongue,
Can lift your blood up with persuasion.

Enter a MESSENGER.

MESSEN. I   My Lord, here are letters for you.
HOTSPUR   I cannot read them now.   [*Exit messenger.* 80
O gentlemen, the time of life is short:
To spend that shortness basely were too long
If life did ride upon a dial's point,
Still ending at the arrival of an hour.
And if we live, we live to tread on kings,
If die, brave death when princes die with us!
Now, for our consciences: the arms are fair,
When the intent of bearing them is just.

Enter another MESSENGER.

MESSEN. 2   My Lord, prepare, the King cómes on apace.   [*Exit.*
HOTSPUR   I thank him that he cuts me from my tale,   90
For I profess not talking. Only this:
Let each man do his best. And here draw I
A sword whose temper I intend to stain
With the best blood that I can meet withal
In the adventure of this perilous day.
Now, Esperance! Percy! And set on!
Sound all the lofty instruments of war,
And by that music let us all embrace,
For, heaven to earth, some of us never shall
A second time do such a courtesy.   100
            [*They embrace as the trumpets sound. Exeunt.*

SCENE 3.

Shrewsbury: the battlefield.

The KING *enters with his* SOLDIERS. *Alarum: exeunt to the battle.*
Then enter SIR WALTER BLUNT, *disguised as the King,*
and the Earl of DOUGLAS, *meeting.*

BLUNT   What is thy name, that in the battle thus
              Thou crossest me? What honour dost thou seek
              Upon my head?

DOUGLAS   Know then my name is Douglas,
              And I do haunt thee in the battle thus
              Because some tell me that thou art a king.

BLUNT   They tell thee true.

DOUGLAS   The Lord of Stafford dear today hath bought
              Thy likeness, for instead of thee, King Harry,
              This sword hath ended him: so shall it thee,
              Unless thou yield thee as my prisoner.   10

BLUNT   I was not born a yielder, thou proud Scot,[56]
              And thou shalt find a king that will revenge
              Lord Stafford's death.

                         [*They fight; Douglas kills Blunt.*

Enter HOTSPUR.

HOTSPUR   O Douglas, hadst thou fought at Holmedon thus,
              I never had triumphed upon a Scot.

DOUGLAS   All's done, all's won: here breathless lies the King.

HOTSPUR   Where?

DOUGLAS   Here.

HOTSPUR   This, Douglas? No, I know this face full well.
              A gallant knight he was – his name was Blunt –   20
              Semblably furnished like the King himself.

DOUGLAS   [*to Blunt:*] A fool go with thy soul, whither it goes![57]
              A borrowed title hast thou bought too dear.
              Why didst thou tell me that thou wert a king?

HOTSPUR   The King hath many marching in his coats.

DOUGLAS   Now, by my sword, I will kill all his coats!
              I'll murder all his wardrobe, piece by piece,
              Until I meet the King.

HOTSPUR   Up and away!
Our soldiers stand full fairly for the day.   [*Exeunt.*

Alarum. Enter FALSTAFF.

FALSTAFF   Though I could scape shot-free at London, I fear the 30
shot here: here's no scoring but upon the pate. – [58]Soft!
Who are you? Sir Walter Blunt: there's honour for
you. Here's no vanity! I am as hot as molten lead, and
as heavy too: God keep lead out of me; I need no more
weight than mine own bowels. I have led my ragamuffins where they are peppered: there's not three of
my hundred-and-fifty left alive; and they are for the
town's end, to beg during life. – But who comes here?

Enter the PRINCE (HAL).

HAL   What, stand'st thou idle here? Lend me thy sword.
Many a noble man lies stark and stiff   40
Under the hooves of vaunting enemies,
Whose deaths are yet unrevenged. I prithee
Lend me thy sword.

FALSTAFF   O Hal, I prithee give me leave to breathe a while.
Turk Gregory[59] never did such deeds in arms as I have
done this day. I have paid Percy, I have made him
sure.

HAL   He is indeed, and living to kill thee.
I prithee lend me thy sword.

FALSTAFF   Nay, before God, Hal, if Percy be alive, thou gets not 50
my sword, but take my pistol if thou wilt.

HAL   Give it me. What, is it in the case?

FALSTAFF   Ay, Hal, 'tis hot, 'tis hot. There's that will sack a city.
                      [*The Prince draws out a bottle of sack.*

HAL   What, is it a time to jest and dally now?
                       [*He throws the bottle at him. Exit.*

FALSTAFF   Well, if Percy be alive, I'll pierce him. If he do come
in my way, so; if he do not, if I come in his willingly,
let him make a carbonado of me. I like not such
grinning honour as Sir Walter hath. Give me life,
which if I can save, so; if not, honour comes unlooked
for, and there's an end.   [*Exit.* 60

SCENE 4.

Shrewsbury: the battlefield.

Alarum. Excursions. Enter the KING, *the* PRINCE (HAL, *wounded*),
LORD JOHN OF LANCASTER *and the* EARL OF WESTMORLAND.

K. HENRY I prithee, Harry, withdraw thyself, thou bleed'st too
                           much.
        – Lord John of Lancaster, go you with him.

JOHN Not I, my Lord, unless I did bleed too.

HAL I beseech your Majesty, make up,
        Lest your retirement do amaze your friends.

K. HENRY I will do so. – My Lord of Westmorland,
        Lead him to his tent.

WEST. [*to Hal:*] Come, my Lord, I'll lead you to your tent.

HAL Lead me, my Lord? I do not need your help,
        And God forbid a shallow scratch should drive   10
        The Prince of Wales from such a field as this,
        Where stained nobility lies trodden on,
        And rebels' arms triumph in massacres.

JOHN We breathe too long: come, cousin Westmorland,
        Our duty this way lies; for God's sake, come.
                [*Exeunt Lancaster and Westmorland.*

HAL By God, thou hast deceived me, Lancaster;
        I did not think thee lord of such a spirit:
        Before, I loved thee as a brother, John,
        But now I do respect thee as my soul.

K. HENRY I saw him hold Lord Percy at the point   20
        With lustier maintenance than I did look for
        Of such an ungrown warrior.

HAL   O, this boy
        Lends mettle to us all!   [*Exit Hal.*

Enter DOUGLAS.

DOUGLAS Another king! They grow like Hydra's heads.[60]
        I am the Douglas, fatal to all those
        That wear those colours on them. What art thou
        That counterfeit'st the person of a king?

K. HENRY The King himself, who, Douglas, grieves at heart

So many of his shadows thou hast met,
And not the very King. I have two boys   30
Seek Percy and thyself about the field,
But, seeing thou fall'st on me so luckily,
I will assay thee: so defend thyself.

DOUGLAS   I fear thou art another counterfeit,
And yet, in faith, thou bear'st thee like a king;
But mine I am sure thou art, whoe'er thou be:
And thus I win thee.

       [*They fight, the King being in danger.*

     Enter the PRINCE OF WALES (HAL).

HAL   Hold up thy head, vile Scot, or thou art like
Never to hold it up again! The spirits
Of valiant Shirley, Stafford, Blunt are in my arms.   40
It is the Prince of Wales that threatens thee,
Who never promiseth but he means to pay.

       [*They fight; Douglas flees.*

Cheerly, my Lord; how fares your Grace?
Sir Nicholas Gawsey hath for succour sent,
And so hath Clifton: I'll to Clifton straight.

K. HENRY   Stay and breathe a while.
Thou hast redeemed thy lost opinion,
And showed thou mak'st some tender of my life
In this fair rescue thou hast brought to me.

HAL   O God, they did me too much injury   50
That ever said I hearkened for your death.
If it were so, I might have let alone
The insulting hand of Douglas over you,
Which would have been as speedy in your end
As all the poisonous potions in the world,
And saved the treacherous labour of your son.

K. HENRY   Make up to Clifton; I'll to Sir Nicholas Gawsey.

           [*Exit King.*

      Enter HOTSPUR.

HOTSPUR   If I mistake not, thou art Harry Monmouth.
HAL   Thou speak'st as if I would deny my name.
HOTSPUR   My name is Harry Percy.
HAL   Why then I see   60

A very valiant rebel of the name.
I am the Prince of Wales, and think not, Percy,
To share with me in glory any more;
Two stars keep not their motion in one sphere,
Nor can one England brook a double reign
Of Harry Percy and the Prince of Wales.

HOTSPUR   Nor shall it, Harry, for the hour is come
To end the one of us; and would to God
Thy name in arms were now as great as mine.

HAL   I'll make it greater ere I part from thee,   70
And all the budding honours on thy crest
I'll crop to make a garland for my head.

HOTSPUR   I can no longer brook thy vanities.   [*They fight.*

Enter FALSTAFF.

FALSTAFF   Well said, Hal! To it, Hal! Nay, you shall find no boy's
play here, I can tell you.

Enter DOUGLAS; *he fights with* FALSTAFF,
who falls down as if he were dead.

[*Exit Douglas.*

The PRINCE *mortally wounds* HOTSPUR.

HOTSPUR   O Harry, thou hast robbed me of my youth!
I better brook the loss of brittle life
Than those proud titles thou hast won of me:
They wound my thoughts worse than thy sword my
                                            flesh.
But thoughts, the slaves of life, and life, time's fool,   80
And time, that takes survey of all the world,
Must have a stop. O, I could prophesy,
But that the earthy and cold hand of death
Lies on my tongue: no, Percy, thou art dust,
And food for –   [*He dies.*

HAL   For worms, brave Percy. Fare thee well, great heart!
Ill-weaved ambition, how much art thou shrunk:
When that this body did contain a spirit,
A kingdom for it was too small a bound;
But now two paces of the vilest earth   90
Is room enough. This earth that bears thee dead

Bears not alive so stout a gentleman.
If thou wert sensible of courtesy
I should not make so dear a show of zeal;
But let my favours hide thy mangled face,
And even in thy behalf I'll thank myself
For doing these fair rites of tenderness.
Adieu, and take thy praise with thee to heaven;
Thy ignomy sleep with thee in the grave,
But not remembered in thy epitaph.   100
    [*Having covered Hotspur's face, he sees the prone Falstaff.*
– What, old acquaintance, could not all this flesh
Keep in a little life? Poor Jack, farewell!
I could have better spared a better man.
O, I should have a heavy miss of thee,
If I were much in love with vanity.
Death hath not struck so fat a deer today,
Though many dearer, in this bloody fray.
Embowelled will I see thee by and by;
Till then, in blood, by noble Percy lie.   [*Exit.*
                                 [*Falstaff stands.*

FALSTAFF   'Embowelled'? If thou embowel me today, I'll give   110
you leave to powder me, and eat me too, tomorrow.
'Sblood, 'twas time to counterfeit, or that hot termagant
Scot had paid me, scot and lot too. 'Counterfeit'? I lie, I
am no counterfeit. To die is to be a counterfeit: for he
is but the counterfeit of a man, who hath not the life of
a man. But to counterfeit dying, when a man thereby
liveth, is to be no counterfeit, but the true and perfect
image of life indeed. The better part of valour is dis-
cretion, in the which better part I have saved my life.
Zounds, I am afraid of this gunpowder Percy, though   120
he be dead. How if he should counterfeit too, and rise?
By my faith, I am afraid he would prove the better
counterfeit; therefore I'll make him sure, yea, and I'll
swear I killed him. Why may not he rise as well as I?
Nothing confutes me but eyes, and nobody sees me:
therefore, sirrah [*stabbing him*], with a new wound in
your thigh, come you along with me.
                        [*He takes up Hotspur on his back.*

Enter the PRINCE (HAL) *and* LORD JOHN OF LANCASTER.

HAL   Come, brother John; full bravely hast thou fleshed
           Thy maiden sword.
JOHN   But soft, whom have we here?
           Did you not tell me this fat man was dead?   130
HAL   I did; I saw him dead,
           Breathless and bleeding on the ground. [*To Falstaff:*]
                                            Art thou alive?
           Or is it fantasy that plays upon our eyesight?
           I prithee speak: we will not trust our eyes
           Without our ears. Thou art not what thou seem'st.
FALSTAFF   No, that's certain: I am not a double man; but if I be
           not Jack Falstaff, then am I a Jack.[61] There is Percy.
                                     [*He throws the body down.*
           If your father will do me any honour, so; if not, let
           him kill the next Percy himself. I look to be either earl
           or duke, I can assure you.   140
HAL   Why, Percy I killed myself, and saw thee dead.
FALSTAFF   Didst thou? Lord, Lord, how this world is given to
           lying! I grant you I was down, and out of breath, and
           so was he, but we rose both at an instant, and fought a
           long hour by Shrewsbury clock. If I may be believed,
           so; if not, let them that should reward valour bear the
           sin upon their own heads. I'll take it upon my death, I
           gave him this wound in the thigh. If the man were
           alive, and would deny it, zounds, I would make him
           eat a piece of my sword.   150
JOHN   This is the strangest tale that ever I heard.
HAL   This is the strangest fellow, brother John.
           [*to Falstaff:*] Come, bring your luggage nobly on your
                                                              back.
           [*Aside to him:*] For my part, if a lie may do thee grace,
           I'll gild it with the happiest terms I have.
                                     [*A retreat is sounded.*
           The trumpet sounds retreat; the day is ours.
           Come, brother, let's to the highest of the field,
           To see what friends are living, who are dead.
                      [*Exeunt the Prince of Wales and John of Lancaster.*
FALSTAFF   I'll follow, as they say, for reward. He that rewards me,

God reward him! If I do grow great, I'll grow less, for 160
I'll purge, and leave sack, and live cleanly, as a noble
man should do.   [*Exit, bearing the body.*

SCENE 5.

Shrewsbury: the battlefield.

The trumpets sound. Enter the KING, *the* PRINCE OF WALES (HAL),
LORD JOHN OF LANCASTER *and the* EARL OF WESTMORLAND,
with WORCESTER *and* VERNON *as prisoners* (*guarded by* SOLDIERS).

K. HENRY   Thus ever did rebellion find rebuke.
Ill-spirited Worcester, did not we send grace,
Pardon, and terms of love to all of you?
And wouldst thou turn our offers contrary?
Misuse the tenor of thy kinsman's trust?
Three knights upon our party slain today,
A noble earl and many a creature else
Had been alive this hour,
If like a Christian thou hadst truly borne
Betwixt our armies true intelligence.   10

WOR'STER   What I have done, my safety urged me to,
And I embrace this fortune patiently,
Since not to be avoided it falls on me.

K. HENRY   Bear Worcester to the death, and Vernon too.
Other offenders we will pause upon.
      [*Exeunt Worcester and Vernon, guarded by soldiers.*
How goes the field?

HAL   The noble Scot, Lord Douglas, when he saw
The fortune of the day quite turned from him,
The noble Percy slain, and all his men
Upon the foot of fear, fled with the rest;   20
And, falling from a hill, he was so bruised
That the pursuers took him. At my tent
The Douglas is, and I beseech your grace
I may dispose of him.

K. HENRY   With all my heart.

HAL   Then, brother John of Lancaster, to you
This honourable bounty shall belong.

Go to the Douglas and deliver him
Up to his pleasure, ransomless and free.
His valours shown upon our crests today
Have taught us how to cherish such high deeds,   30
Even in the bosom of our adversaries.

JOHN   I thank your Grace for this high courtesy,
Which I shall give away immediately.

K. HENRY   Then this remains, that we divide our power.
You, son John, and my cousin Westmorland
Towards York shall bend you with your dearest speed
To meet Northumberland and the prelate Scroop,
Who, as we hear, are busily in arms.
Myself and you, son Harry, will towards Wales,
To fight with Glendower and the Earl of March.   40
Rebellion in this land shall lose his sway,
Meeting the check of such another day;
And since this business so fair is done,
Let us not leave till all our own be won.   [*Exeunt.*

FINIS.

HENRY IV, PART TWO

CHARACTERS:

RUMOUR, *speaker of the* INDUCTION

The King's Alliance:

King HENRY IV, *formerly Henry Bullingbrooke*
HENRY (HAL), PRINCE OF WALES, *the King's eldest son;*
   later King HENRY V
PRINCE JOHN *of Lancaster, a younger son of the King*
Humphrey, Duke of GLOUCESTER, *another son*
Thomas, Duke of CLARENCE, *another son*
The Earl of WARWICK
The Earl of WESTMORLAND
The Earl of SURREY
Sir John BLUNT
HARCOURT
The King's PAGE

Rebels and Their Relatives:

The Earl of NORTHUMBERLAND
LADY NORTHUMBERLAND, *his wife*
LADY PERCY, *widow of Hotspur*
The ARCHBISHOP *of* YORK
Lord MOWBRAY
Lord HASTINGS
LORD BARDOLPH
TRAVERS
MORTON
Sir John COLEVILE

The Falstaff Group:

Sir John FALSTAFF
Edward (Ned) POINS
BARDOLPH
Ancient PISTOL
PETO

Falstaff's PAGE
HOSTESS, *Mistress Quickly*
DOLL *Tearsheet*

Others:
The Lord Chief JUSTICE
A SERVANT *of the Lord Chief Justice*
Robert SHALLOW, *a rural Justice*
SILENCE, *another Justice*
DAVY, *Shallow's servant*
Ralph MOULDY
Simon SHADOW
Thomas WART
Francis FEEBLE
Peter BULLCALF
FANG, *an officer*
SNARE, *another officer*
FRANCIS *and two other* DRAWERS *(waiters)*
Two GROOMS
PORTER
GOWER, *a messenger*
Another MESSENGER, OFFICERS, MUSICIANS,
SOLDIERS, LORDS, BEADLES *and* ATTENDANTS

Speakers of the EPILOGUE

HENRY IV, PART TWO

INDUCTION

Northumberland: Warkworth Castle.

Enter RUMOUR, *in a robe painted full of tongues.*

RUMOUR   Open your ears: for which of you will stop
The vent of hearing when loud Rumour speaks?
I, from the orient to the drooping west,
Making the wind my post-horse, still unfold
The acts commencèd on this ball of earth.
Upon my tongues continual slanders ride,
The which in every language I pronounce,
Stuffing the ears of men with false reports.
I speak of peace, while covert enmity,
Under the smile of safety, wounds the world;   10
And who but Rumour, who but only I,
Make fearful musters and prepared defence,
Whiles the big year, swoll'n with some other grief,
Is thought with child by the stern tyrant War,
And no such matter? Rumour is a pipe
Blown by surmises, jealousies, conjectures,
And of so easy and so plain a stop[1]
That the blunt monster with uncounted heads,
The still-discordant wav'ring multitude,
Can play upon it. But what need I thus   20
My well-known body to anatomize
Among my household? Why is Rumour here?
I run before King Harry's victory,
Who in a bloody field by Shrewsbury
Hath beaten down young Hotspur and his troops,
Quenching the flame of bold rebellion
Even with the rebels' blood. But what mean I
To speak so true at first? My office is
To noise abroad that Harry Monmouth[2] fell
Under the wrath of noble Hotspur's sword,   30

And that the King before the Douglas' rage
Stooped his anointed head as low as death.
This have I rumoured through the peasant towns
Between that royal field of Shrewsbury
And this worm-eaten hold of raggèd stone,
Where Hotspur's father, old Northumberland,
Lies crafty-sick. The posts come tiring on,
And not a man of them brings other news
Than they have learnt of me. From Rumour's tongues
They bring smooth comforts false, worse than true
                         wrongs. 40
                          [*Exit.*

ACT I, SCENE I.

Northumberland: Warkworth Castle.

Enter the LORD BARDOLPH *at the outer door.*

LORD B. Who keeps the gate here, ho?

Enter the PORTER *from within.*

Where is the Earl?

PORTER What shall I say you are?

LORD B.   Tell thou the Earl
That the Lord Bardolph doth attend him here.

PORTER His Lordship is walked forth into the orchard.
Please it your honour knock but at the gate,
And he himself will answer.

Enter NORTHUMBERLAND, *wearing a nightcap and using a crutch.*

LORD B.   Here comes the Earl.

[*Exit porter.*

NORTH. What news, Lord Bardolph? Every minute now
Should be the father of some stratagem.
The times are wild; contention, like a horse
Full of high feeding, madly hath broke loose   10
And bears down all before him.

LORD B.   Noble Earl,
I bring you certain news from Shrewsbury.

NORTH. Good, and God will!

LORD B.   As good as heart can wish.
The King is almost wounded to the death,
And, in the fortune of my Lord your son,
Prince Harry slain outright; and both the Blunts
Killed by the hand of Douglas; young Prince John
And Westmorland and Stafford fled the field;
And Harry Monmouth's brawn, the hulk Sir John,
Is prisoner to your son. O, such a day,   20
So fought, so followed, and so fairly won,
Came not till now to dignify the times
Since Cæsar's fortunes!

NORTH.   How is this derived?

	Saw you the field? Came you from Shrewsbury?
LORD B.	I spake with one, my Lord, that came from thence,
	A gentleman well bred, and of good name,
	That freely rendered me these news for true.

Enter TRAVERS.

NORTH.	Here comes my servant Travers, whom I sent
	On Tuesday last to listen after news.
LORD B.	My Lord, I over-rode him on the way, 30
	And he is furnished with no certainties
	More than he haply may retail from me.
NORTH.	Now, Travers, what good tidings comes with you?
TRAVERS	My Lord, Sir John Umfrevile turned me back
	With joyful tidings, and, being better horsed,
	Out-rode me. After him came spurring hard
	A gentleman almost forspent with speed,
	That stopped by me to breathe his bloodied horse.
	He asked the way to Chester, and of him
	I did demand what news from Shrewsbury. 40
	He told me that rebellion had ill luck,
	And that young Harry Percy's spur was cold.
	With that he gave his able horse the head,
	And, bending forward, struck his armèd heels
	Against the panting sides of his poor jade,
	Up to the rowel-head; and starting so,
	He seemed in running to devour the way,
	Staying no longer question.
NORTH.	Ha? Again!
	Said he young Harry Percy's spur was cold?
	Of Hotspur, Coldspur? That rebellion 50
	Had met ill luck?
LORD B.	My Lord, I'll tell you what.
	If my young Lord, your son, have not the day,
	Upon mine honour, for a silken point
	I'll give my barony; never talk of it.
NORTH.	Why should that gentleman that rode by Travers
	Give then such instances of loss?
LORD B.	Who, he?
	He was some hilding fellow that had stol'n

The horse he rode on, and, upon my life,
Spoke at a venture. – Look, here comes more news.

Enter MORTON.

NORTH. Yea, this man's brow, like to a title-leaf,   60
Foretells the nature of a tragic volume.
So looks the strand whereon the imperious flood
Hath left a witnessed usurpation.
– Say, Morton, didst thou come from Shrewsbury?

MORTON I ran from Shrewsbury, my noble Lord,
Where hateful death put on his ugliest mask
To fright our party.

NORTH.   How doth my son, and brother?
Thou tremblest, and the whiteness in thy cheek
Is apter than thy tongue to tell thy errand.
Even such a man, so faint, so spiritless,   70
So dull, so dead in look, so woe-begone,
Drew Priam's curtain in the dead of night,
And would have told him half his Troy was burnt;
But Priam found the fire ere he his tongue,
And I my Percy's death ere thou report'st it.
This thou wouldst say, 'Your son did thus and thus;
Your brother thus; so fought the noble Douglas',
Stopping my greedy ear with their bold deeds.
But in the end, to stop my ear indeed,
Thou hast a sigh to blow away this praise,   80
Ending with 'Brother, son, and all are dead.'

MORTON Douglas is living, and your brother, yet;
But, for my Lord your son –

NORTH.   Why, he is dead!
See what a ready tongue suspicion hath!
He that but fears the thing he would not know
Hath, by instinct, knowledge from others' eyes
That what he feared is chanced. Yet speak, Morton:
Tell thou an earl his divination lies,
And I will take it as a sweet disgrace,
And make thee rich for doing me such wrong.   90

MORTON You are too great to be by me gainsaid;
Your spirit is too true, your fears too certain.

NORTH.   Yet, for all this, say not that Percy's dead.
           I see a strange confession in thine eye:
           Thou shak'st thy head, and hold'st it fear or sin
           To speak a truth. If he be slain, say so.
           The tongue offends not that reports his death;
           And he doth sin that doth belie the dead,
           Not he which says the dead is not alive.
           Yet the first bringer of unwelcome news   100
           Hath but a losing office, and his tongue
           Sounds ever after as a sullen bell
           Remembered tolling a departing friend.
LORD B.   I cannot think, my Lord, your son is dead.
MORTON   I am sorry I should force you to believe
           That which I would to God I had not seen;
           But these mine eyes saw him in bloody state,
           Rend'ring faint quittance, wearied and out-breathed,
           To Harry Monmouth, whose swift wrath beat down
           The never-daunted Percy to the earth,   110
           From whence with life he never more sprung up.
           In few, his death, whose spirit lent a fire
           Even to the dullest peasant in his camp,
           Being bruited once, took fire and heat away
           From the best-tempered courage in his troops;
           For from his metal was his party steeled,
           Which once in him abated, all the rest
           Turned on themselves, like dull and heavy lead;
           And as the thing that's heavy in itself
           Upon enforcement flies with greatest speed,   120
           So did our men, heavy in Hotspur's loss,
           Lend to this weight such lightness with their fear
           That arrows fled not swifter toward their aim
           Than did our soldiers, aiming at their safety,
           Fly from the field. Then was that noble Worcester
           So soon tane prisoner, and that furious Scot,
           The bloody Douglas, whose well-labouring sword
           Had three times slain th'appearance of the King,
           Gan vail his stomach, and did grace the shame
           Of those that turned their backs, and in his flight,   130
           Stumbling in fear, was took. The sum of all

Is that the King hath won, and hath sent out
A speedy power to encounter you, my Lord,
Under the conduct of young Lancaster
And Westmorland. This is the news at full.

NORTH.   For this I shall have time enough to mourn.
In poison there is physic, and these news,
Having been well, that would have made me sick,
Being sick, have in some measure made me well;
And, as the wretch – whose fever-weakened joints,   140
Like strengthless hinges, buckle under life –
Impatient of his fit, breaks like a fire
Out of his keeper's arms, even so my limbs,
Weakened with grief, being now enraged with grief,
Are thrice themselves. Hence, therefore, thou
                            nice crutch!
A scaly gauntlet now with joints of steel
Must glove this hand. And hence, thou sickly coif!
Thou art a guard too wanton for the head
Which princes, fleshed with conquest, aim to hit.
Now bind my brows with iron, and approach   150
The raggèd'st hour that time and spite dare bring
To frown upon th'enraged Northumberland!
Let heaven kiss earth! Now let not Nature's hand
Keep the wild flood confined! Let order die!
And let this world no longer be a stage
To feed contention in a ling'ring act;
But let one spirit of the first-born Cain
Reign in all bosoms, that, each heart being set
On bloody courses, the rude scene may end,
And darkness be the burier of the dead!   160

LORD B.   This strainèd passion doth you wrong, my Lord.
MORTON   Sweet Earl, divorce not wisdom from your honour;
The lives of all your loving complices
Lean on your health, the which, if you give o'er
To stormy passion, must perforce decay.
You cast th'event of war, my noble Lord,
And summed the account of chance before you said
'Let us make head'. It was your pre-surmise
That in the dole of blows your son might drop.

You knew he walked o'er perils, on an edge, 170
More likely to fall in than to get o'er.
You were advised his flesh was capable
Of wounds and scars, and that his forward spirit
Would lift him where most trade of danger ranged.
Yet did you say 'Go forth'; and none of this,
Though strongly apprehended, could restrain
The stiff-borne action. What hath then befall'n,
Or what hath this bold enterprise brought forth,
More than that being which was like to be?[3]

LORD B.   We all that are engagèd to this loss 180
Knew that we ventured on such dangerous seas
That if we wrought out life, 'twas ten to one;
And yet we ventured for the gain proposed,
Choked the respect of likely peril feared;
And since we are o'erset, venture again.
Come, we will all put forth, body and goods.

MORTON   'Tis more than time. – And, my most noble Lord,
I hear for certain, and dare speak the truth,
The gentle Archbishop of York is up
With well-appointed powers. He is a man 190
Who with a double surety binds his followers.
My Lord, your son had only but the corpse,
But shadows and the shows of men, to fight;
For that same word 'rebellion' did divide
The action of their bodies from their souls,
And they did fight with queasiness, constrained,
As men drink potions, that their weapons only
Seemed on our side; but, for their spirits and souls,
This word 'rebellion' – it had froze them up
As fish are in a pond. But now the Bishop 200
Turns insurrection to religion;
Supposed sincere and holy in his thoughts,
He's followed both with body and with mind,
And doth enlarge his rising with the blood
Of fair King Richard, scraped from Pomfret stones;
Derives from heaven his quarrel and his cause;
Tells them he doth bestride a bleeding land
Gasping for life under great Bullingbrooke;

And more and less do flock to follow him.

NORTH. I knew of this before, but, to speak truth,   210
This present grief had wiped it from my mind.
Go in with me, and counsel every man
The aptest way for safety and revenge.
Get posts and letters, and make friends with speed –
Never so few, and never yet more need.   [*Exeunt.*

SCENE 2.

London: a street.

Enter SIR JOHN FALSTAFF, *followed by his* PAGE
bearing his sword and buckler.

FALSTAFF Sirrah, you giant, what says the doctor to my water?
PAGE He said, sir, the water itself was a good healthy water;
but, for the party that owed it, he might have more
diseases than he knew for.
FALSTAFF Men of all sorts take a pride to gird at me. The brain
of this foolish-compounded clay, man, is not able to
invent anything that intends to laughter more than I
invent, or is invented on me; I am not only witty in
myself, but the cause that wit is in other men. I do here
walk before thee, like a sow that hath overwhelmed all   10
her litter but one. If the Prince put thee into my
service for any other reason than to set me off, why
then I have no judgement. Thou whoreson mandrake,
thou art fitter to be worn in my cap than to wait at my
heels. I was never manned with an agate till now, but I
will inset you neither in gold nor silver, but in vile
apparel, and send you back again to your master for a
jewel – the juvenal the Prince your master, whose chin
is not yet fledge. I will sooner have a beard grow in
the palm of my hand than he shall get one off his   20
cheek; and yet he will not stick to say his face is a face-
royal. God may finish it when He will, 'tis not a hair
amiss yet. He may keep it still at a face-royal, for a
barber shall never earn sixpence out of it. And yet he'll
be crowing as if he had writ man ever since his father

was a bachelor. He may keep his own grace, but he's almost out of mine, I can assure him. What said Master Dommelton about the satin for my short cloak and my slops?

PAGE   He said, sir, you should procure him better assurance   30 than Bardolph. He would not take his bond and yours; he liked not the security.

FALSTAFF   Let him be damned like the glutton! Pray God his tongue be hotter! A whoreson Achitophel![4] A rascally 'yea-forsooth' knave, to bear a gentleman in hand, and then stand upon security! The whoreson smoothy-pates do now wear nothing but high shoes and bunches of keys at their girdles; and if a man is through with them in honest taking-up, then they must stand upon security. I had as lief they would put ratsbane in my   40 mouth as offer to stop it with security. I looked a should have sent me two-and-twenty yards of satin, as I am a true knight, and he sends me 'security'! Well, he may sleep in security, for he hath the horn of abundance, and the lightness of his wife shines through it; and yet cannot he see, though he have his own lanthorn to light him.[5] Where's Bardolph?

PAGE   He's gone in Smithfield to buy your worship a horse.

FALSTAFF   I bought him in Paul's, and he'll buy me a horse in Smithfield. And I could get me but a wife in the stews,   50 I were manned, horsed, and wived.

Enter the LORD CHIEF JUSTICE *and his* SERVANT.

PAGE   Sir, here comes the nobleman that committed the Prince for striking him about Bardolph.[6]

FALSTAFF   Wait close; I will not see him.

JUSTICE   [*to his servant:*] What's he that goes there?

SERVANT   Falstaff, an't please your Lordship.

JUSTICE   He that was in question for the robbery?

SERVANT   He, my Lord; but he hath since done good service at Shrewsbury, and, as I hear, is now going with some charge to the Lord John of Lancaster.   60

JUSTICE   What, to York? Call him back again.

SERVANT   Sir John Falstaff!

FALSTAFF   Boy, tell him I am deaf.

PAGE   You must speak louder; my master is deaf.

JUSTICE   I am sure he is, to the hearing of anything good. — Go pluck him by the elbow; I must speak with him.

SERVANT   Sir John!

FALSTAFF   What? A young knave, and begging? Is there not wars? Is there not employment? Doth not the King lack subjects? Do not the rebels need soldiers? Though it be 70 a shame to be on any side but one, it is worse shame to beg than to be on the worst side, were it worse than the name of rebellion can tell how to make it.

SERVANT   You mistake me, sir.

FALSTAFF   Why, sir, did I say you were an honest man? Setting my knighthood and my soldiership aside, I had lied in my throat if I had said so.

SERVANT   I pray you, sir, then set your knighthood and your soldiership aside, and give me leave to tell you, you lie in your throat if you say I am any other than an honest 80 man.

FALSTAFF   I give thee leave to tell me so? I lay aside that which grows to me? If thou gett'st any leave of me, hang me. If thou tak'st leave, thou wert better be hanged. You hunt counter. Hence! Avaunt!

SERVANT   Sir, my Lord would speak with you.

JUSTICE   Sir John Falstaff, a word with you.

FALSTAFF   My good Lord! God give your Lordship good time of day. I am glad to see your Lordship abroad; I heard say your Lordship was sick. I hope your Lordship goes 90 abroad by advice. Your Lordship, though not clean past your youth, have yet some smack of age in you, some relish of the saltness of time in you; and I most humbly beseech your Lordship to have a reverend care of your health.

JUSTICE   Sir John, I sent for you before your expedition to Shrewsbury.

FALSTAFF   An't please your Lordship, I hear his Majesty is returned with some discomfort from Wales.

JUSTICE   I talk not of his Majesty. You would not come when I 100 sent for you.

FALSTAFF   And I hear, moreover, his Highness is fallen into this same whoreson apoplexy.

JUSTICE   Well, God mend him! I pray you, let me speak with you.

FALSTAFF   This apoplexy, as I take it, is a kind of lethargy, an't please your Lordship, a kind of sleeping in the blood, a whoreson tingling.

JUSTICE   What tell you me of it? Be it as it is.

FALSTAFF   It hath it original from much grief, from study, and perturbation of the brain. I have read the cause of his 110 effects in Galen;[7] it is a kind of deafness.

JUSTICE   I think you are fallen into the disease, for you hear not what I say to you.

FALSTAFF   Very well, my Lord, very well. Rather, an't please you, it is the disease of not listening, the malady of not marking, that I am troubled withal.

JUSTICE   To punish you by the heels would amend the attention of your ears, and I care not if I do become your physician.

FALSTAFF   I am as poor as Job, my Lord, but not so patient.[8] Your 120 Lordship may minister the potion of imprisonment to me in respect of poverty; but how I should be your patient to follow your prescriptions, the wise may make some dram of a scruple, or indeed a scruple itself.

JUSTICE   I sent for you, when there were matters against you for your life, to come speak with me.

FALSTAFF   As I was then advised by my learned counsel in the laws of this land-service, I did not come.

JUSTICE   Well, the truth is, Sir John, you live in great infamy.

FALSTAFF   He that buckles himself in my belt cannot live in less. 130

JUSTICE   Your means are very slender, and your waste is great.

FALSTAFF   I would it were otherwise; I would my means were greater and my waist slenderer.

JUSTICE   You have misled the youthful Prince.

FALSTAFF   The young Prince hath misled me. I am the fellow with the great belly, and he my dog.

JUSTICE   Well, I am loath to gall a new-healed wound. Your day's service at Shrewsbury hath a little gilded over your night's exploit on Gad's Hill. You may thank th'unquiet time for your quiet o'erposting that action. 140

FALSTAFF   My Lord —

JUSTICE   But since all is well, keep it so. Wake not a sleeping wolf.

FALSTAFF   To wake a wolf is as bad as smell a fox.

JUSTICE   What! You are as a candle, the better part burnt out.

FALSTAFF   A wassail candle, my Lord, all tallow. If I did say of wax, my growth would approve the truth.

JUSTICE   There is not a white hair in your face but should have his effect of gravity.

FALSTAFF   His effect of gravy, gravy, gravy.   150

JUSTICE   You follow the young Prince up and down, like his ill angel.

FALSTAFF   Not so, my Lord; your ill angel is light, but I hope he that looks upon me will take me without weighing. And yet in some respects, I grant, I cannot go. I cannot tell. Virtue is of so little regard in these coster-mongers' times that true valour is turned bear-herd; pregnancy is made a tapster, and his quick wit wasted in giving reckonings; all the other gifts appertinent to man, as the malice of this age shapes them, are not 160 worth a gooseberry. You that are old consider not the capacities of us that are young; you do measure the heat of our livers with the bitterness of your galls;[9] and we that are in the vaward of our youth, I must confess, are wags too.

JUSTICE   Do you set down your name in the scroll of youth, that are written down old with all the characters of age? Have you not a moist eye, a dry hand, a yellow cheek, a white beard, a decreasing leg, an increasing belly? Is not your voice broken, your wind short, your 170 chin double, your wit single, and every part about you blasted with antiquity? And will you yet call yourself young? Fie, fie, fie, Sir John!

FALSTAFF   My Lord, I was born about three of the clock in the afternoon, with a white head, and something a round belly. For my voice, I have lost it with hallowing, and singing of anthems. To approve my youth further, I will not. The truth is, I am only old in judgement and understanding; and he that will caper with me for a

thousand marks, let him lend me the money, and have 180
at him! For the box of the ear that the Prince gave
you, he gave it like a rude prince, and you took it like
a sensible lord. I have checked him for it, and the
young lion repents – [aside:] marry, not in ashes and
sackcloth, but in new silk and old sack.

JUSTICE   Well, God send the Prince a better companion!

FALSTAFF   God send the companion a better prince! I cannot rid
my hands of him.

JUSTICE   Well, the King hath severed you and Prince Harry. I
hear you are going with Lord John of Lancaster against 190
the Archbishop and the Earl of Northumberland.

FALSTAFF   Yea, I thank your pretty sweet wit for it. But look
you pray, all you that kiss my lady Peace at home, that
our armies join not in a hot day; for, by the Lord, I
take but two shirts out with me, and I mean not to
sweat extraordinarily. If it be a hot day, and I brandish
anything but a bottle, I would I might never spit
white again. There is not a dangerous action can peep
out his head but I am thrust upon it. Well, I cannot
last ever; but it was alway yet the trick of our English 200
nation, if they have a good thing, to make it too
common. If ye will needs say I am an old man, you
should give me rest. I would to God my name were
not so terrible to the enemy as it is. I were better to be
eaten to death with a rust than to be scoured to
nothing with perpetual motion.

JUSTICE   Well, be honest, be honest, and God bless your
expedition!

FALSTAFF   Will your Lordship lend me a thousand pound to
furnish me forth?   210

JUSTICE   Not a penny, not a penny! You are too impatient to
bear crosses. Fare you well. Commend me to my cousin
Westmorland.   [Exeunt Lord Chief Justice and servant.

FALSTAFF   If I do, fillip me with a three-man beetle. A man can
no more separate age and covetousness than a can part
young limbs and lechery; but the gout galls the one,
and the pox pinches the other; and so both the degrees
prevent my curses. – Boy!

PAGE   Sir?

FALSTAFF What money is in my purse?   220

PAGE   Seven groats and two pence.

FALSTAFF I can get no remedy against this consumption of the
purse; borrowing only lingers and lingers it out, but
the disease is incurable. Go bear this letter to my Lord
of Lancaster; this to the Prince; this to the Earl of
Westmorland; and this to old Mistress Ursula, whom I
have weekly sworn to marry since I perceived the first
white hair of my chin. About it! You know where to
find me.   [*Exit the page.*

A pox of this gout! Or a gout of this pox! For the one 230
or the other plays the rogue with my great toe. 'Tis no
matter if I do halt; I have the wars for my colour, and
my pension shall seem the more reasonable. A good
wit will make use of anything; I will turn diseases to
commodity.   [*Exit.*

SCENE 3.

York: the Archbishop's palace.

Enter the ARCHBISHOP OF YORK,
THOMAS MOWBRAY (*the Earl Marshal*),
LORD HASTINGS *and* LORD BARDOLPH.

ARCHB.   Thus have you heard our cause, and known our means,
And, my most noble friends, I pray you all
Speak plainly your opinions of our hopes.
And first, Lord Marshal, what say you to it?

MOWBRAY I well allow the occasion of our arms,
But gladly would be better satisfied
How in our means we should advance ourselves
To look with forehead bold and big enough
Upon the power and puissance of the King.

HASTINGS Our present musters grow upon the file   10
To five-and-twenty thousand men of choice;
And our supplies live largely in the hope
Of great Northumberland, whose bosom burns
With an incensèd fire of injuries.

LORD B.   The question then, Lord Hastings, standeth thus:
            Whether our present five-and-twenty thousand
            May hold up head without Northumberland.
HASTINGS   With him we may.
LORD B.   Yea, marry, there's the point;
            But if without him we be thought too feeble,
            My judgement is, we should not step too far   20
            Till we had his assistance by the hand;
            For in a theme so bloody-faced as this,
            Conjecture, expectation, and surmise
            Of aids incertain should not be admitted.[10]
ARCHB.   'Tis very true, Lord Bardolph, for indeed
            It was young Hotspur's cause at Shrewsbury.
LORD B.   It was, my Lord; who lined himself with hope,
            Eating the air and promise of supply,
            Flatt'ring himself in project of a power
            Much smaller than the smallest of his thoughts;   30
            And so, with great imagination
            Proper to madmen, led his powers to death,
            And, winking, leaped into destruction.
HASTINGS   But, by your leave, it never yet did hurt
            To lay down likelihoods and forms of hope.
LORD B.   Yes, if this present quality of war —
            Indeed, the instant action, a cause on foot —
            Lives so in hope, as in an early spring
            We see th'appearing buds, which to prove fruit
            Hope gives not so much warrant, as despair   40
            That frosts will bite them. When we mean to build,
            We first survey the plot, then draw the model;
            And when we see the figure of the house,
            Then must we rate the cost of the erection,
            Which if we find outweighs ability,
            What do we then but draw anew the model
            In fewer offices, or at least desist
            To build at all? Much more, in this great work —
            Which is almost to pluck a kingdom down
            And set another up — should we survey   50
            The plot of situation and the model,
            Consent upon a sure foundation,

            Question surveyors, know our own estate,
            How able such a work to undergo,
            To weigh against his opposite; or else
            We fortify in paper and in figures,
            Using the names of men instead of men,
            Like one that draws the model of an house
            Beyond his power to build it, who, half-through,
            Gives o'er, and leaves his part-created cost   60
            A naked subject to the weeping clouds,
            And waste for churlish winter's tyranny.[11]
HASTINGS Grant that our hopes, yet likely of fair birth,
            Should be still-born, and that we now possessed
            The utmost man of expectation,
            I think we are a body strong enough,
            Even as we are, to equal with the King.
LORD B. What, is the King but five-and-twenty thousand?
HASTINGS To us no more, nay, not so much, Lord Bardolph;
            For his divisions, as the times do brawl,   70
            Are in three heads: one power against the French;
            And one against Glendower; perforce a third
            Must take up us. So is the unfirm King
            In three divided, and his coffers sound
            With hollow poverty and emptiness.
ARCHB. That he should draw his several strengths together
            And come against us in full puissance
            Need not be dreaded.
HASTINGS   If he should do so,
            He leaves his back unarmed, the French and Welsh
            Baying him at the heels; never fear that.   80
LORD B. Who is it like should lead his forces hither?
HASTINGS The Duke of Lancaster, and Westmorland;
            Against the Welsh, himself and Harry Monmouth;
            But who is substituted 'gainst the French
            I have no certain notice.
ARCHB.   Let us on,
            And publish the occasion of our arms.
            The commonwealth is sick of their own choice;
            Their over-greedy love hath surfeited.
            An habitation giddy and unsure

Hath he that buildeth on the vulgar heart.   90
O thou fond many, with what loud applause
Didst thou beat heaven with blessing Bullingbrooke,
Before he was what thou wouldst have him be!
And being now trimmed in thine own desires,
Thou, beastly feeder, art so full of him
That thou provok'st thyself to cast him up.
So, so, thou common dog, didst thou disgorge
Thy glutton bosom of the royal Richard;
And now thou wouldst eat thy dead vomit up,
And howl'st to find it. What trust is in these times?   100
They that, when Richard lived, would have him die
Are now become enamoured on his grave.
Thou that threw'st dust upon his goodly head,
When through proud London he came sighing on
After th'admired heels of Bullingbrooke,
Cry'st now 'O earth, yield us that king again,
And take thou this!' O thoughts of men accursed!
Past and to come seems best; things present, worst.[12]
MOWBRAY Shall we go draw our numbers and set on?
HASTINGS We are time's subjects, and time bids be gone.   110
                                        [*Exeunt.*

ACT 2, SCENE 1.

London: a street in Eastcheap.

Enter MISTRESS QUICKLY, *the* HOSTESS *of a tavern,*
with two officers, FANG *and (at a distance)* SNARE.

HOSTESS   Master Fang, have you entered the action?
FANG   It is entered.
HOSTESS   Where's your yeoman? Is't a lusty yeoman? Will a
   stand to't?
FANG   Sirrah! – Where's Snare?
HOSTESS   O Lord, ay! Good Master Snare.
SNARE   [*coming forward:*] Here, here!
FANG   Snare, we must arrest Sir John Falstaff.
HOSTESS   Yea, good Master Snare, I have entered him and all.
SNARE   It may chance cost some of us our lives, for he will stab.   10
HOSTESS   Alas the day, take heed of him: he stabbed me in mine
   own house, most beastly, in good faith. A cares not
   what mischief he does, if his weapon be out. He will
   foin like any devil; he will spare neither man, woman,
   nor child.[13]
FANG   If I can close with him, I care not for his thrust.
HOSTESS   No, nor I neither; I'll be at your elbow.
FANG   And I but fist him once, an a come but within my
   vice –
HOSTESS   I am undone by his going, I warrant you; he's an   20
   infinitive thing upon my score. Good Master Fang,
   hold him sure; good Master Snare, let him not scape.
   A comes continuantly to Pie Corner (saving your man-
   hoods) to buy a saddle, and he is indited to dinner
   to the Lubber's Head in Lumbert Street to Master
   Smooth's the silk-man. I pray you, since my exion is
   entered, and my case so openly known to the world,
   let him be brought in to his answer. A hundred mark is
   a long one for a poor lone woman to bear, and I have
   borne, and borne, and borne, and have been fubbed   30
   off, and fubbed off, and fubbed off, from this day to
   that day, that it is a shame to be thought on.[14] There is

no honesty in such dealing, unless a woman should be made an ass, and a beast, to bear every knave's wrong.

Enter FALSTAFF, BARDOLPH *and the* PAGE.

Yonder he comes, and that arrant malmsey-nose knave Bardolph with him. Do your offices, do your offices, Master Fang and Master Snare, do me, do me, do me your offices.

FALSTAFF   How now, whose mare's dead? What's the matter?

FANG   Sir John, I arrest you at the suit of Mistress Quickly.   40

FALSTAFF   Away, varlets! Draw, Bardolph! Cut me off the villain's head! Throw the quean in the channel!

[*A brawl ensues.*

HOSTESS   Throw me in the channel? I'll throw thee in the channel! Wilt thou, wilt thou, thou bastardly rogue? Murder! Murder! Ah, thou honeysuckle villain, wilt thou kill God's officers and the King's? Ah, thou honeyseed rogue! Thou art a honeyseed, a man-queller, and a woman-queller.

FALSTAFF   Keep them off, Bardolph!

FANG   A rescue! A rescue!   50

HOSTESS   Good people, bring a rescue or two. Thou wot, wot thou, thou, thou wot, wot ta? Do, do, thou rogue! Do, thou hempseed!

PAGE   Away, you scullion! You rampallian! You fustilarian! I'll tickle your catastrophe!

Enter the LORD CHIEF JUSTICE *and his* MEN.

JUSTICE   What is the matter? Keep the peace here, ho!

[*The brawl ends. Fang holds Falstaff.*

HOSTESS   Good my Lord, be good to me; I beseech you, stand to me.

JUSTICE   How now, Sir John? What, are you brawling here? Doth this become your place, your time and business?   60
You should have been well on your way to York.
[*To Fang:*] Stand from him, fellow; wherefore hang'st
                                    thou upon him?

HOSTESS   O my most worshipful Lord, an't please your Grace, I am a poor widow of Eastcheap, and he is arrested at my suit.

JUSTICE   For what sum?

HOSTESS   It is more than for some, my Lord, it is for all: all I
            have. He hath eaten me out of house and home; he
            hath put all my substance into that fat belly of his; [to
            Falstaff:] but I will have some of it out again, or I will   70
            ride thee a–nights like the mare.

FALSTAFF   I think I am as like to ride the mare, if I have any
            vantage of ground to get up.

JUSTICE   How comes this, Sir John? What man of good temper
            would endure this tempest of exclamation? Are you
            not ashamed to enforce a poor widow to so rough a
            course to come by her own?

FALSTAFF   [to hostess:] What is the gross sum that I owe thee?

HOSTESS   Marry, if thou wert an honest man, thyself and the
            money too. Thou didst swear to me upon a parcel–gilt   80
            goblet, sitting in my Dolphin chamber, at the round
            table, by a sea–coal fire, upon Wednesday in Wheeson
            week, when the Prince broke thy head for liking his
            father to a singing–man of Windsor, thou didst swear to
            me then, as I was washing thy wound, to marry me, and
            make me my lady thy wife. Canst thou deny it? Did not
            goodwife Keech the butcher's wife come in then and
            call me 'gossip Quickly'? – coming in to borrow a mess
            of vinegar, telling us she had a good dish of prawns,
            whereby thou didst desire to eat some, whereby I told   90
            thee they were ill for a green wound? And didst thou
            not, when she was gone downstairs, desire me to be no
            more so familiarity with such poor people, saying that
            ere long they should call me 'madam'? And didst thou
            not kiss me, and bid me fetch thee thirty shillings? I put
            thee now to thy book–oath; deny it if thou canst.

FALSTAFF   My Lord, this is a poor mad soul, and she says up and
            down the town that her eldest son is like you. She hath
            been in good case, and the truth is, poverty hath
            distracted her. But, for these foolish officers, I beseech   100
            you I may have redress against them.

JUSTICE   Sir John, Sir John, I am well acquainted with your
            manner of wrenching the true cause the false way. It is
            not a confident brow, nor the throng of words that

come with such more than impudent sauciness from you, can thrust me from a level consideration. You have, as it appears to me, practised upon the easy-yielding spirit of this woman, and made her serve your uses both in purse and in person.

HOSTESS   Yea, in truth, my Lord.   110

JUSTICE   Pray thee, peace. [*To Falstaff:*] Pay her the debt you owe her, and unpay the villainy you have done with her. The one you may do with sterling money, and the other with current repentance.

FALSTAFF   My Lord, I will not undergo this sneap without reply. You call honourable boldness 'impudent sauciness'; if a man will make curtsy and say nothing, he is virtuous. No, my Lord, my humble duty remembered, I will not be your suitor. I say to you I do desire deliverance from these officers, being upon hasty employment in   120 the King's affairs.

JUSTICE   You speak as having power to do wrong; but answer in the effect of your reputation, and satisfy the poor woman.

FALSTAFF   Come hither, hostess.

[*He takes her aside for private persuasion.*

Enter GOWER, *a messenger.*

JUSTICE   Now, Master Gower, what news?

GOWER   The King, my Lord, and Harry Prince of Wales
           Are near at hand; the rest the paper tells.
           [*Gower gives him a letter, which he peruses.*]

FALSTAFF   [*to hostesss, concluding:*] As I am a gentleman!

HOSTESS   Faith, you said so before.   130

FALSTAFF   As I am a gentleman! Come, no more words of it.

HOSTESS   By this heavenly ground I tread on, I must be fain to pawn both my plate and the tapestry of my dining-chambers.

FALSTAFF   Glasses, glasses, is the only drinking; and for thy walls, a pretty slight drollery, or the story of the Prodigal, or the German hunting, in waterwork, is worth a thousand of these bed-hangers and these fly-bitten tapestries. Let it be ten pound if thou canst. Come,

and 'twere not for thy humours, there's not a better 140
wench in England: Go, wash thy face, and draw the
action. Come, thou must not be in this humour with
me; dost not know me? Come, come, I know thou
wast set on to this.

HOSTESS   Pray thee, Sir John, let it be but twenty nobles; i'faith,
I am loath to pawn my plate, so God save me, law!

FALSTAFF   Let it alone; I'll make other shift; you'll be a fool still.

HOSTESS   Well, you shall have it, though I pawn my gown.
I hope you'll come to supper. You'll pay me all
together?   150

FALSTAFF   Will I live? [*To Bardolph:*] Go, with her, with her!
Hook on, hook on!

HOSTESS   Will you have Doll Tearsheet meet you at supper?

FALSTAFF   No more words; let's have her.
                [Exeunt hostess, Fang, Snare, Bardolph and the page.

JUSTICE   [*to Gower:*] I have heard better news.

FALSTAFF   What's the news, my Lord?

JUSTICE   [*to Gower:*] Where lay the King tonight?

GOWER   At Basingstoke, my Lord.

FALSTAFF   I hope, my Lord, all's well. What is the news, my Lord?

JUSTICE   [*to Gower:*] Come all his forces back?   160

GOWER   No, fifteen hundred foot, five hundred horse
Are marched up to my Lord of Lancaster,
Against Northumberland and the Archbishop.

FALSTAFF   Comes the King back from Wales, my noble Lord?

JUSTICE   [*to Gower:*] You shall have letters of me presently.
Come, go along with me, good Master Gower.

FALSTAFF   My Lord!

JUSTICE   What's the matter?

FALSTAFF   Master Gower, shall I entreat you with me to dinner?

GOWER   I must wait upon my good Lord here, I thank you, 170
good Sir John.

JUSTICE   Sir John, you loiter here too long, being you are to
take soldiers up in counties as you go.

FALSTAFF   Will you sup with me, Master Gower?

JUSTICE   What foolish master taught you these manners, Sir
John?

FALSTAFF   Master Gower, if they become me not, he was a fool

that taught them me. [*To Justice:*] This is the right
fencing grace, my Lord: tap for tap, and so part fair.

JUSTICE   Now the Lord lighten thee: thou art a great fool.   180

[*Exeunt, Falstaff separately.*]

SCENE 2.

London: Prince Henry's residence.

Enter PRINCE HENRY (HAL) *and* POINS.

HAL   Before God, I am exceeding weary.

POINS   Is't come to that? I had thought weariness durst not
have attached one of so high blood.

HAL   Faith, it does me, though it discolour the complexion
of my greatness to acknowledge it. Doth it not show
vilely in me, to desire small beer?

POINS   Why, a prince should not be so loosely studied as to
remember so weak a composition.

HAL   Belike then my appetite was not princely got, for, by
my troth, I do now remember the poor creature, small   10
beer. But indeed, these humble considerations make
me out of love with my greatness. What a disgrace is it
to me to remember thy name! Or to know thy face
tomorrow! Or to take note how many pair of silk
stockings thou hast – viz. these, and those that were
thy peach-coloured ones! Or to bear the inventory of
thy shirts, as, one for superfluity, and another for use!
But that the tennis-court keeper knows better than I,
for it is a low ebb of linen with thee when thou keepest
not racket there – as thou hast not done a great while,   20
because the rest of thy low countries have made a shift
to eat up thy holland. And God knows whether those
that bawl out the ruins of thy linen shall inherit His
kingdom; but the midwives say the children are not in
the fault; whereupon the world increases, and kindreds
are mightily strengthened.[15]

POINS   How ill it follows, after you have laboured so hard,
you should talk so idly! Tell me, how many good
young princes would do so, their fathers being so sick
as yours at this time is?   30

HAL	Shall I tell thee one thing, Poins?
POINS	Yes, faith, and let it be an excellent good thing.
HAL	It shall serve, among wits of no higher breeding than thine.
POINS	Go to, I stand the push of your one thing that you will tell.
HAL	Marry, I tell thee it is not meet that I should be sad now my father is sick; albeit I could tell to thee, as to one it pleases me for fault of a better to call my friend, I could be sad, and sad indeed too.
POINS	Very hardly, upon such a subject.
HAL	By this hand, thou thinkest me as far in the devil's book as thou and Falstaff, for obduracy and persistency. Let the end try the man. But I tell thee, my heart bleeds inwardly that my father is so sick; and keeping such vile company as thou art hath in reason taken from me all ostentation of sorrow.
POINS	The reason?
HAL	What wouldst thou think of me if I should weep?
POINS	I would think thee a most princely hypocrite.
HAL	It would be every man's thought; and thou art a blessèd fellow, to think as every man thinks. Never a man's thought in the world keeps the roadway better than thine. Every man would think me an hypocrite indeed; and what accites your most worshipful thought to think so?
POINS	Why, because you have been so lewd, and so much engraffed to Falstaff.
HAL	And to thee.
POINS	By this light, I am well spoke on; I can hear it with mine own ears. The worst that they can say of me is that I am a second brother, and that I am a proper fellow of my hands; and those two things I confess I cannot help. By the Mass, here comes Bardolph.

Enter BARDOLPH *and the* PAGE.

HAL	And the boy that I gave Falstaff: a had him from me Christian, and look if the fat villain have not transformed him ape.

BARDOLPH God save your Grace!

HAL   And yours, most noble Bardolph!

POINS   [*to Bardolph:*] Come, you virtuous ass, you bashful fool, 70
          must you be blushing? Wherefore blush you now?
          What a maidenly man-at-arms are you become! Is't
          such a matter to get a pottle-pot's maidenhead?

PAGE   A calls me e'en now, my Lord, through a red lattice,
          and I could discern no part of his face from the
          window. At last I spied his eyes, and methought he
          had made two holes in the ale-wife's petticoat, and so
          peeped through.

HAL   [*to Poins:*] Has not the boy profited?

BARDOLPH [*to page:*] Away, you whoreson upright rabbit, away! 80

PAGE   Away, you rascally Althaea's dream, away!

HAL   Instruct us, boy: what dream, boy?

PAGE   Marry, my Lord, Althaea dreamt she was delivered of a
          firebrand; and therefore I call him her dream.[16]

HAL   A crown's-worth of good interpretation! There 'tis,
          boy.   [*Hal gives the page a crown coin.*

POINS   O that this blossom could be kept from cankers! Well,
          there is sixpence to preserve thee.   [*He pays the page.*

BARDOLPH And you do not make him be hanged among you, the
          gallows shall be wronged.   90

HAL   And how doth thy master, Bardolph?

BARDOLPH Well, my Lord. He heard of your Grace's coming to
          town: there's a letter for you.

POINS   Delivered with good respect. And how doth the Martle-
          mas, your master?

BARDOLPH In bodily health, sir.

POINS   Marry, the immortal part needs a physician, but that
          moves not him: though that be sick, it dies not.

HAL   I do allow this wen to be as familiar with me as my
          dog; and he holds his place, for look you how he 100
          writes –   [*He gives the letter to Poins.*

POINS   [*reading the letter.*] 'John Falstaff, Knight' – Every man
          must know that, as oft as he has occasion to name
          himself; even like those that are kin to the King, for
          they never prick their finger but they say 'There's
          some of the King's blood spilt.' 'How comes that?',

says he that takes upon him not to conceive. The answer is as ready as a borrower's cap: 'I am the King's poor cousin, sir.'

HAL   Nay, they will be kin to us, or they will fetch it from 110 Japhet. But the letter: 'Sir John Falstaff, Knight, to the son of the King nearest his father, Harry Prince of Wales, greeting.'

POINS   Why, this is a certificate!

HAL   Peace! 'I will imitate the honourable Romans in brevity.'

POINS   He sure means brevity in breath, short-winded.

HAL   'I commend me to thee, I commend thee, and I leave thee. Be not too familiar with Poins, for he misuses thy favours so much that he swears thou art to marry 120 his sister Nell. Repent at idle times as thou mayst, and so farewell.

> Thine by yea and no – which is as much
> as to say, as thou usest him – Jack Falstaff
> with my familiars, John with my brothers
> and sisters, and Sir John with all Europe.'

POINS   My lord, I'll steep this letter in sack and make him eat it.

HAL   That's to make him eat twenty of his words. But *do* you use me thus, Ned? Must I marry your sister? 130

POINS   God send the wench no worse fortune! But I never said so.

HAL   Well, thus we play the fools with the time, and the spirits of the wise sit in the clouds and mock us. [*To Bardolph:*] Is your master here in London?

BARDOLPH Yea, my Lord.

HAL   Where sups he? Doth the old boar feed in the old frank?

BARDOLPH At the old place, my Lord, in Eastcheap.

HAL   What company? 140

PAGE   Ephesians, my Lord, of the old church.[17]

HAL   Sup any women with him?

PAGE   None, my Lord, but old Mistress Quickly, and Mistress Doll Tearsheet.

HAL   What pagan may that be?

PAGE	A proper gentlewoman, sir, and a kinswoman of my master's.
HAL	Even such kin as the parish heifers are to the town bull. – Shall we steal upon them, Ned, at supper?
POINS	I am your shadow, my Lord; I'll follow you.
HAL	Sirrah, you boy, and Bardolph, no word to your master that I am yet come to town. There's for your silence.

150

[He gives them money.

BARDOLPH	I have no tongue, sir.
PAGE	And for mine, sir, I will govern it.
HAL	Fare you well; go. *[Exeunt Bardolph and the page.*

This Doll Tearsheet should be some road.

POINS	I warrant you, as common as the way between Saint Albans and London.
HAL	How might we see Falstaff bestow himself tonight in his true colours, and not ourselves be seen?
POINS	Put on two leathern jerkins and aprons, and wait upon him at his table as drawers.
HAL	From a god to a bull? A heavy descension! It was Jove's case.[18] From a prince to a prentice? A low transformation, that shall be mine; for in everything the purpose must weigh with the folly. Follow me, Ned. *[Exeunt.*

160

SCENE 3.

Warkworth: Northumberland's castle.

Enter NORTHUMBERLAND, LADY NORTHUMBERLAND
and LADY PERCY.

NORTH.	I pray thee, loving wife, and gentle daughter,
	Give even way unto my rough affairs;
	Put not you on the visage of the times
	And be like them to Percy troublesome.
L. NORTH.	I have given over; I will speak no more.
	Do what you will; your wisdom be your guide.
NORTH.	Alas, sweet wife, my honour is at pawn,
	And, but my going, nothing can redeem it.
L. PERCY	O, yet, for God's sake, go not to these wars!

The time was, father, that you broke your word   10
When you were more endeared to it than now,
When your own Percy, when my heart's dear Harry,
Threw many a northward look to see his father
Bring up his powers; but he did long in vain.
Who then persuaded you to stay at home?
There were two honours lost, yours and your son's.
For yours, the God of Heaven brighten it!
For his, it stuck upon him as the sun
In the grey vault of heaven, and by his light
Did all the chivalry of England move   20
To do brave acts. He was indeed the glass
Wherein the noble youth did dress themselves.
He had no legs that practised not his gait;
And speaking thick, which nature made his blemish,
Became the accents of the valiant:
For those that could speak low and tardily
Would turn their own perfection to abuse,
To seem like him. So that in speech, in gait,
In diet, in affections of delight,
In military rules, humours of blood,   30
He was the mark and glass, copy and book,
That fashioned others. And him – O wondrous him!
O miracle of men! – him did you leave,
Second to none, unseconded by you,
To look upon the hideous god of war
In disadvantage, to abide a field
Where nothing but the sound of Hotspur's name
Did seem defensible. So you left him.
Never, O never, do his ghost the wrong
To hold your honour more precise and nice   40
With others than with him! Let them alone.
The Marshal and the Archbishop are strong;
Had my sweet Harry had but half their numbers,
Today might I, hanging on Hotspur's neck,
Have talked of Monmouth's grave.[19]

NORTH.   Beshrew your heart,
Fair daughter, you do draw my spirits from me
With new lamenting ancient oversights.

But I must go and meet with danger there,
Or it will seek me in another place
And find me worse provided.

L. NORTH.   O, fly to Scotland,   50
Till that the nobles and the armèd commons
Have of their puissance made a little taste.

L. PERCY   If they get ground and vantage of the King,
Then join you with them like a rib of steel,
To make strength stronger; but, for all our loves,
First let them try themselves. So did your son;
He was so suffered; so came I a widow,
And never shall have length of life enough
To rain upon remembrance with mine eyes,
That it may grow and sprout as high as heaven   60
For recordation to my noble husband.

NORTH.   Come, come, go in with me. 'Tis with my mind
As with the tide swelled up unto his height,
That makes a still-stand, running neither way.
Fain would I go to meet the Archbishop,
But many thousand reasons hold me back.
I will resolve for Scotland. There am I,
Till time and vantage crave my company. ·   [*Exeunt.*

SCENE 4.

London: Eastcheap: a tavern.

Enter FRANCIS *and a second* DRAWER.

FRANCIS   What the devil hast thou brought there – apple-johns?
Thou knowest Sir John cannot endure an apple-john.

DRAWER 2 Mass, thou sayst true. The Prince once set a dish of
apple-johns before him, and told him there were five
more Sir Johns, and, putting off his hat, said 'I will now
take my leave of these six dry, round, old, withered
knights.' It angered him to the heart; but he hath
forgot that.

FRANCIS   Why then, cover, and set them down, and see if thou
canst find out Sneak's noise. Mistress Tearsheet would   10
fain hear some music.

Enter a third DRAWER.

DRAWER 3 Dispatch! The room where they supped is too hot; they'll come in straight.

FRANCIS Sirrah, here will be the Prince and Master Poins anon, and they will put on two of our jerkins and aprons, and Sir John must not know of it. Bardolph hath brought word.

DRAWER 3 By the Mass, here will be old utis. It will be an excellent stratagem.

DRAWER 2 I'll see if I can find out Sneak.   [*Exeunt drawers 2 and 3.* 20

Enter HOSTESS *and* DOLL TEARSHEET, *drunk.*

HOSTESS I'faith, sweetheart, methinks now you are in an excellent good temperality. Your pulsidge beats as extraordinarily as heart would desire, and your colour, I warrant you, is as red as any rose, in good truth, law! But, i'faith, you have drunk too much canaries, and that's a marvellous searching wine, and it perfumes the blood ere one can say 'What's this?'. How do you now?

DOLL Better than I was – hem!

HOSTESS Why, that's well said – a good heart's worth gold. Lo, 30 here comes Sir John.

Enter FALSTAFF, *singing, and holding a chamber-pot.*

FALSTAFF 'When Arthur first in court' – Empty the jordan! –
                                    [*Exit Francis with chamber-pot.*
'And was a worthy king' – How now, Mistress Doll?

HOSTESS Sick of a qualm; yea, good faith.

FALSTAFF So is all her sect: and they be once in a calm, they are sick.

DOLL A pox damn you, you muddy rascal, is that all the comfort you give me?

FALSTAFF You make fat rascals, Mistress Doll.

DOLL *I* make them? Gluttony and diseases make them; I 40 make them not.

FALSTAFF If the cook help to make the gluttony, you help to make the diseases, Doll; we catch of you, Doll, we catch of you. Grant that, my poor virtue, grant that.

DOLL Ay, marry, our chains and our jewels –

FALSTAFF   Your brooches, pearls, and ouches – for to serve
           bravely is to come halting off, you know; to come off
           the breach, with his pike bent bravely; and to surgery
           bravely; to venture upon the charged chambers
           bravely.[20]   50

DOLL   Hang yourself, you muddy conger, hang yourself!

HOSTESS   By my troth, this is the old fashion: you two never
           meet but you fall to some discord. You are both,
           i'good truth, as rheumatic as two dry toasts; you cannot
           one bear with another's confirmities. What the good-
           year! One must bear, and that [to Doll:] must be you;
           you are the weaker vessel, as they say, the emptier
           vessel.

DOLL   Can a weak empty vessel bear such a huge full hogs-
           head?[21] There's a whole merchant's venture of Bordeaux   60
           stuff in him: you have not seen a hulk better stuffed in
           the hold. – Come, I'll be friends with thee, Jack; thou
           art going to the wars; and, whether I shall ever see thee
           again or no, there is nobody cares.

                       Enter DRAWER 3.

DRAWER 3   Sir, Ancient Pistol's below, and would speak with you.

DOLL   Hang him, swaggering rascal. Let him not come hither;
           it is the foul-mouthed'st rogue in England.

HOSTESS   If he swagger, let him not come here. No, by my faith!
           I must live among my neighbours; I'll no swaggerers; I
           am in good name and fame with the very best. Shut   70
           the door; there comes no swaggerers here. I have not
           lived all this while to have swaggering now. Shut the
           door, I pray you.

FALSTAFF   Dost thou hear, hostess?

HOSTESS   Pray ye, pacify yourself, Sir John; there comes no
           swaggerers here.

FALSTAFF   Dost thou hear? It is mine ancient.

HOSTESS   Tilly-fally, Sir John, ne'er tell me; and your ancient
           swagger, a comes not in my doors. I was before Maister
           Tisick the debuty t'other day, and, as he said to me –   80
           'twas no longer ago than Wednesday last, i'good faith
           – 'Neighbour Quickly,' says he – Maister Dumb our
           minister was by then – 'Neighbour Quickly,' says he,

'receive those that are civil, for,' said he, 'you are in an ill name': now a said so, I can tell whereupon. 'For', says he, 'you are an honest woman, and well thought on; therefore take heed what guests you receive; receive', says he, 'no swaggering companions.' There comes none here. You would bless you to hear what he said. No, I'll no swaggerers.   90

FALSTAFF   He's no swaggerer, hostess; a tame cheater, i'faith. You may stroke him as gently as a puppy greyhound. He'll not swagger with a Barbary hen, if her feathers turn back in any show of resistance. – Call him up, drawer.

                                              [*Exit drawer 3.*

HOSTESS   'Cheater', call you him? I will bar no honest man my house, nor no cheater, but I do not love swaggering; by my troth, I am the worse when one says 'swagger'. Feel, masters, how I shake, look you, I warrant you.

DOLL   So you do, hostess.

HOSTESS   Do I? Yea, in very truth, do I, and 'twere an aspen leaf.   100
            I cannot abide swaggerers.

            Enter ANCIENT PISTOL, BARDOLPH *and the* PAGE.

PISTOL   God save you, Sir John!

FALSTAFF   Welcome, Ancient Pistol! Here, Pistol, I charge you with a cup of sack; do you discharge upon mine hostess.

PISTOL   I will discharge upon her, Sir John, with two bullets.[22]

FALSTAFF   She is pistol-proof, sir; you shall not hardly offend her.

HOSTESS   Come, I'll drink no proofs, nor no bullets. I'll drink no more than will do me good, for no man's pleasure, I.

PISTOL   Then, to you, Mistress Dorothy! I will charge you.   110

DOLL   Charge me? I scorn you, scurvy companion. What, you poor, base, rascally, cheating, lack-linen mate! Away, you mouldy rogue, away! I am meat for your master.

PISTOL   I know you, Mistress Dorothy.

DOLL   Away, you cutpurse rascal, you filthy bung, away! By this wine, I'll thrust my knife in your mouldy chaps, and you play the saucy cuttle with me. Away, you bottle-ale rascal, you basket-hilt stale juggler, you! Since when, I pray you, sir? God's light, with two points on your shoulder? Much!   120

PISTOL   God let me not live but I will murder your ruff for this.

FALSTAFF   No more, Pistol! I would not have you go off here.
            Discharge yourself of our company, Pistol.[23]

HOSTESS   No, good Captain Pistol, not here, sweet captain!

DOLL   'Captain'? Thou abominable damned cheater, art thou
            not ashamed to be called 'captain'? And captains were
            of my mind, they would truncheon you out, for taking
            their names upon you before you have earned them.
            You a captain? You slave! For what? For tearing a
            poor whore's ruff in a bawdy-house? He a captain!   130
            Hang him, rogue, he lives upon mouldy stewed prunes
            and dried cakes. A captain? God's light, these villains
            will make the word as odious as the word 'occupy',
            which was an excellent good word before it was ill-
            sorted. Therefore captains had need look to't.[24]

BARDOLPH   Pray thee go down, good ancient.

FALSTAFF   Hark thee hither, Mistress Doll.   [He takes her aside.

PISTOL   Not I: I tell thee what, Corporal Bardolph, I could tear
            her! I'll be revenged of her.

PAGE   Pray thee, go down.   140

PISTOL   I'll see her damned first! To Pluto's damnèd lake, by
            this hand, to th'infernal deep, with Erebus and tortures
            vile also! Hold hook and line, say I! Down, down,
            dogs! Down, faitours! Have we not Hiren here?
                                        [He brandishes his sword.

HOSTESS   Good Captain Peesel, be quiet; 'tis very late, i'faith. I
            beseek you now, aggravate your choler.

PISTOL   These be good humours indeed! Shall pack-horses,
            And hollow pampered jades of Asia,
            Which cannot go but thirty mile a day,
            Compare with Cæsars and with Cannibals,   150
            And Troyant Greeks? Nay, rather damn them with
            King Cerberus, and let the welkin roar!
            Shall we fall foul for toys?[25]

HOSTESS   By my troth, Captain, these are very bitter words.

BARDOLPH   Be gone, good ancient; this will grow to a brawl anon.

PISTOL   Die men like dogs! Give crowns like pins! Have we
            not Hiren here?

HOSTESS   O' my word, captain, there's none such here. What the

	goodyear, do you think I would deny her? For God's sake, be quiet.

        goodyear, do you think I would deny her? For God's
        sake, be quiet.   160

PISTOL   Then feed and be fat, my fair Calipolis!
                  Come, give's some sack.
                  '*Si fortune me tormente sperato me contento.*'
                  Fear we broadsides? No, let the fiend give fire!
                  Give me some sack; – and, sweetheart, lie thou there!
                                         [*He lays down his sword.*
                  Come we to full points here? And are etceteras
                                       nothings?[26]

FALSTAFF   Pistol, I would be quiet.

PISTOL   Sweet knight, I kiss thy neaf. What! We have seen the
                  seven stars!

DOLL   For God's sake, thrust him downstairs; I cannot endure   170
                  such a fustian rascal.

PISTOL   'Thrust him downstairs'? Know we not Galloway nags?

FALSTAFF   Quoit him down, Bardolph, like a shove-groat shilling.
                  Nay, and a do nothing but speak nothing, a shall be
                  nothing here.

BARDOLPH   [*to Pistol:*] Come, get you downstairs.

PISTOL   What! Shall we have incision? Shall we imbrue?
                                         [*He wields his sword.*
                  Then death rock me asleep, abridge my doleful days!
                  Why then, let grievous, ghastly, gaping wounds
                  Untwind the Sisters Three! Come, Atropos, I say!   180

HOSTESS   Here's goodly stuff toward!

FALSTAFF   Give me my rapier, boy.

DOLL   I pray thee, Jack, I pray thee, do not draw.

FALSTAFF   [*draws his rapier. To Pistol:*] Get you downstairs.

HOSTESS   Here's a goodly tumult! I'll forswear keeping house
                  afore I'll be in these tirrits and frights!
                                     [*Falstaff thrusts at Pistol.*
                  So, murder, I warrant now! Alas, alas, put up your
                  naked weapons, put up your naked weapons!
                                 [*Exit Pistol, pursued by Bardolph.*

DOLL   I pray thee, Jack, be quiet; the rascal's gone. Ah, you
                  whoreson little valiant villain, you!   190

HOSTESS   [*to Falstaff:*] Are you not hurt i'th'groin? Methought
                  a made a shrewd thrust at your belly.

Enter BARDOLPH.

FALSTAFF   Have you turned him out o'doors?

BARDOLPH   Yea sir; the rascal's drunk. You have hurt him, sir, i'th'shoulder.

FALSTAFF   A rascal, to brave me!

DOLL   Ah, you sweet little rogue, you! Alas, poor ape, how thou sweat'st! Come, let me wipe thy face; come on, you whoreson chops. Ah, rogue, i'faith, I love thee. Thou art as valorous as Hector of Troy, worth five of 200 Agamemnon, and ten times better than the Nine Worthies.[27] Ah, villain!

FALSTAFF   A rascally slave! I will toss the rogue in a blanket.

DOLL   Do, and thou darest for thy heart. And thou dost, I'll canvass thee between a pair of sheets.

Enter MUSICIANS.

PAGE   The music is come, sir.

FALSTAFF   Let them play. – Play, sirs!   [*Music ensues.*
Sit on my knee, Doll. A rascal bragging slave! The rogue fled from me like quicksilver.

DOLL   I'faith, and thou followed'st him like a church. Thou 210 whoreson little tidy Bartholomew boar-pig, when wilt thou leave fighting a-days, and foining a-nights, and begin to patch up thine old body for heaven?

Enter, behind, the PRINCE (HAL) *and* POINS, *disguised as drawers.*

FALSTAFF   Peace, good Doll, do not speak like a death's-head; do not bid me remember mine end.

DOLL   Sirrah, what humour's the Prince of?

FALSTAFF   A good shallow young fellow. A would have made a good pantler; a would ha' chipped bread well.

DOLL   They say Poins has a good wit.

FALSTAFF   He a good wit? Hang him, baboon! His wit's as thick 220 as Tewkesbury mustard: there's no more conceit in him than is in a mallet.

DOLL   Why does the Prince love him so, then?

FALSTAFF   Because their legs are both of a bigness, and a plays at quoits well, and eats conger and fennel, and drinks off candles' ends for flap-dragons, and rides the wild mare

with the boys, and jumps upon joint-stools, and swears
with a good grace, and wears his boots very smooth like
unto the sign of the leg, and breeds no bate with telling
of discreet stories, and such other gambol faculties a has   230
that show a weak mind and an able body, for the which
the Prince admits him: for the Prince himself is such
another – the weight of a hair will turn the scales
between their avoirdupois.

HAL   [aside to Poins:] Would not this nave of a wheel have his
           ears cut off?

POINS   Let's beat him before his whore.

HAL   Look whe'er the withered elder hath not his poll
           clawed like a parrot.

POINS   Is it not strange that desire should so many years out-   240
           live performance?

FALSTAFF   Kiss me, Doll.

HAL   Saturn and Venus this year in conjunction! What says
           th'almanac to that?

POINS   And look whether the fiery trigon, his man, be not
           lisping to his master's old tables, his note-book, his
           counsel-keeper.[28]

FALSTAFF   Thou dost give me flattering busses.

DOLL   By my troth, I kiss thee with a most constant heart.

FALSTAFF   I am old, I am old.   250

DOLL   I love thee better than I love e'er a scurvy young boy
           of them all.

FALSTAFF   What stuff wilt have a kirtle of? I shall receive money
           a Thursday; shalt have a cap tomorrow. – A merry
           song! – Come, it grows late; we'll to bed. Thou'lt
           forget me when I am gone.

DOLL   By my troth, thou'lt set me a-weeping and thou sayst
           so. Prove that ever I dress myself handsome till thy
           return – well, hearken a'th'end.

FALSTAFF   – Some sack, Francis.   260

HAL and POINS [coming forward:] Anon, anon, sir!

FALSTAFF   Ha! A bastard son of the King's? – And art not thou
           Poins his brother?

HAL   Why, thou globe of sinful continents, what a life dost
           thou lead!

FALSTAFF	A better than thou – I am a gentleman; thou art a drawer.
HAL	Very true, sir, and I come to draw you out by the ears.
HOSTESS	O, the Lord preserve thy Grace! By my troth, welcome to London! Now the Lord bless that sweet face of 270 thine! O Jesu, are you come from Wales?
FALSTAFF	Thou whoreson mad compound of majesty, by this light – flesh and corrupt blood [*indicating Doll*], thou art welcome.
DOLL	How? You fat fool, I scorn you.
POINS	My Lord, he will drive you out of your revenge and turn all to a merriment, if you take not the heat.
HAL	[*to Falstaff:*] You whoreson candle-mine you, how vilely did you speak of me now, before this honest, virtuous, civil gentlewoman! 280
HOSTESS	God's blessing of your good heart, and so she is, by my troth!
FALSTAFF	[*to Hal:*] Didst thou hear me?
HAL	Yea, and you knew me, as you did when you ran away by Gad's Hill; you knew I was at your back, and spoke it on purpose to try my patience.
FALSTAFF	No, no, no, not so; I did not think thou wast within hearing.
HAL	I shall drive you then to confess the wilful abuse, and then I know how to handle you. 290
FALSTAFF	No abuse, Hal, o' mine honour, no abuse.
HAL	Not? To dispraise me, and call me 'pantler', and 'bread-chipper', and I know not what?
FALSTAFF	No abuse, Hal.
POINS	No abuse?
FALSTAFF	No abuse, Ned, i'th'world, honest Ned, none. I dispraised him before the wicked, that the wicked might not fall in love with [*turning to Prince Henry*] thee – in which doing, I have done the part of a careful friend and a true subject, and thy father is to give me thanks 300 for it. No abuse, Hal; none, Ned, none; no, faith, boys, none.
HAL	See now whether pure fear and entire cowardice doth not make thee wrong this virtuous gentlewoman to

close with us. Is she of the wicked? Is thine hostess here
of the wicked? Or is thy boy of the wicked? Or honest
Bardolph, whose zeal burns in his nose, of the wicked?

POINS   Answer, thou dead elm, answer.

FALSTAFF   The fiend hath pricked down Bardolph irrecoverable,
and his face is Lucifer's privy-kitchen, where he doth   310
nothing but roast malt-worms. For the boy, there is a
good angel about him, but the devil binds him too.

HAL   For the women?

FALSTAFF   For one of them, she's in hell already, and burns poor
souls. For th'other, I owe her money, and whether she
be damned for that I know not.

HOSTESS   No, I warrant you.

FALSTAFF   No, I think thou art not; I think thou art quit for that.
Marry, there is another indictment upon thee, for
suffering flesh to be eaten in thy house, contrary to   320
the law, for the which I think thou wilt howl.

HOSTESS   All victuallers do so. What's a joint of mutton or two
in a whole Lent?

HAL   You, gentlewoman –

DOLL   What says your Grace?

FALSTAFF   His Grace says that which his flesh rebels against.[29]

                 [Peto, outside, knocks at the door.

HOSTESS   Who knocks so loud at door? Look to th'door there,
Francis.

Enter PETO.

HAL   Peto, how now, what news?

PETO   The King your father is at Westminster,   330
And there are twenty weak and wearied posts
Come from the north; and as I came along
I met and overtook a dozen captains,
Bare-headed, sweating, knocking at the taverns,
And asking every one for Sir John Falstaff.

HAL   By heaven, Poins, I feel me much to blame,
So idly to profane the precious time,
When tempest of commotion, like the south
Borne with black vapour, doth begin to melt   340
And drop upon our bare unarmèd heads.
Give me my sword and cloak. – Falstaff, good night.

        [Exeunt the Prince and Poins.

FALSTAFF Now comes in the sweetest morsel of the night, and
we must hence and leave it unpicked.

      [Knocking at the door. Exit Bardolph.
More knocking at the door?

      Enter BARDOLPH.

 – How now, what's the matter?

BARDOLPH You must away to court, sir, presently.
A dozen captains stay at door for you.

FALSTAFF *[to page:]* Pay the musicians, sirrah. – Farewell, hostess;
farewell, Doll. You see, my good wenches, how men
of merit are sought after; the undeserver may sleep,   350
when the man of action is called on. Farewell, good
wenches. If I be not sent away post, I will see you
again ere I go.

DOLL I cannot speak; if my heart be not ready to burst –
well, sweet Jack, have a care of thyself.

FALSTAFF Farewell, farewell.

    [Exit with Bardolph, Peto, the page and musicians.

HOSTESS Well, fare thee well. I have known thee these twenty-
nine years, come peascod-time, but an honester and
truer-hearted man – well, fare thee well.

BARDOLPH *[at the door:]* Mistress Tearsheet!   360

HOSTESS What's the matter?

BARDOLPH Bid Mistress Tearsheet come to my master.

HOSTESS O, run, Doll, run! Run, good Doll! Come! – She comes
blubbered. – Yea, will you come, Doll?   *[Exeunt.*

ACT 3, SCENE 1.

Westminster: the palace.

Enter the KING *in his dressing-gown, followed by a* PAGE.

HENRY IV   Go, call the Earls of Surrey and of Warwick;
But, ere they come, bid them o'er-read these letters
And well consider of them. Make good speed.

                                            [*Exit the page.*

How many thousand of my poorest subjects
Are at this hour asleep! O sleep, O gentle sleep,
Nature's soft nurse, how have I frighted thee,
That thou no more wilt weigh my eyelids down,
And steep my senses in forgetfulness?
Why rather, sleep, li'st thou in smoky cribs,
Upon uneasy pallets stretching thee,   10
And hushed with buzzing night-flies to thy slumber,
Than in the perfumed chambers of the great,
Under the canopies of costly state,
And lulled with sound of sweetest melody?
O thou dull god, why li'st thou with the vile
In loathsome beds, and leav'st the kingly couch
A watch-case, or a common 'larum-bell?
Wilt thou upon the high and giddy mast
Seal up the ship-boy's eyes, and rock his brains
In cradle of the rude imperious surge,   20
And in the visitation of the winds,
Who take the ruffian billows by the top,
Curling their monstrous heads, and hanging them
With deafing clamour in the slippery clouds,
That, with the hurly, death itself awakes?
Canst thou, O partial sleep, give thy repose
To the wet sea-son in an hour so rude,
And in the calmest and most stillest night,
With all appliances and means to boot,
Deny it to a king? Then happy low, lie down!   30
Uneasy lies the head that wears a crown.

    Enter the Earls of WARWICK *and* SURREY.

WARWICK Many good morrows to your Majesty!
HENRY IV Is it good morrow, lords?
WARWICK   'Tis one o'clock, and past.
HENRY IV Why then, good morrow to you all, my lords.
          Have you read o'er the letters that I sent you?
WARWICK We have, my liege.
HENRY IV Then you perceive the body of our kingdom,
          How foul it is, what rank diseases grow,
          And with what danger, near the heart of it.
WARWICK It is but as a body yet distempered,   40
          Which to his former strength may be restored
          With good advice and little medicine.
          My lord Northumberland will soon be cooled.
HENRY IV O God, that one might read the book of Fate,
          And see the revolution of the times
          Make mountains level, and the continent,
          Weary of solid firmness, melt itself
          Into the sea; and other times to see
          The beachy girdle of the ocean
          Too wide for Neptune's hips; how chance's mocks   50
          And changes fill the cup of alteration
          With divers liquors. O, if this were seen,
          The happiest youth, viewing his progress through,
          What perils past, what crosses to ensue,
          Would shut the book, and sit him down and die.[30]
          'Tis not ten years gone
          Since Richard and Northumberland, great friends,
          Did feast together, and in two years after
          Were they at wars. It is but eight years since
          This Percy was the man nearest my soul,   60
          Who like a brother toiled in my affairs
          And laid his love and life under my foot;
          Yea, for my sake, even to the eyes of Richard
          Gave him defiance. But which of you was by −
          [to Warwick:] You, cousin Nevil, as I may remember −
          When Richard, with his eye brimful of tears,
          Then checked and rated by Northumberland,
          Did speak these words, now proved a prophecy?
          'Northumberland, thou ladder by the which

My cousin Bullingbrooke ascends my throne'   70
(Though then, God knows, I had no such intent,
But that necessity so bowed the state
That I and greatness were compelled to kiss),
'The time shall come' – thus did he follow it –
'The time will come, that foul sin, gathering head,
Shall break into corruption' – so went on,
Foretelling this same time's condition,
And the division of our amity.[31]

WARWICK There is a history in all men's lives
Figuring the natures of the times deceased,   80
The which observed, a man may prophesy,
With a near aim, of the main chance of things
As yet not come to life, who in their seeds
And weak beginning lie intreasured.
Such things become the hatch and brood of time;
And by the necessary form of this,
King Richard might create a perfect guess
That great Northumberland, then false to him,
Would of that seed grow to a greater falseness,
Which should not find a ground to root upon   90
Unless on you.

HENRY IV   Are these things then necessities?
Then let us meet them like necessities,
And that same word even now cries out on us.
They say the Bishop and Northumberland
Are fifty thousand strong.

WARWICK   It cannot be, my Lord.
Rumour doth double, like the voice and echo,
The numbers of the feared. Please it your Grace
To go to bed. Upon my soul, my Lord,
The powers that you already have sent forth
Shall bring this prize in very easily.   100
To comfort you the more, I have received
A certain instance that Glendower is dead.[32]
Your Majesty hath been this fortnight ill,
And these unseasoned hours perforce must add
Unto your sickness.

HENRY IV   I will take your counsel.

And were these inward wars once out of hand,
We would, dear lords, unto the Holy Land.   [*Exeunt.*

SCENE 2.

Gloucestershire: outside Shallow's house.

Enter Justice SHALLOW *and Justice* SILENCE.

SHALLOW   Come on, come on, come on, sir! Give me your hand,
sir, give me your hand, sir! An early stirrer, by the
rood! And how doth my good cousin Silence?

SILENCE   Good morrow, good cousin Shallow.

SHALLOW   And how doth my cousin your bedfellow? And your
fairest daughter and mine, my god-daughter Ellen?

SILENCE   Alas, a black woosel, cousin Shallow.

SHALLOW   By yea and no, sir. I dare say my cousin William is
become a good scholar — he is at Oxford still, is he
not?   10

SILENCE   Indeed, sir, to my cost.

SHALLOW   A must then to the Inns o'Court shortly. I was once of
Clement's Inn, where I think they will talk of 'mad
Shallow' yet.

SILENCE   You were called 'lusty Shallow' then, cousin.

SHALLOW   By the Mass, I was called anything, and I would have
done anything indeed, too, and roundly, too. There
was I, and little John Doit of Staffordshire, and black
George Barnes, and Francis Pickbone, and Will Squele,
a Cotsole man — you had not four such swinge-bucklers   20
in all the Inns o'Court again. And I may say to you, we
knew where the bona-robas were, and had the best of
them all at commandment. Then was Jack Falstaff (now
Sir John) a boy, and page to Thomas Mowbray, Duke
of Norfolk.

SILENCE   This Sir John, cousin, that comes hither anon about
soldiers?

SHALLOW   The same Sir John, the very same. I see him break
Scoggin's head at the court gate, when a was a crack,
not thus high; and the very same day did I fight with   30
one Samson Stockfish, a fruiterer, behind Gray's Inn.

Jesu, Jesu, the mad days that I have spent! And to see
how many of my old acquaintance are dead!

SILENCE   We shall all follow, cousin.

SHALLOW   Certain, 'tis certain, very sure, very sure. Death (as the
Psalmist saith) is certain to all: all shall die. How a
good yoke of bullocks at Stamford fair?[33]

SILENCE   By my troth, I was not there.

SHALLOW   Death is certain. Is old Double of your town living
yet?   40

SILENCE   Dead, sir.

SHALLOW   Jesu, Jesu, dead! A drew a good bow, and dead! A shot
a fine shoot: John a Gaunt loved him well, and betted
much money on his head. Dead! A would have clapped
i'th'clout at twelve score, and carried you a forehand
shaft a fourteen and fourteen and a half,[34] that it would
have done a man's heart good to see. How a score of
ewes now?

SILENCE   Thereafter as they be; a score of good ewes may be
worth ten pounds.   50

SHALLOW   And is old Double dead?

SILENCE   Here come two of Sir John Falstaff's men, as I think.

Enter BARDOLPH *and Falstaff's* PAGE.

SHALLOW   Good morrow, honest gentlemen.

BARDOLPH   I beseech you, which is Justice Shallow?

SHALLOW   I am Robert Shallow, sir, a poor esquire of this county,
and one of the King's Justices of the Peace. What is
your good pleasure with me?

BARDOLPH   My captain, sir, commends him to you, my captain Sir
John Falstaff, a tall gentleman, by heaven, and a most
gallant leader.   60

SHALLOW   He greets me well, sir; I knew him a good back-sword
man. How doth the good knight? May I ask how my
lady his wife doth?

BARDOLPH   Sir, pardon; a soldier is better accommodated than with
a wife.

SHALLOW   It is well said, in faith, sir, and it is well said indeed,
too. 'Better accommodated'! It is good, yea indeed
is it. Good phrases are surely, and ever were, very

commendable. 'Accommodated': it comes of '*accommodo*'. Very good, a good phrase.   70

BARDOLPH Pardon, sir, I have heard the word – phrase call you it? By this day, I know not the phrase, but I will maintain the word with my sword to be a soldier-like word, and a word of exceeding good command, by heaven. 'Accommodated': that is, when a man is, as they say, accommodated, or when a man is being whereby a may be thought to be accommodated; which is an excellent thing.

SHALLOW It is very just.

Enter FALSTAFF.

Look, here comes good Sir John. [*To Falstaff:*] Give me   80
your good hand, give me your worship's good hand. By my troth, you like well, and bear your years very well. Welcome, good Sir John.

FALSTAFF I am glad to see you well, good Master Robert Shallow. [*To Silence:*] Master Surecard, as I think?

SHALLOW No, Sir John, it is my cousin Silence, in commission with me.

FALSTAFF Good Master Silence, it well befits you should be of the peace.

SILENCE Your good worship is welcome.   90

FALSTAFF Fie, this is hot weather, gentlemen. Have you provided me here half a dozen sufficient men?

SHALLOW Marry, have we, sir. Will you sit?

FALSTAFF Let me see them, I beseech you.

SHALLOW Where's the roll? Where's the roll? Where's the roll? Let me see, let me see, let me see. So, so, so, so, so, so, so. Yea, marry, sir. – Rafe Mouldy! – Let them appear as I call, let them do so, let them do so. Let me see – where is Mouldy?

Enter MOULDY.

MOULDY Here, and it please you.   100

SHALLOW What think you, Sir John? A good-limbed fellow, young, strong, and of good friends.

FALSTAFF Is thy name 'Mouldy'?

MOULDY Yea, an't please you.

FALSTAFF   'Tis the more time thou wert used.

SHALLOW   Ha, ha, ha! Most excellent, i'faith! Things that are mouldy lack use! Very singular good, in faith; well said, Sir John, very well said.

FALSTAFF   Prick him.

MOULDY   I was pricked well enough before, and you could have   110
let me alone. My old dame will be undone now for one to do her husbandry and her drudgery.[35] You need not to have pricked me; there are other men fitter to go out than I.

FALSTAFF   Go to! Peace, Mouldy; you shall go, Mouldy; it is time you were spent.

MOULDY   'Spent'?

SHALLOW   Peace, fellow, peace: stand aside. Know you where you are? For th'other, Sir John – let me see. – Simon Shadow!   120

FALSTAFF   Yea, marry, let me have him to sit under. He's like to be a cold soldier.

SHALLOW   Where's Shadow?

Enter SHADOW.

SHADOW   Here, sir.

FALSTAFF   Shadow, whose son art thou?

SHADOW   My mother's son, sir.

FALSTAFF   Thy mother's son! Like enough, and thy father's shadow. So the son of the female is the shadow of the male; it is often so, indeed – but not of the father's substance![36]   130

SHALLOW   Do you like him, Sir John?

FALSTAFF   Shadow will serve for summer. Prick him, for we have a number of shadows fill up the muster-book.[37]

SHALLOW   – Thomas Wart!

FALSTAFF   Where's he?

Enter WART.

WART   Here, sir.

FALSTAFF   Is thy name 'Wart'?

WART   Yea, sir.

FALSTAFF   Thou art a very ragged Wart.

SHALLOW   Shall I prick him, Sir John?   140

FALSTAFF It were superfluous, for his apparel is built upon his
back, and the whole frame stands upon pins.[38] Prick
him no more.

SHALLOW Ha, ha, ha! You can do it, sir, you can do it; I commend
you well. – Francis Feeble!

Enter FEEBLE.

FEEBLE Here, sir.

SHALLOW What trade art thou, Feeble?

FEEBLE A woman's tailor, sir.

SHALLOW Shall I prick him, sir?

FALSTAFF You may; but if he had been a man's tailor, he'd ha'   150
pricked *you*. – Wilt thou make as many holes in an
enemy's battle as thou hast done in a woman's petticoat?

FEEBLE I will do my good will, sir; you can have no more.

FALSTAFF Well, said, good woman's tailor! Well said, courageous
Feeble! Thou wilt be as valiant as the wrathful dove,
or most magnanimous mouse. – Prick the woman's
tailor well, Master Shallow; deep, Master Shallow.

FEEBLE I would Wart might have gone, sir.

FALSTAFF I would thou wert a man's tailor, that thou mightst
mend him and make him fit to go. I cannot put him to a   160
private soldier, that is the leader of so many thousands.[39]
Let that suffice, most forcible Feeble.

FEEBLE It shall suffice, sir.

FALSTAFF I am bound to thee, reverend Feeble. – Who is next?

SHALLOW – Peter Bullcalf o'th'green!

FALSTAFF Yea, marry, let's see Bullcalf.

Enter BULLCALF.

BULLCALF Here, sir.

FALSTAFF 'Fore God, a likely fellow! Come, prick Bullcalf till he
roar again.

BULLCALF O Lord, good my Lord Captain –   170

FALSTAFF What, dost thou roar before thou art pricked?

BULLCALF O Lord, sir, I am a diseased man.

FALSTAFF What disease hast thou?

BULLCALF A whoreson cold, sir, a cough, sir, which I caught
with ringing in the King's affairs upon his coronation
day, sir.

FALSTAFF　Come, thou shalt go to the wars in a gown. We will have away thy cold, and I will take such order that thy friends shall ring for thee.[40] – Is here all?

SHALLOW　Here is two more called than your number. You must 180 have but four here, sir; and so, I pray you, go in with me to dinner.

FALSTAFF　Come, I will go drink with you, but I cannot tarry dinner. I am glad to see you, by my troth, Master Shallow.

SHALLOW　O, Sir John, do you remember since we lay all night in the Windmill in Saint George's Field?

FALSTAFF　No more of that, good Master Shallow, no more of that.

SHALLOW　Ha, 'twas a merry night! And is Jane Nightwork alive?

FALSTAFF　She lives, Master Shallow. 190

SHALLOW　She never could away with me.

FALSTAFF　Never, never. She would always say she could not abide Master Shallow.

SHALLOW　By the Mass, I could anger her to th'heart. She was then a bona-roba. Doth she hold her own well?

FALSTAFF　Old, old, Master Shallow.

SHALLOW　Nay, she must be old; she cannot choose but be old; certain she's old; and had Robin Nightwork by old Nightwork before I came to Clement's Inn.

SILENCE　That's fifty-five year ago. 200

SHALLOW　Ha, cousin Silence, that thou hadst seen that that this knight and I have seen! – Ha, Sir John, said I well?

FALSTAFF　We have heard the chimes at midnight, Master Shallow.

SHALLOW　That we have, that we have, that we have! In faith, Sir John, we have. Our watchword was 'Hem, boys!'. Come, let's to dinner; come, let's to dinner. Jesus, the days that we have seen! Come, come.

　　　　　　　　　　[*Exeunt Falstaff, Shallow and Silence.*

BULLCALF　Good Master Corporate Bardolph, stand my friend – and here's four Harry ten-shillings in French crowns for you. In very truth, sir, I had as lief be hanged, sir, 210 as go. And yet for mine own part, sir, I do not care; but rather because I am unwilling, and, for mine own part, have a desire to stay with my friends; else, sir, I did not care, for mine own part, so much.

BARDOLPH *[taking the money:]* Go to; stand aside.

MOULDY   And, good Master Corporal Captain, for my old dame's
           sake stand my friend. She has nobody to do anything
           about her when I am gone, and she is old and cannot
           help herself. You shall have forty, sir.

BARDOLPH Go to; stand aside.   220

FEEBLE   By my troth, I care not; a man can die but once; we
           owe God a death. I'll ne'er bear a base mind. An't be
           my destiny, so; an't be not, so. No man's too good to
           serve's prince; and, let it go which way it will, he that
           dies this year is quit for the next.

BARDOLPH Well said; th'art a good fellow.

FEEBLE   Faith, I'll bear no base mind.

                 Enter FALSTAFF, SHALLOW *and* SILENCE.

FALSTAFF   Come, sir, which men shall I have?

SHALLOW Four of which you please.

BARDOLPH *[aside to Falstaff:]* Sir, a word with you. I have three   230
         pound to free Mouldy and Bullcalf.

FALSTAFF   Go to, well.

SHALLOW Come, Sir John, which four will you have?

FALSTAFF   Do you choose for me.

SHALLOW Marry, then, Mouldy, Bullcalf, Feeble, and Shadow.

FALSTAFF   Mouldy and Bullcalf: for you, Mouldy, stay at home
           till you are past service; and for your part, Bullcalf,
           grow till you come unto it. I will none of you.

                              [Exeunt Mouldy and Bullcalf.

SHALLOW Sir John, Sir John, do not yourself wrong; they are
           your likeliest men, and I would have you served with   240
           the best.

FALSTAFF   Will you tell me, Master Shallow, how to choose a
           man? Care I for the limb, the thews, the stature, bulk,
           and big assemblance of a man? Give me the spirit,
           Master Shallow. Here's Wart; you see what a ragged
           appearance it is. A shall charge you, and discharge you,
           with the motion of a pewterer's hammer, come off and
           on swifter than he that gibbets on the brewer's bucket.⁴¹
           And this same half-faced fellow, Shadow: give me this
           man; he presents no mark to the enemy: the foeman   250
           may with as great aim level at the edge of a pen-knife.

And for a retreat, how swiftly will this Feeble, the
woman's tailor, run off! O, give me the spare men, and
spare me the great ones. – Put me a caliver into Wart's
hand, Bardolph.   [*Bardolph does so.*

BARDOLPH Hold, Wart; traverse. Thas! Thas! Thas!⁴²

FALSTAFF Come, manage me your caliver. So, very well! Go to,
very good, exceeding good! O, give me always a little,
lean, old, chopped, bald shot. Well said, i'faith! Wart,
th'art a good scab. Hold, there's a tester for thee.   260

SHALLOW He is not his craft's master; he doth not do it right. I
remember at Mile-End Green, when I lay at Clement's
Inn – I was then Sir Dagonet in Arthur's show⁴³ – there
was a little quiver fellow, and a would manage you his
piece thus, and a would about and about, and come
you in, and come you in. 'Rah, tah, tah!' would a say.
'Bounce!' would a say. And away again would a go,
and again would a come. I shall ne'er see such a fellow.

FALSTAFF These fellows will do well, Master Shallow. – God
keep you, Master Silence; I will not use many words   270
with you. – Fare you well, gentlemen both; I thank
you. I must a dozen mile tonight. – Bardolph, give the
soldiers coats.

SHALLOW Sir John, the Lord bless you! God prosper your affairs!
God send us peace! At your return, visit my house; let
our old acquaintance be renewed. Peradventure I will
with ye to the court.

FALSTAFF 'Fore God, would you would.

SHALLOW Go to; I have spoke at a word. God keep you!

FALSTAFF Fare you well, gentle gentlemen.   280
                    [*Exeunt Shallow and Silence.*
On, Bardolph, lead the men away.
              [*Exeunt Bardolph, Wart, Shadow and Feeble.*
As I return, I will fetch off these justices. I do see the
bottom of Justice Shallow. Lord, Lord, how subject
we old men are to this vice of lying! This same starved
justice hath done nothing but prate to me of the wildness of his youth, and the feats he hath done about
Turnbull Street, and every third word a lie, duer paid
to the hearer than the Turk's tribute.⁴⁴ I do remember

him at Clement's Inn, like a man made after supper of
a cheese-paring. When a was naked, he was for all the   290
world like a forked radish, with a head fantastically
carved upon it with a knife. A was so forlorn that his
dimensions to any thick sight were invincible; a was
the very genius of famine, yet lecherous as a monkey,
and the whores called him 'Mandrake'. A came ever in
the rearward of the fashion, and sung those tunes to
the overscutched housewives that he heard the carmen
whistle, and sware they were his fancies or his good-
nights.[45] And now is this Vice's dagger become a squire,
and talks as familiarly of John a Gaunt as if he had been   300
sworn brother to him, and I'll be sworn a ne'er saw
him but once in the tilt-yard, and then he burst his
head for crowding among the marshal's men. I saw it,
and told John a Gaunt he beat his own name, for you
might have thrust him and all his apparel into an eel-
skin – the case of a treble hautboy was a mansion for
him, a court. And now has he land and beefs. Well, I'll
be acquainted with him if I return, and't shall go hard
but I'll make him a philosopher's two stones to me.[46] If
the young dace be a bait for the old pike, I see no   310
reason in the law of nature but I may snap at him. Let
time shape, and there an end.   [*Exit.*

Yorkshire: Gaultree Forest.

Enter the ARCHBISHOP, MOWBRAY *and* HASTINGS,
with their SOLDIERS.

ARCHB.   What is this forest called?
HASTINGS 'Tis Gaultree Forest, an't shall please your Grace.
ARCHB.   Here stand, my lords, and send discoverers forth
                   To know the numbers of our enemies.
HASTINGS We have sent forth already.
ARCHB.   'Tis well done.
                   My friends and brethren in these great affairs,
                   I must acquaint you that I have received
                   New-dated letters from Northumberland,
                   Their cold intent, tenure and substance, thus:
                   Here doth he wish his person, with such powers   10
                   As might hold sortance with his quality,
                   The which he could not levy; whereupon
                   He is retired, to ripe his growing fortunes,
                   To Scotland; and concludes in hearty prayers
                   That your attempts may overlive the hazard
                   And fearful meeting of their opposite.
MOWBRAY Thus do the hopes we have in him touch ground,
                   And dash themselves to pieces.

Enter a MESSENGER.

HASTINGS   Now, what news?
MESSENGER West of this forest, scarcely off a mile,
                   In goodly form comes on the enemy,   20
                   And, by the ground they hide, I judge their number
                   Upon or near the rate of thirty thousand.
MOWBRAY The just proportion that we gave them out.
                   Let us sway on, and face them in the field.

Enter WESTMORLAND.

ARCHB.   What well-appointed leader fronts us here?
MOWBRAY I think it is my Lord of Westmorland.
WEST.   Health and fair greeting from our general,

The Prince, Lord John and Duke of Lancaster.

ARCHB. Say on, my Lord of Westmorland, in peace,
What doth concern your coming.

WEST.   Then, my lord,   30
Unto your Grace do I in chief address
The substance of my speech. If that rebellion
Came like itself, in base and abject routs,
Led on by bloody youth, guarded with rage,
And countenanced by boys and beggary;
I say, if damned commotion so appeared
In his true, native, and most proper shape,
You, reverend father, and these noble lords
Had not been here to dress the ugly form
Of base and bloody insurrection   40
With your fair honours. You, Lord Archbishop,
Whose see is by a civil peace maintained,
Whose beard the silver hand of peace hath touched,
Whose learning and good letters peace hath tutored,
Whose white investments figure innocence,
The dove and very blessèd spirit of peace:
Wherefore do you so ill translate yourself
Out of the speech of peace that bears such grace
Into the harsh and boist'rous tongue of war,
Turning your books to graves, your ink to blood,   50
Your pens to lances, and your tongue divine
To a loud trumpet and a point of war?

ARCHB. Wherefore do I this? So the question stands.
Briefly, to this end: we are all diseased,
And with our surfeiting and wanton hours
Have brought ourselves into a burning fever,
And we must bleed for it; of which disease
Our late King Richard, being infected, died.
But, my most noble Lord of Westmorland,
I take not on me here as a physician,   60
Nor do I as an enemy to peace
Troop in the throngs of military men,
But rather show awhile like fearful war
To diet rank minds sick of happiness,
And purge th'obstructions which begin to stop

Our very veins of life. Hear me more plainly.
I have in equal balance justly weighed
What wrongs our arms may do, what wrongs we suffer,
And find our griefs heavier than our offences.
We see which way the stream of time doth run,   70
And are enforced from our most quiet there
By the rough torrent of occasion,
And have the summary of all our griefs,
When time shall serve, to show in articles,
Which long ere this we offered to the King,
And might by no suit gain our audience.
When we are wronged, and would unfold our griefs,
We are denied access unto his person
Even by those men that most have done us wrong.[47]
The dangers of the days but newly gone,   80
Whose memory is written on the earth
With yet-appearing blood, and the examples
Of every minute's instance, present now,
Hath put us in these ill-beseeming arms,
Not to break peace, or any branch of it,
But to establish here a peace indeed,
Concurring both in name and quality.

WEST.   Whenever yet was your appeal denied?
Wherein have you been gallèd by the King?
What peer hath been suborned to grate on you,   90
That you should seal this lawless bloody book
Of forged rebellion with a seal divine,
And consecrate commotion's bitter edge?

ARCHB.   My brother general, the commonwealth,
To brother born an household cruelty,
I make my quarrel in particular.[48]

WEST.   There is no need of any such redress,
Or if there were, it not belongs to you.

MOWBRAY Why not to him in part, and to us all
That feel the bruises of the days before,   100
And suffer the condition of these times
To lay a heavy and unequal hand
Upon our honours?

WEST.   O, my good Lord Mowbray,

Construe the times to their necessities,
And you shall say, indeed, it is the time,
And not the King, that doth you injuries.
Yet for your part, it not appears to me
Either from the King or in the present time
That you should have an inch of any ground
To build a grief on. Were you not restored   110
To all the Duke of Norfolk's signories,
Your noble and right well-remembered father's?

MOWBRAY What thing, in honour, had my father lost
That need to be revived and breathed in me?
The King that loved him, as the state stood then,
Was force perforce compelled to banish him;
And then that Henry Bullingbrooke and he,
Being mounted and both rousèd in their seats,
Their neighing coursers daring of the spur,
Their armèd staves in charge, their beavers down,   120
Their eyes of fire sparkling through sights of steel,
And the loud trumpet blowing them together:
Then, then, when there was nothing could have stayed
My father from the breast of Bullingbrooke –
O, when the King did throw his warder down,
His own life hung upon the staff he threw.
Then threw he down himself and all their lives
That by indictment and by dint of sword
Have since miscarried under Bullingbrooke.

WEST.   You speak, Lord Mowbray, now you know not what.   130
The Earl of Her'ford was reputed then
In England the most valiant gentleman.
Who knows on whom fortune would then have smiled?
But if your father had been victor there,
He ne'er had borne it out of Coventry;
For all the country, in a general voice,
Cried hate upon him, and all their prayers and love
Were set on Her'ford, whom they doted on,
And blessed and graced, indeed, more than the King.[49]
But this is mere digression from my purpose.   140
Here come I from our princely general
To know your griefs, to tell you from his Grace

That he will give you audience; and wherein
It shall appear that your demands are just,
You shall enjoy them, every thing set off
That might so much as think you enemies.

MOWBRAY But he hath forced us to compel this offer,
And it proceeds from policy, not love.

WEST.   Mowbray, you overween to take it so.
This offer comes from mercy, not from fear;   150
For lo, within a ken our army lies,
Upon mine honour, all too confident
To give admittance to a thought of fear.
Our battle is more full of names than yours,
Our men more perfect in the use of arms,
Our armour all as strong, our cause the best;
Then reason will our hearts should be as good.
Say you not, then, our offer is compelled.

MOWBRAY Well, by my will we shall admit no parley.

WEST.   That argues but the shame of your offence;   160
A rotten case abides no handling.

HASTINGS Hath the Prince John a full commission,
In very ample virtue of his father,
To hear and absolutely to determine
Of what conditions we shall stand upon?

WEST.   That is intended in the general's name.
I muse you make so slight a question.

ARCHB.   Then take, my Lord of Westmorland, this schedule,
For this contains our general grievances.
Each several article herein redressed,   170
All members of our cause, both here and hence,
That are ensinewed to this action
Acquitted by a true substantial form,
And present execution of our wills
To us and to our purposes confined:
We come within our aweful banks again,
And knit our powers to the arm of peace.[50]

WEST.   This will I show the general. Please you, lords,
In sight of both our battles we may meet,
And either end in peace – which God so frame! –   180
Or to the place of diff'rence call the swords

Which must decide it.

ARCHB.   My Lord, we will do so.
                                        [*Exit Westmorland.*

MOWBRAY There is a thing within my bosom tells me
That no conditions of our peace can stand.

HASTINGS Fear you not that. If we can make our peace
Upon such large terms, and so absolute,
As our conditions shall consist upon,
Our peace shall stand as firm as rocky mountains.

MOWBRAY Yea, but our valuation shall be such
That every slight and false-derivèd cause,   190
Yea, every idle, nice and wanton reason,
Shall to the King taste of this action;
That, were our royal faiths martyrs in love,
We shall be winnowed with so rough a wind
That even our corn shall seem as light as chaff,
And good from bad find no partition.

ARCHB.   No, no, my Lord. Note this: the King is weary
Of dainty and such picking grievances;
For he hath found, to end one doubt by death
Revives two greater in the heirs of life;   200
And therefore will he wipe his tables clean,
And keep no tell-tale to his memory
That may repeat and history his loss
To new remembrance; for full well he knows
He cannot so precisely weed this land
As his misdoubts present occasion.
His foes are so enrooted with his friends
That, plucking to unfix an enemy,
He doth unfasten so and shake a friend;
So that this land, like an offensive wife   210
That hath enragèd him on to offer strokes,
As he is striking, holds his infant up,
And hangs resolved correction in the arm
That was upreared to execution.

HASTINGS Besides, the King hath wasted all his rods
On late offenders, that he now doth lack
The very instruments of chastisement,
So that his power, like to a fangless lion,

ARCHB.   May offer, but not hold.

                                   'Tis very true;

And therefore be assured, my good Lord Marshal,   220

If we do now make our atonement well,

Our peace will, like a broken limb united,

Grow stronger for the breaking.

MOWBRAY   Be it so.

Here is returned my Lord of Westmorland.

Enter WESTMORLAND.

WEST.   The Prince is here at hand. Pleaseth your Lordship

To meet his Grace just distance 'tween our armies?

MOWBRAY Your Grace of York, in God's name then, set forward.

ARCHB.   Before, and greet his Grace! My Lord, we come.

                                                     [Exeunt.

SCENE 2.

Yorkshire: Gaultree Forest.

Enter PRINCE JOHN OF LANCASTER *with* WESTMORLAND
and a SOLDIER *who bears wine, meeting the* ARCHBISHOP,
MOWBRAY, HASTINGS *and a* CAPTAIN.

PR. JOHN   You are well encountered here, my cousin Mowbray;

          – Good day to you, gentle Lord Archbishop;

          – And so to you, Lord Hastings, – and to all.

          – My Lord of York, it better showed with you

When that your flock, assembled by the bell,

Encircled you to hear with reverence

Your exposition on the holy text,

Than now to see you here an iron man talking,

Cheering a rout of rebels with your drum,

Turning the word to sword, and life to death.   10

That man that sits within a monarch's heart

And ripens in the sunshine of his favour,

Would he abuse the countenance of the King,

Alack, what mischiefs might he set abroach

In shadow of such greatness! With you, Lord Bishop,

It is even so. Who hath not heard it spoken

How deep you were within the books of God?

To us the speaker in His parliament,
To us th'imagined voice of God himself,
The very opener and intelligencer   20
Between the grace, the sanctities, of heaven
And our dull workings. O, who shall believe
But you misuse the reverence of your place,
Employ the countenance and grace of heaven,
As a false favourite doth his prince's name,
In deeds dishonourable? You have tane up,
Under the counterfeited zeal of God,
The subjects of His substitute, my father,
And both against the peace of heaven and him
Have here up-swarmed them.

ARCHB.   Good my Lord of Lancaster, 30
I am not here against your father's peace,
But, as I told my Lord of Westmorland,
The time misordered doth, in common sense,
Crowd us and crush us to this monstrous form
To hold our safety up. I sent your Grace
The parcels and particulars of our grief,
The which hath been with scorn shoved from the court,
Whereon this Hydra son of war is born,
Whose dangerous eyes may well be charmed asleep
With grant of our most just and right desires,[51]   40
And true obedience, of this madness cured,
Stoop tamely to the foot of majesty.

MOWBRAY If not, we ready are to try our fortunes
To the last man.

HASTINGS   And though we here fall down,
We have supplies to second our attempt.
If they miscarry, theirs shall second them,
And so success of mischief shall be born,
And heir from heir shall hold this quarrel up
Whiles England shall have generation.

PR. JOHN You are too shallow, Hastings, much too shallow, 50
To sound the bottom of the after-times.

WEST.   Pleaseth your Grace to answer them directly
How far forth you do like their articles.

PR. JOHN I like them all, and do allow them well,

And swear here, by the honour of my blood,
My father's purposes have been mistook,
And some about him have too lavishly
Wrested his meaning and authority.
[*To Archbishop:*] My Lord, these griefs shall be with
                              speed redressed;
Upon my soul, they shall. If this may please you,   60
Discharge your powers unto their several counties,
As we will ours; and here, between the armies,
Let's drink together friendly and embrace,
That all their eyes may bear those tokens home
Of our restorèd love and amity.

ARCHB.   I take your princely word for these redresses.

PR. JOHN   I give it you, and will maintain my word;
And thereupon I drink unto your Grace.   [*He drinks.*

HASTINGS   Go, captain, and deliver to the army
This news of peace. Let them have pay, and part.   70
I know it will well please them. Hie thee, captain!
                                   [*Exit captain.*

ARCHB.   [*toasting:*] To you, my noble Lord of Westmorland!

WEST.   [*returning the toast:*] I pledge your Grace; and if you
                             knew what pains
I have bestowed to breed this present peace,
You would drink freely; but my love to ye
Shall show itself more openly hereafter.

ARCHB.   I do not doubt you.

WEST.   I am glad of it.
      – Health to my Lord and gentle cousin, Mowbray.

MOWBRAY You wish me health in very happy season,
For I am on the sudden something ill.   80

ARCHB.   Against ill chances men are ever merry,
But heaviness fore-runs the good event.

WEST.   Therefore be merry, coz, since sudden sorrow
Serves to say thus, 'Some good thing comes tomorrow.'

ARCHB.   Believe me, I am passing light in spirit.

MOWBRAY So much the worse, if your own rule be true.
                       [*Shouting from the rebels' army.*

PR. JOHN   The word of peace is rendered. Hark how they shout!

MOWBRAY This had been cheerful after victory.

ARCHB.   A peace is of the nature of a conquest,
            For then both parties nobly are subdued,   90
            And neither party loser.

PR. JOHN   [*to Westmorland:*]   Go, my Lord,
            And let our army be dischargèd too. [*Exit Westmorland.*
            [*To Archbishop:*] And, good my Lord, so please you,
                                                    let our trains
            March by us, that we may peruse the men
            We should have coped withal.

ARCHB.   Go, good Lord Hastings,
            And, ere they be dismissed, let them march by.
                                            [*Exit Hastings.*

PR. JOHN   I trust, lords, we shall lie tonight together.

                Enter WESTMORLAND *with* SOLDIERS.

            Now, cousin, wherefore stands our army still?

WEST.   The leaders, having charge from you to stand,
            Will not go off until they hear you speak.   100

PR. JOHN   They know their duties.

                        Enter HASTINGS.

HASTINGS   [*to Archbishop:*] My Lord, our army is dispersed already.
            Like youthful steers unyoked, they take their courses
            East, west, north, south; or, like a school broke up,
            Each hurries toward his home and sporting-place.

WEST.   Good tidings, my Lord Hastings – for the which
            I do arrest thee, traitor, of high treason;
            And you, Lord Archbishop, and you, Lord Mowbray,
            Of capital treason I attach you both.
                [*The soldiers seize Hastings, the Archbishop and Mowbray.*

MOWBRAY   Is this proceeding just and honourable?   110

WEST.   Is your assembly so?

ARCHB.   Will you thus break your faith?

PR. JOHN   I pawned thee none.
            I promised you redress of these same grievances
            Whereof you did complain; which, by mine honour,
            I will perform with a most Christian care.
            But, for you rebels, look to taste the due
            Meet for rebellion and such acts as yours.
            Most shallowly did you these arms commence,

Fondly brought here, and foolishly sent hence.
– Strike up our drums, pursue the scattered stray;   120
God, and not we, hath safely fought today.
Some guard these traitors to the block of death,
Treason's true bed and yielder–up of breath.   [*Exeunt.*

SCENE 3.

Yorkshire: Gaultree Forest.

Alarum. Excursions.

Enter FALSTAFF *and* SIR JOHN COLEVILE, *meeting.*

FALSTAFF   What's your name, sir? Of what condition are you, and of what place, I pray?

COLEVILE   I am a knight, sir, and my name is Colevile of the Dale.

FALSTAFF   Well then, Colevile is your name, a knight is your degree, and your place the Dale. Colevile shall be still your name, a traitor your degree, and the dungeon your place – a place deep enough; so shall you be still Colevile of the Dale.

COLEVILE   Are not you Sir John Falstaff?   10

FALSTAFF   As good a man as he, sir, whoe'er I am. Do ye yield, sir, or shall I sweat for you? If I do sweat, they are the drops of thy lovers, and they weep for thy death; therefore rouse up fear and trembling, and do observance to my mercy.

COLEVILE   I think you are Sir John Falstaff, and in that thought yield me.   [*He kneels.*

FALSTAFF   I have a whole school of tongues in this belly of mine, and not a tongue of them all speaks any other word but my name. And I had but a belly of any indifferency,   20 I were simply the most active fellow in Europe; my womb, my womb, my womb undoes me. Here comes our general.   [*Retreat sounded.*

Enter PRINCE JOHN, WESTMORLAND *and* BLUNT, *with* SOLDIERS.

PR. JOHN   The heat is past; follow no further now.
Call in the powers, good cousin Westmorland.
     [*Exit Westmorland.*

      – Now, Falstaff, where have you been all this while?
      When everything is ended, then you come:
      These tardy tricks of yours will, on my life,
      One time or other break some gallows' back.

FALSTAFF   I would be sorry, my Lord, but it should be thus. I 30
never knew yet but rebuke and check was the reward
of valour. Do you think me a swallow, an arrow, or a
bullet? Have I in my poor and old motion the
expedition of thought? I have speeded hither with the
very extremest inch of possibility; I have foundered
nine score and odd posts; and here, travel-tainted as I
am, have in my pure and immaculate valour taken Sir
John Colevile of the Dale, a most furious knight and
valorous enemy. But what of that? He saw me, and
yielded; that I may justly say, with the hook-nosed 40
fellow of Rome, three words, 'I came, saw, and overcame.'[52]

PR. JOHN   It was more of his courtesy than your deserving.

FALSTAFF   I know not. Here he is, and here I yield him. And I
beseech your Grace, let it be booked with the rest of
this day's deeds, or, by the Lord, I will have it in a
particular ballad else, with mine own picture on the
top on't, Colevile kissing my foot; to the which course
if I be enforced, if you do not all show like gilt two-
pences to me, and I in the clear sky of fame o'ershine 50
you as much as the full moon doth the cinders of the
element (which show like pins' heads to her), believe
not the word of the noble.[53] Therefore let me have
right, and let desert mount.

PR. JOHN   Thine's too heavy to mount.

FALSTAFF   Let it shine, then.

PR. JOHN   Thine's too thick to shine.

FALSTAFF   Let it do something, my good Lord, that may do me
good, and call it what you will.

PR. JOHN   Is thy name Colèvile?

COLEVILE   It is, my Lord. 60

PR. JOHN   A famous rebel art thou, Colèvile.

FALSTAFF   And a famous true subject took him.

COLEVILE   I am, my Lord, but as my betters are

That led me hither. Had they been ruled by me,
You should have won them dearer than you have.

FALSTAFF I know not how they sold themselves, but thou, like a
kind fellow, gav'st thyself away gratis, and I thank thee
for thee.

Enter WESTMORLAND.

PR. JOHN Now, have you left pursuit?
WEST. Retreat is made and execution stayed.   70
PR. JOHN Send Colèvile with his confederates
To York, to present execution.
– Blunt, lead him hence, and see you guard him sure.
                              [*Exit Blunt with Colevile.*
And now dispatch we toward the court, my lords.
I hear the King my father is sore sick.
[*To Westmorland:*] Our news shall go before us to his
                                             Majesty,
Which, cousin, you shall bear to comfort him,
And we with sober speed will follow you.
FALSTAFF My Lord, I beseech you, give me leave to go
Through Gloucestershire and, when you come to court, 80
Stand, my good Lord, pray, in your good report.
PR. JOHN Fare you well, Falstaff. I, in my condition,
Shall better speak of you than you deserve.
                              [*Exeunt all but Falstaff.*
FALSTAFF I would you had the wit; 'twere better than your dukedom. Good faith, this same young sober-blooded boy
doth not love me, nor a man cannot make him laugh;
but that's no marvel, he drinks no wine. There's never
none of these demure boys come to any proof, for thin
drink doth so over-cool their blood, and making many
fish meals, that they fall into a kind of male green- 90
sickness; and then when they marry, they get wenches.
They are generally fools and cowards; which some of us
should be too, but for inflammation. A good sherris-
sack hath a twofold operation in it. It ascends me into
the brain, dries me there all the foolish and dull and
crudy vapours which environ it, makes it apprehensive,
quick, forgetive, full of nimble, fiery, and delectable
shapes, which delivered o'er to the voice, the tongue,

which is the birth, becomes excellent wit. The second property of your excellent sherris is the warming of the 100 blood, which before, cold and settled, left the liver white and pale, which is the badge of pusillanimity and cowardice; but the sherris warms it, and makes it course from the inwards to the parts' extremes. It illumineth the face, which, as a beacon, gives warning to all the rest of this little kingdom, man, to arm; and then the vital commoners, and inland petty spirits, muster me all to their captain, the heart, who, great and puffed up with this retinue, doth any deed of courage; and this valour comes of sherris. So that skill in the weapon 110 is nothing without sack, for that sets it a-work; and learning, a mere hoard of gold kept by a devil, till sack commences it and sets it in act and use. Hereof comes it that Prince Harry is valiant; for the cold blood he did naturally inherit of his father he hath like lean, sterile and bare land manured, husbanded and tilled, with excellent endeavour of drinking good (and good store of) fertile sherris, that he is become very hot and valiant. If I had a thousand sons, the first human principle I would teach them should be to forswear thin potations, 120 and to addict themselves to sack.

Enter BARDOLPH.

How now, Bardolph?

BARDOLPH The army is dischargèd all and gone.

FALSTAFF Let them go. I'll through Gloucestershire, and there will I visit Master Robert Shallow, Esquire. I have him already tempering between my finger and my thumb, and shortly will I seal with him. Come away. [*Exeunt.*

SCENE 4.

Westminster: the Jerusalem Chamber of the palace.

Enter the KING, *carried in a chair,* WARWICK,
THOMAS (DUKE OF CLARENCE), HUMPHREY (DUKE OF GLOUCESTER),
and attendant LORDS.

HENRY IV Now, lords, if God doth give successful end
To this debate that bleedeth at our doors,
We will our youth lead on to higher fields,
And draw no swords but what are sanctified.
Our navy is addressed, our power collected,
Our substitutes in absence well invested,
And everything lies level to our wish;
Only we want a little personal strength,
And pause us till these rebels now afoot
Come underneath the yoke of government.   10
WARWICK Both which we doubt not but your Majesty
Shall soon enjoy.
HENRY IV   Humphrey, my son of Gloucester,
Where is the Prince your brother?
GLO'STER I think he's gone to hunt, my Lord, at Windsor.
HENRY IV And how accompanied?
GLO'STER   I do not know, my Lord.
HENRY IV Is not his brother Thomas of Clarence with him?
GLO'STER No, my good Lord, he is in presence here.
CLARENCE What would my Lord and father?
HENRY IV Nothing but well to thee, Thomas of Clarence.
How chance thou art not with the Prince thy brother? 20
He loves thee, and thou dost neglect him, Thomas.
Thou hast a better place in his affection
Than all thy brothers; cherish it, my boy,
And noble offices thou mayst effect
Of mediation, after I am dead,
Between his greatness and thy other brethren.
Therefore omit him not; blunt not his love,
Nor lose the good advantage of his grace
By seeming cold, or careless of his will;

For he is gracious, if he be observed: 30
He hath a tear for pity, and a hand
Open as day for melting charity.
Yet notwithstanding, being incensed, he is flint,
As humorous as winter, and as sudden
As flaws congealed in the spring of day.
His temper therefore must be well observed.
Chide him for faults, and do it reverently,
When you perceive his blood inclined to mirth;
But, being moody, give him time and scope,
Till that his passions, like a whale on ground,   40
Confound themselves with working. Learn this,
                                        Thomas,
And thou shalt prove a shelter to thy friends,
A hoop of gold to bind thy brothers in,
That the united vessel of their blood,
Mingled with venom of suggestion
(As force perforce the age will pour it in),
Shall never leak, though it do work as strong
As aconitum or rash gunpowder.

CLARENCE I shall observe him with all care and love.
HENRY IV Why art thou not at Windsor with him, Thomas?   50
CLARENCE He is not there today; he dines in London.
HENRY IV And how accompanied? Canst thou tell that?
CLARENCE With Poins and other his continual followers.
HENRY IV Most subject is the fattest soil to weeds,
          And he, the noble image of my youth,
          Is overspread with them; therefore my grief
          Stretches itself beyond the hour of death.
          The blood weeps from my heart when I do shape,
          In forms imaginary, th'unguided days
          And rotten times that you shall look upon   60
          When I am sleeping with my ancestors:
          For when his headstrong riot hath no curb,
          When rage and hot blood are his counsellors,
          When means and lavish manners meet together,
          O, with what wings shall his affections fly
          Towards fronting peril and opposed decay!
WARWICK My gracious Lord, you look beyond him quite.

The Prince but studies his companions
Like a strange tongue, wherein, to gain the language,
'Tis needful that the most immodest word   70
Be looked upon and learnt; which, once attained,
Your Highness knows, comes to no further use
But to be known and hated. So, like gross terms,
The Prince will, in the perfectness of time,
Cast off his followers; and their memory
Shall as a pattern or a measure live
By which his Grace must mete the lives of other,
Turning past evils to advantages.

HENRY IV 'Tis seldom when the bee doth leave her comb
In the dead carrion.[54]

Enter WESTMORLAND.

                    Who's here? Westmorland?   80
WEST.   Health to my sovereign, and new happiness
Added to that that I am to deliver!
Prince John, your son, doth kiss your Grace's hand.
Mowbray, the Bishop Scroop, Hastings and all
Are brought to the correction of your law.
There is not now a rebel's sword unsheathed,
But Peace puts forth her olive everywhere.
The manner how this action hath been borne
Here at more leisure may your Highness read,
With every course in his particular.   90

HENRY IV O Westmorland, thou art a summer bird
Which ever in the haunch of winter sings
The lifting up of day.

Enter HARCOURT.

                    Look, here's more news.
HARCOURT From enemies heaven keep your Majesty,
And, when they stand against you, may they fall
As those that I am come to tell you of!
The Earl Northumberland and the Lord Bardolph,
With a great power of English and of Scots,
Are by the Shrieve of Yorkshire overthrown.
The manner and true order of the fight   100
This packet, please it you, contains at large.

HENRY IV	And wherefore should these good news make me sick?
	Will Fortune never come with both hands full,
	But write her fair words still in foulest letters?
	She either gives a stomach and no food:
	Such are the poor, in health; or else a feast
	And takes away the stomach: such are the rich
	That have abundance and enjoy it not.
	I should rejoice now at this happy news,
	And now my sight fails, and my brain is giddy. 110
	O me! Come near me. Now I am much ill.
GLO'STER	Comfort, your Majesty!
CLARENCE	O my royal father!
WEST.	My sovereign Lord, cheer up yourself, look up.
WARWICK	Be patient, Princes. You do know these fits
	Are with his Highness very ordinary.
	Stand from him, give him air; he'll straight be well.
CLARENCE	No, no, he cannot long hold out these pangs.
	Th'incessant care and labour of his mind
	Hath wrought the mure that should confine it in
	So thin that life looks through and will break out. 120
GLO'STER	The people fear me, for they do observe
	Unfathered heirs and loathly births of nature;
	The seasons change their manners, as the year
	Had found some months asleep and leaped them over.
CLARENCE	The river hath thrice flowed, no ebb between,
	And the old folk, time's doting chronicles,
	Say it did so a little time before
	That our great-grandsire, Edward, sicked and died.
WARWICK	Speak lower, Princes, for the King recovers.
GLO'STER	This apoplexy will certain be his end. 130
HENRY IV	I pray you take me up, and bear me hence
	Into some other chamber. Softly, pray.

[*The King is carried to an adjacent visible chamber.*

SCENE 5.

Westminster: another chamber of the palace.

The KING is laid upon a bed. He is attended by the same LORDS
as in the previous scene, the action being continuous.

HENRY IV Let there be no noise made, my gentle friends,
          Unless some dull and favourable hand
          Will whisper music to my weary spirit.

WARWICK – Call for the music in the other room.

                              [*Exit one person. Soft music ensues.*

HENRY IV Set me the crown upon my pillow here.

                              [*The crown is placed on a pillow.*

CLARENCE His eye is hollow, and he changes much.

                              [*Noise within.*

WARWICK Less noise, less noise!

Enter PRINCE HENRY (HAL).

HAL   Who saw the Duke of Clarence?

CLARENCE I am here, brother, full of heaviness.

HAL How now, rain within doors, and none abroad?
     How doth the King?   10

GLO'STER Exceeding ill.

HAL   Heard he the good news yet?
     Tell it him.

GLO'STER He altered much upon the hearing it.

HAL If he be sick with joy, he'll recover without physic.

WARWICK Not so much noise, my lords. Sweet Prince, speak low;
         The King your father is disposed to sleep.

CLARENCE Let us withdraw into the other room.

WARWICK Will't please your Grace to go along with us?

HAL No, I will sit and watch here by the King.

                              [*Exeunt all but the King and Prince Henry.*

     Why doth the crown lie there upon his pillow,   20
     Being so troublesome a bedfellow?
     O polished perturbation, golden care,
     That keep'st the ports of slumber open wide
     To many a watchful night! Sleep with it now!
     Yet not so sound, and half so deeply sweet,

As he whose brow with homely biggen bound
Snores out the watch of night. O majesty!
When thou dost pinch thy bearer, thou dost sit
Like a rich armour worn in heat of day,
That scald'st with safety. By his gates of breath   30
There lies a downy feather which stirs not;
Did he suspire, that light and weightless down
Perforce must move. – My gracious Lord! My father!
– This sleep is sound indeed; this is a sleep
That from this golden rigol hath divorced
So many English kings. – Thy due from me
Is tears and heavy sorrows of the blood,
Which nature, love and filial tenderness
Shall, O dear father, pay thee plenteously.
My due from thee is this imperial crown,   40
Which, as immediate from thy place and blood,
Derives itself to me.   [*He puts the crown on his head.*
                    Lo where it sits,
Which God shall guard; and put the world's whole
                                        strength

Into one giant arm, it shall not force
This lineal honour from me. This from thee
Will I to mine leave, as 'tis left to me.
                    [*Exit. Music ceases. The King awakens.*

HENRY IV Warwick! Gloucester! Clarence!

Enter WARWICK, GLOUCESTER, CLARENCE *and attendant* LORDS.

CLARENCE Doth the King call?
WARWICK What would your Majesty? How fares your Grace?
HENRY IV Why did you leave me here alone, my lords?   50
CLARENCE We left the Prince my brother here, my liege,
          Who undertook to sit and watch by you.
HENRY IV The Prince of Wales? Where is he? Let me see him.
          He is not here.
WARWICK This door is open; he is gone this way.
GLO'STER He came not through the chamber where we stayed.
HENRY IV Where is the crown? Who took it from my pillow?
WARWICK When we withdrew, my liege, we left it here.
HENRY IV The Prince hath tane it hence. Go, seek him out.

Is he so hasty that he doth suppose   60
My sleep my death?
Find him, my lord of Warwick; chide him hither.

                                    [*Exit Warwick.*

This part of his conjoins with my disease,
And helps to end me. See, sons, what things you are.
How quickly nature falls into revolt
When gold becomes her object!
For this the foolish over-careful fathers
Have broke their sleep with thoughts,
Their brains with care, their bones with industry;
For this they have engrossed and piled up   70
The cankered heaps of strange-achievèd gold;
For this they have been thoughtful to invest
Their sons with arts and martial exercises;
When, like the bee culling from every flower
The virtuous sweets,
Our thighs packed with wax, our mouths with honey,
We bring it to the hive; and like the bees
Are murdered for our pains. This bitter taste
Yields his engrossments to the ending father.[55]

                   Enter WARWICK.

Now where is he that will not stay so long   80
Till his friend, sickness, have determined me?
WARWICK My lord, I found the Prince in the next room,
Washing with kindly tears his gentle cheeks,
With such a deep demeanour in great sorrow,
That tyranny which never quaffed but blood
Would, by beholding him, have washed his knife
With gentle eye-drops. He is coming hither.
HENRY IV But wherefore did he take away the crown?

Enter PRINCE HENRY (HAL), *holding the crown.*

Lo where he comes. – Come hither to me, Harry. –
[*To lords:*] Depart the chamber, leave us here alone.   90
       [*Exeunt all except King Henry IV and Prince Henry.*
HAL   I never thought to hear you speak again.
HENRY IV Thy wish was father, Harry, to that thought.
I stay too long by thee; I weary thee.

Dost thou so hunger for mine empty chair
That thou wilt needs invest thee with my honours
Before thy hour be ripe? O foolish youth!
Thou seek'st the greatness that will overwhelm thee.
Stay but a little, for my cloud of dignity
Is held from falling with so weak a wind
That it will quickly drop; my day is dim.   100
Thou hast stol'n that which after some few hours
Were thine without offence, and at my death
Thou hast sealed up my expectation.
Thy life did manifest thou lov'dst me not,
And thou wilt have me die assured of it.
Thou hid'st a thousand daggers in thy thoughts,
Which thou hast whetted on thy stony heart,
To stab at half an hour of my life.
What, canst thou not forbear me half an hour?
Then get thee gone, and dig my grave thyself,   110
And bid the merry bells ring to thine ear
That thou art crownèd, not that I am dead.
Let all the tears that should bedew my hearse
Be drops of balm to sanctify thy head;
Only compound me with forgotten dust.
Give that which gave thee life unto the worms;
Pluck down my officers, break my decrees;
For now a time is come to mock at form:
Harry the Fifth is crowned! Up, vanity!
Down, royal state! All you sage counsellors, hence!   120
And to the English court assemble now,
From every region, apes of idleness!
Now, neighbour confines, purge you of your scum!
Have you a ruffian that will swear, drink, dance,
Revel the night, rob, murder, and commit
The oldest sins the newest kind of ways?
Be happy, he will trouble you no more.
England shall double gild his treble guilt;
England shall give him office, honour, might;
For the fifth Harry from curbed licence plucks   130
The muzzle of restraint, and the wild dog
Shall flesh his tooth on every innocent.

O my poor kingdom, sick with civil blows!
When that my care could not withhold thy riots,
What wilt thou do when riot is thy care?
O, thou wilt be a wilderness again,
Peopled with wolves, thy old inhabitants![56]

HAL O, pardon me, my liege! But for my tears,
The moist impediments unto my speech,
I had forestalled this dear and deep rebuke   140
Ere you with grief had spoke and I had heard
The course of it so far. There is your crown,

                    [He returns the crown, and kneels.

And He that wears the crown immortally
Long guard it yours! If I affect it more
Than as your honour and as your renown,
Let me no more from this obedience rise,
Which my most inward true and duteous spirit
Teacheth this prostrate and exterior bending.
God witness with me: when I here came in
And found no course of breath within your Majesty,   150
How cold it struck my heart! If I do feign,
O let me in my present wildness die,
And never live to show th'incredulous world
The noble change that I have purposèd!
Coming to look on you, thinking you dead,
And dead almost, my liege, to think you were,
I spake unto this crown as having sense,
And thus upbraided it: 'The care on thee depending
Hath fed upon the body of my father;
Therefore thou best of gold art worse than gold.   160
Other, less fine in carat, is more precious,
Preserving life in med'cine potable;[57]
But thou, most fine, most honoured, most renowned,
Hast eat thy bearer up.' Thus, my most royal liege,
Accusing it, I put it on my head,
To try with it, as with an enemy
That had before my face murdered my father,
The quarrel of a true inheritor;
But if it did infect my blood with joy
Or swell my thoughts to any strain of pride,   170

If any rebel or vain spirit of mine
Did with the least affection of a welcome
Give entertainment to the might of it,
Let God for ever keep it from my head,
And make me as the poorest vassal is
That doth with awe and terror kneel to it!

HENRY IV Oh my son,
God put it in thy mind to take it hence,
That thou mightst win the more thy father's love,
Pleading so wisely in excuse of it.   180
Come hither, Harry; sit thou by my bed,

                    [*Hal rises, and sits by the bed.*

And hear, I think, the very latest counsel
That ever I shall breathe. God knows, my son,
By what by-paths and indirect crook'd ways
I met this crown; and I myself know well
How troublesome it sat upon my head.
To thee it shall descend with better quiet,
Better opinion, better confirmation;
For all the soil of the achievement goes
With me into the earth. It seemed in me   190
But as an honour snatched with boist'rous hand,
And I had many living to upbraid
My gain of it by their assistances,
Which daily grew to quarrel and to bloodshed,
Wounding supposèd peace. All these bold fears
Thou seest with peril I have answerèd,
For all my reign hath been but as a scene
Acting that argument. And now my death
Changes the mood, for what in me was purchased
Falls upon thee in a more fairer sort,   200
So thou the garland wear'st successively.
Yet though thou stand'st more sure than I could do,
Thou art not firm enough, since griefs are green;
And all my friends, which thou must make thy friends,
Have but their stings and teeth newly tane out,
By whose fell working I was first advanced,
And by whose power I well might lodge a fear
To be again displaced; which to avoid,

I cut them off, and had a purpose now
To lead out many to the Holy Land,   210
Lest rest and lying still might make them look
Too near unto my state. Therefore, my Harry,
Be it thy course to busy giddy minds
With foreign quarrels, that action hence borne out
May waste the memory of the former days.
More would I, but my lungs are wasted so,
That strength of speech is utterly denied me.
How I came by the crown, O God forgive,
And grant it may with thee in true peace live!

HAL   My gracious liege,   220
You won it, wore it, kept it, gave it me;
Then plain and right must my possession be,
Which I with more than with a common pain
'Gainst all the world will rightfully maintain.

       Enter PRINCE JOHN OF LANCASTER,
       WARWICK *and attendant* LORDS.

HENRY IV   Look, look, here comes my John of Lancaster.
PR. JOHN   Health, peace and happiness to my royal father!
HENRY IV   Thou bring'st me happiness and peace, son John,
But health, alack, with youthful wings is flown
From this bare withered trunk. Upon thy sight
My worldly business makes a period.   230
Where is my Lord of Warwick?

HAL   My Lord of Warwick!
                         [*Warwick approaches the King.*

HENRY IV   Doth any name particular belong
Unto the lodging where I first did swoon?
WARWICK   'Tis called 'Jerusalem', my noble Lord.
HENRY IV   Laud be to God! Even there my life must end.
It hath been prophesied to me, many years,
I should not die but in Jerusalem,
Which vainly I supposed the Holy Land.
But bear me to that chamber; there I'll lie;
In that Jerusalem shall Harry die.   240
                       [*Exeunt, lords bearing the King.*

Gloucestershire: Shallow's house.

Enter SHALLOW, SILENCE, BARDOLPH, FALSTAFF *and his* PAGE.

SHALLOW   By cock and pie, sir, you shall not away tonight. −
     What, Davy, I say!

FALSTAFF   You must excuse me, Master Robert Shallow.

SHALLOW   I will not excuse you; you shall not be excused; excuses
     shall not be admitted; there is no excuse shall serve;
     you shall not be excused. − Why, Davy!

Enter DAVY.

DAVY   Here, sir.

SHALLOW   Davy, Davy, Davy, Davy! Let me see, Davy; let me
     see, Davy; let me see. Yea, marry, William cook, bid
     him come hither. − Sir John, you shall not be excused. 10

DAVY   Marry, sir, thus: those precepts cannot be served; and
    again, sir, shall we sow the hade land with wheat?

SHALLOW   With red wheat, Davy. But for William cook: are
     there no young pigeons?

DAVY   Yes, sir. Here is now the smith's note for shoeing and
    plough-irons.

SHALLOW   Let it be cast and paid. − Sir John, you shall not be
     excused.

DAVY   Now, sir, a new link to the bucket must needs be had.
    And, sir, do you mean to stop any of William's wages, 20
    about the sack he lost at Hinckley fair?

SHALLOW   A shall answer it. Some pigeons, Davy, a couple of
     short-legged hens, a joint of mutton, and any pretty
     little tiny kickshaws, tell William cook.

DAVY   Doth the man of war stay all night, sir?

SHALLOW   Yea, Davy. I will use him well; a friend i'th'court is
     better than a penny in purse. Use his men well, Davy,
     for they are arrant knaves, and will backbite.

DAVY   No worse than they are backbitten, sir, for they have
    marvellous foul linen. 30

SHALLOW   Well conceited, Davy.⁵⁸ About thy business, Davy.

DAVY   I beseech you, sir, to countenance William Visor of
    Woncot against Clement Perkes o'th'Hill.

SHALLOW   There is many complaints, Davy, against that Visor; that Visor is an arrant knave, on my knowledge.

DAVY   I grant your worship that he is a knave, sir; but yet God forbid, sir, but a knave should have some countenance at his friend's request. An honest man, sir, is able to speak for himself, when a knave is not. I have served your worship truly, sir, this eight years, and if I cannot 40 once or twice in a quarter bear out a knave against an honest man, I have little credit with your worship. The knave is mine honest friend, sir; therefore, I beseech you, let him be countenanced.

SHALLOW   Go to; I say he shall have no wrong. Look about, Davy.
                               [*Exit Davy.*
Where are you, Sir John? Come, come, come, off with your boots. – Give me your hand, Master Bardolph.

BARDOLPH I am glad to see your worship.

SHALLOW   I thank thee with all my heart, kind Master Bardolph;
          [*to the page:*] And welcome, my tall fellow. Come, Sir
                                           John. 50

FALSTAFF   I'll follow you, good Master Robert Shallow.
                               [*Exit Shallow.*
Bardolph, look to our horses.
                 [*Exeunt Bardolph and the page.*
If I were sawed into quantities, I should make four dozen of such bearded hermits' staves as Master Shallow. It is a wonderful thing to see the semblable coherence of his men's spirits and his. They, by observing him, do bear themselves like foolish justices; he, by conversing with them, is turned into a justice-like servingman. Their spirits are so married in con-junction, with the participation of society, that they 60 flock together in consent, like so many wild geese. If I had a suit to Master Shallow, I would humour his men with the mputation of being near their master; if to his men, I would curry with Master Shallow that no man could better command his servants. It is certain that either wise bearing or ignorant carriage is caught, as men take diseases, one of another; therefore let men take heed of their company. I will devise matter

enough out of this Shallow to keep Prince Harry in
continual laughter the wearing out of six fashions,   70
which is four terms, or two actions, and a shall laugh
without intervallums.[59] O, it is much that a lie with a
slight oath, and a jest with a sad brow, will do with a
fellow that never had the ache in his shoulders! O, you
shall see him laugh till his face be like a wet cloak ill
laid up.

SHALLOW   [*within:*] Sir John!

FALSTAFF   I come, Master Shallow, I come, Master Shallow.

                                                 [*Exit.*

SCENE 2.

Westminster: the palace.

Enter WARWICK *and the* LORD CHIEF JUSTICE.

WARWICK   How now, my Lord Chief Justice, whither away?

JUSTICE   How doth the King?

WARWICK   Exceeding well; his cares are now all ended.

JUSTICE   I hope, not dead.

WARWICK   He's walked the way of nature,
And to our purposes he lives no more.

JUSTICE   I would his Majesty had called me with him:
The service that I truly did his life
Hath left me open to all injuries.

WARWICK   Indeed I think the young King loves you not.

JUSTICE   I know he doth not, and do arm myself   10
To welcome the condition of the time,
Which cannot look more hideously upon me
Than I have drawn it in my fantasy.[60]

Enter PRINCE JOHN OF LANCASTER, CLARENCE, GLOUCESTER
and OTHERS.

WARWICK   Here come the heavy issue of dead Harry.
O that the living Harry had the temper
Of he, the worst of these three gentlemen!
How many nobles then should hold their places
That must strike sail to spirits of vile sort!

JUSTICE   O God, I fear all will be overturned.

PR. JOHN   Good morrow, cousin Warwick, good morrow.   20

GLO'STER *and* CLARENCE   Good morrow, cousin.
PR. JOHN   We meet like men that had forgot to speak.
WARWICK   We do remember, but our argument
          Is all too heavy to admit much talk.
PR. JOHN   Well, peace be with him that hath made us heavy.
JUSTICE   Peace be with us, lest we be heavier.
GLO'STER   O, good my Lord, you have lost a friend indeed,
          And I dare swear you borrow not that face
          Of seeming sorrow: it is sure your own.
PR. JOHN   [*to Justice:*] Though no man be assured what grace to find,   30
          You stand in coldest expectation.
          I am the sorrier; would 'twere otherwise.
CLARENCE   [*to Justice:*] Well, you must now speak Sir John Falstaff fair,
          Which swims against your stream of quality.
JUSTICE   Sweet Princes, what I did, I did in honour,
          Led by th'impartial conduct of my soul.
          And never shall you see that I will beg
          A raggèd and forestalled remission.
          If truth and upright innocency fail me,
          I'll to the King my master that is dead,   40
          And tell him who hath sent me after him.
WARWICK   Here comes the Prince.

Enter HAL *as* KING KENRY V, *attended by* BLUNT *and* OTHERS.

JUSTICE   Good morrow, and God save your Majesty!
HENRY V   This new and gorgeous garment, majesty,
          Sits not so easy on me as you think.
          Brothers, you mix your sadness with some fear.
          This is the English, not the Turkish court;
          Not Amurath an Amurath succeeds,[61]
          But Harry Harry. Yet be sad, good brothers,
          For, by my faith, it very well becomes you.   50
          Sorrow so royally in you appears
          That I will deeply put the fashion on
          And wear it in my heart. Why then, be sad;
          But entertain no more of it, good brothers,
          Than a joint burden laid upon us all.
          For me, by heaven, I bid you be assured,
          I'll be your father and your brother too.
          Let me but bear your love, I'll bear your cares.

Yet weep that Harry's dead, and so will I;
But Harry lives, that shall convert those tears   60
By number into hours of happiness.

PRINCES   We hope no otherwise from your Majesty.

HENRY V   You all look strangely on me – and
            [*to Justice:*]   you most;
            You are, I think, assured I love you not.

JUSTICE   I am assured, if I be measured rightly,
            Your Majesty hath no just cause to hate me.

HENRY V   How might a prince of my great hopes forget
            So great indignities you laid upon me?
            What! Rate, rebuke, and roughly send to prison
            Th'immediate heir of England? Was this easy?   70
            May this be washed in Lethe and forgotten?

JUSTICE   I then did use the person of your father:
            The image of his power lay then in me;
            And in th'administration of his law,
            Whiles I was busy for the commonwealth,
            Your Highness pleasèd to forget my place,
            The majesty and power of law and justice,
            The image of the King whom I presented,
            And struck me in my very seat of judgement;
            Whereon, as an offender to your father,   80
            I gave bold way to my authority
            And did commit you. If the deed were ill,
            Be you contented, wearing now the garland,
            To have a son set your decrees at naught?
            To pluck down justice from your aweful bench?
            To trip the course of law, and blunt the sword
            That guards the peace and safety of your person?
            Nay, more, to spurn at your most royal image,
            And mock your workings in a second body?
            Question your royal thoughts, make the case yours;   90
            Be now the father and propose a son,
            Hear your own dignity so much profaned,
            See your most dreadful laws so loosely slighted,
            Behold yourself so by a son disdained;
            And then imagine me taking your part,
            And in your power soft silencing your son.

After this cold considerance, sentence me;
And, as you are a king, speak in your state
What I have done that misbecame my place,
My person, or my liege's sovereignty.   100

HENRY V   You are right, Justice, and you weigh this well.
Therefore still bear the balance and the sword,
And I do wish your honours may increase
Till you do live to see a son of mine
Offend you and obey you, as I did.
So shall I live to speak my father's words:
'Happy am I, that have a man so bold
That dares do justice on my proper son;
And not less happy, having such a son
That would deliver up his greatness so   110
Into the hands of justice.' You did commit me;
For which I do commit into your hand
The unstained sword that you have used to bear,
With this remembrance: that you use the same
With the like bold, just and impartial spirit
As you have done 'gainst me. There is my hand.
You shall be as a father to my youth;
My voice shall sound as you do prompt mine ear,
And I will stoop and humble my intents
To your well-practised wise directions.   120
– And, Princes all, believe me, I beseech you:
My father is gone wild into his grave,
For in his tomb lie my affections;
And with his spirits sadly I survive
To mock the expectation of the world,
To frustrate prophecies, and to raze out
Rotten opinion, who hath writ me down
After my seeming. The tide of blood in me
Hath proudly flowed in vanity till now;
Now doth it turn, and ebb back to the sea,   130
Where it shall mingle with the state of floods,
And flow henceforth in formal majesty.
Now call we our high court of parliament,
And let us choose such limbs of noble counsel
That the great body of our state may go

In equal rank with the best-governed nation;
That war, or peace, or both at once, may be
As things acquainted and familiar to us;
[*to Justice:*] In which you, father, shall have foremost hand.
[*To all:*] Our coronation done, we will accite,   140
As I before remembered, all our state;[62]
And, God consigning to my good intents,
No prince nor peer shall have just cause to say,
'God shorten Harry's happy life one day!'   [*Exeunt.*

SCENE 3.

Gloucestershire: Shallow's garden.

Enter FALSTAFF, SHALLOW, SILENCE, DAVY,
BARDOLPH, *and Falstaff's* PAGE.

SHALLOW   Nay, you shall see my orchard, where, in an arbour, we
will eat a last year's pippin of mine own graffing, with a
dish of caraways, and so forth – come, cousin Silence –
and then to bed.

FALSTAFF   'Fore God, you have here a goodly dwelling, and a
rich.

SHALLOW   Barren, barren, barren; beggars all, beggars all, Sir John.
Marry, good air. – Spread, Davy, spread, Davy; well
said, Davy.

FALSTAFF   This Davy serves you for good uses: he is your serving-   10
man and your husband.

SHALLOW   A good varlet, a good varlet, a very good varlet, Sir
John – by the Mass, I have drunk too much sack at
supper – a good varlet. Now sit down, now sit down.
– Come, cousin.

SILENCE   Ah, sirrah! quoth a, we shall
[*sings:*]   'Do nothing but eat, and make good cheer,
                 And praise God for the merry year,
                 When flesh is cheap and females dear,
                 And lusty lads roam here and there,   20
                    So merrily,
                 And ever among so merrily.'

FALSTAFF   There's a merry heart, good Master Silence! I'll give
you a health for that anon.

SHALLOW   Give Master Bardolph some wine, Davy.

DAVY   Sweet sir, sit. I'll be with you anon. Most sweet sir, sit;
          master page, good master page, sit. Proface! What you
          want in meat, we'll have in drink; but you must bear;
          the heart's all.   [*Exit.*

SHALLOW   Be merry, Master Bardolph; and, my little soldier there,   30
          be merry.

SILENCE   [*sings:*]   'Be merry, be merry, my wife has all,
                       For women are shrews, both short and tall.
                       'Tis merry in hall, when beards wags all,
                       And welcome merry Shrovetide!
                       Be merry, be merry.'

FALSTAFF I did not think Master Silence had been a man of this
          mettle.

SILENCE   Who, I? I have been merry twice and once ere now.

                  Enter DAVY *with a dish of apples.*

DAVY   [*to Bardolph:*] There's a dish of leather-coats for you.   40

SHALLOW   Davy!

DAVY   Your worship? I'll be with you straight. [*To Bardolph:*]
          A cup of wine, sir?

SILENCE   [*sings:*]   'A cup of wine that's brisk and fine,
                       And drink unto thee, leman mine,
                       And a merry heart lives long-a.'

FALSTAFF Well said, Master Silence.

SILENCE   And we shall be merry, now comes in the sweet o'th'
          night.

FALSTAFF Health and long life to you, Master Silence.   50

SILENCE   [*sings:*]   'Fill the cup, and let it come,
                       I'll pledge you a mile to th'bottom.'

SHALLOW   Honest Bardolph, welcome! If thou want'st anything
          and wilt not call, beshrew thy heart. [*To the page:*]
          Welcome, my little tiny thief, and welcome indeed,
          too! – I'll drink to Master Bardolph, and to all the
          cabileros about London.

DAVY   I hope to see London once ere I die.

BARDOLPH And I might see you there, Davy –

SHALLOW   By the Mass, you'll crack a quart together – ha! will   60
          you not, Master Bardolph?

BARDOLPH Yea, sir, in a pottle-pot.

SHALLOW By God's liggens, I thank thee. The knave will stick by thee, I can assure thee that; a will not out, a; 'tis true bred!

BARDOLPH And I'll stick by him, sir.

SHALLOW Why, there spoke a king. Lack nothing! Be merry!
                              [*Urgent knocking can be heard.*
        Look who's at door there, ho! Who knocks?
                                        [*Exit Davy.*

FALSTAFF [*to Silence, seeing him drink:*] Why, now you have done me right.   70

SILENCE [*sings:*]   'Do me right,
                    And dub me knight:
                    Samingo.'
        Is't not so?

FALSTAFF 'Tis so.

SILENCE Is't so? Why then, say an old man can do somewhat.

                    Enter DAVY.

DAVY   An't please your worship, there's one Pistol come from the court with news.

FALSTAFF From the court? Let him come in.

                    Enter PISTOL.

        How now, Pistol?   80

PISTOL   Sir John, God save you!

FALSTAFF What wind blew you hither, Pistol?

PISTOL   Not the ill wind which blows no man to good. Sweet knight, thou art now one of the greatest men in this realm.

SILENCE Birlady, I think a be, but goodman Puff of Barson.

PISTOL   Puff?
        Puff i'thy teeth, most recreant coward base!
        – Sir John, I am thy Pistol and thy friend,
        And helter-skelter have I rode to thee,   90
        And tidings do I bring, and lucky joys,
        And golden times, and happy news of price.

FALSTAFF I pray thee now, deliver them like a man of this world.

PISTOL   A *foutre* for the world and worldlings base!
        I speak of Africa and golden joys.

FALSTAFF   O base Assyrian knight, what is thy news?
            Let King Cophetua know the truth thereof.
SILENCE   [*sings:*] 'And Robin Hood, Scarlet, and John.'
PISTOL   Shall dunghill curs confront the Helicons?
            And shall good news be baffled?   100
            Then, Pistol, lay thy head in Furies' lap.[63]
SHALLOW   Honest gentleman, I know not your breeding.
PISTOL   Why then, lament therefor.
SHALLOW   Give me pardon, sir. If, sir, you come with news from
            the court, I take it there's but two ways: either to utter
            them, or conceal them. I am, sir, under the King, in
            some authority.
PISTOL   Under *which* king, besonian? Speak, or die.
SHALLOW   Under King Harry.
PISTOL   Harry the Fourth, or Fifth?
SHALLOW   Harry the Fourth.
PISTOL   A *foutre* for thine office!   110
            – Sir John, thy tender lambkin now is King;
            Harry the Fifth's the man. I speak the truth:
            When Pistol lies, do this, [*he gestures*] and fig me, like
            The bragging Spaniard.[64]
FALSTAFF   What, is the old King dead?
PISTOL   As nail in door! The things I speak are just.
FALSTAFF   Away, Bardolph: saddle my horse! Master Robert
            Shallow, choose what office thou wilt in the land, 'tis
            thine. Pistol, I will double-charge thee with dignities.
BARDOLPH   O joyful day! I would not take a knighthood for my
            fortune.   120
PISTOL   What, I do bring good news?
FALSTAFF   [*to Davy:*] Carry Master Silence to bed. – Master
            Shallow, my lord Shallow, be what thou wilt, I am
            Fortune's steward! Get on thy boots; we'll ride all night.
            – O sweet Pistol! – Away, Bardolph!   [*Exit Bardolph.*
            Come, Pistol, utter more to me, and withal devise
            something to do thyself good. – Boot, boot, Master
            Shallow! I know the young King is sick for me. Let us
            take any man's horses: the laws of England are at my
            commandment. Blessed are they that have been my   130
            friends, and woe to my Lord Chief Justice!

PISTOL   Let vultures vile seize on his lungs also!
           'Where is the life that late I led?', say they;
           Why, here it is; welcome these pleasant days! [*Exeunt.*

SCENE 4.

London: a street.

Enter BEADLES *dragging in* HOSTESS QUICKLY *and* DOLL TEARSHEET.

HOSTESS   No, thou arrant knave! I would to God that I might
           die, that I might have thee hanged. Thou hast drawn
           my shoulder out of joint.
BEADLE 1   The constables have delivered her over to me, and she
           shall have whipping-cheer enough, I warrant her;
           there hath been a man or two killed about her.
DOLL   Nut-hook, nut-hook, you lie![65] Come on, I'll tell thee
           what, thou damned tripe-visaged rascal, and the child I
           go with do miscarry, thou wert better thou hadst
           struck thy mother, thou paper-faced villain.   10
HOSTESS   O the Lord, that Sir John were come! He would make
           this a bloody day to somebody. But I pray God the
           fruit of her womb miscarry!
BEADLE 1   If it do, you shall have a dozen of cushions again; you
           have but eleven now.[66] Come, I charge you both, go
           with me, for the man is dead that you and Pistol beat
           amongst you.
DOLL   I'll tell you what, you thin man in a censer, I will have
           you as soundly swinged for this, you bluebottle rogue,
           you filthy famished correctioner. If you be not swinged, 20
           I'll forswear half-kirtles.
BEADLE 1   Come, come, you she-knight-errant, come!
HOSTESS   O God, that right should thus overcome might! Well,
           of sufferance comes ease.
DOLL   Come, you rogue; come, bring me to a justice.
HOSTESS   Ay, come, you starved bloodhound.
DOLL   Goodman death, goodman bones!
HOSTESS   Thou atomy, thou![67]
DOLL   Come, you thin thing, come, you rascal!
BEADLE 1   Very well.   [*Exeunt.* 30

SCENE 5.

Westminster: near the Abbey.

Enter TWO GROOMS, *strewing rushes.*

GROOM 1   More rushes, more rushes!

GROOM 2   The trumpets have sounded twice.

GROOM 1   'Twill be two o'clock ere they come from the
           coronation. Dispatch, dispatch!   [*Exeunt.*

Trumpets sound, and the KING *and his* TRAIN *pass over the stage.
After them, enter* FALSTAFF *and his* PAGE, SHALLOW,
PISTOL *and* BARDOLPH.

FALSTAFF   Stand here by me, Master Shallow; I will make the
           King do you grace. I will leer upon him as a comes by,
           and do but mark the countenance that he will give me.

PISTOL   God bless thy lungs, good knight!

FALSTAFF   Come here, Pistol; stand behind me. [*To Shallow:*] O,
           if I had had time to have made new liveries, I would   10
           have bestowed the thousand pound I borrowed of
           you. But 'tis no matter; this poor show doth better:
           this doth infer the zeal I had to see him.

SHALLOW   It doth so.

FALSTAFF   It shows my earnestness of affection –

PISTOL   It doth so.

FALSTAFF   My devotion –

PISTOL   It doth, it doth, it doth!

FALSTAFF   As it were, to ride day and night, and not to deliberate,
           not to remember, not to have patience to shift me –   20

SHALLOW   It is best, certain.

FALSTAFF   But to stand stained with travel, and sweating with
           desire to see him, thinking of nothing else, putting all
           affairs else in oblivion, as if there were nothing else to
           be done but to see him.

PISTOL   'Tis *semper idem*, for *absque hoc nihil est*;[68] 'tis all in every
           part.

SHALLOW   'Tis so, indeed.

PISTOL   My knight, I will inflame thy noble liver,
           And make thee rage.   30

Thy Doll, and Helen of thy noble thoughts,
Is in base durance and contagious prison,
Haled thither
By most mechanical and dirty hand.
Rouse up Revenge from ebon den with fell
                           Alecto's snake,
For Doll is in. Pistol speaks naught but truth.[69]

FALSTAFF I will deliver her.   [*Shouting heard. Trumpets sound.*
PISTOL   There roared the sea, and trumpet-clangour sounds.

Enter KING HENRY V, PRINCE JOHN OF LANCASTER,
     the LORD CHIEF JUSTICE *and* OTHERS.

FALSTAFF God save thy Grace, King Hal, my royal Hal!
PISTOL   The heavens thee guard and keep, most royal imp of
                                   fame! 40

FALSTAFF God save thee, my sweet boy!
HENRY V   My Lord Chief Justice, speak to that vain man.
JUSTICE   [*to Falstaff:*] Have you your wits? Know you what 'tis
                              you speak?

FALSTAFF My King! My Jove! I speak to thee, my heart!
HENRY V   I know thee not, old man. Fall to thy prayers.
How ill white hairs becomes a fool and jester!
I have long dreamt of such a kind of man,
So surfeit-swelled, so old, and so profane;
But, being awaked, I do despise my dream.
Make less thy body hence, and more thy grace;   50
Leave gormandizing; know the grave doth gape
For thee thrice wider than for other men.
Reply not to me with a fool-born jest.
Presume not that I am the thing I was;
For God doth know, so shall the world perceive,
That I have turned away my former self;
So will I those that kept me company.
When thou dost hear I am as I have been,
Approach me, and thou shalt be as thou wast,
The tutor and the feeder of my riots;   60
Till then I banish thee, on pain of death,
As I have done the rest of my misleaders,
Not to come near our person by ten mile.
For competence of life, I will allow you,

That lack of means enforce you not to evils;
And as we hear you do reform yourselves,
We will, according to your strengths and qualities,
Give you advancement.
[*To the Lord Chief Justice:*] Be it your charge, my Lord,
To see performed the tenor of my word.
– Set on.   [*Exeunt the King and his train.* 70

FALSTAFF   Master Shallow, I owe you a thousand pound.

SHALLOW   Yea, marry, Sir John; which I beseech you to let me
have home with me.

FALSTAFF   That can hardly be, Master Shallow. Do not you
grieve at this. I shall be sent for in private to him.
Look you, he must seem thus to the world. Fear not
your advancements: I will be the man yet that shall
make you great.

SHALLOW   I cannot perceive how, unless you give me your
doublet, and stuff me out with straw. I beseech you, 80
good Sir John, let me have five hundred of my
thousand.

FALSTAFF   Sir, I will be as good as my word. This that you heard
was but a colour.

SHALLOW   A colour that I fear you will die in, Sir John.

FALSTAFF   Fear no colours.[70] Go with me to dinner. – Come,
Lieutenant Pistol; come, Bardolph. – I shall be sent for
soon at night.

Enter the LORD CHIEF JUSTICE *and* PRINCE JOHN, *with* OFFICERS.

JUSTICE   [*to officers:*] Go, carry Sir John Falstaff to the Fleet.
Take all his company along with him.   90

FALSTAFF   My Lord, my Lord –

JUSTICE   I cannot now speak; I will hear you soon.
– Take them away.

PISTOL   '*Si fortuna me tormenta, spero me contenta.*'[71]
            [*Exeunt all but Prince John and the Lord Chief Justice.*

PR. JOHN   I like this fair proceeding of the King's.
He hath intent his wonted followers
Shall all be very well provided for;
But all are banished till their conversations
Appear more wise and modest to the world.

JUSTICE   And so they are.   100

PR. JOHN   The King hath called his parliament, my Lord.
JUSTICE   He hath.
PR. JOHN   I will lay odds that, ere this year expire,
           We bear our civil swords and native fire
           As far as France. I heard a bird so sing,
           Whose music, to my thinking, pleased the King.
           Come, will you hence?   [*Exeunt.*

EPILOGUE.[72]

First, my fear; then, my curtsy; last, my speech.

My fear is your displeasure; my curtsy, my duty; and my speech, to beg your pardons. If you look for a good speech now, you undo me: for what I have to say is of mine own making; and what indeed I should say will, I doubt, prove mine own marring. But to the purpose, and so to the venture. Be it known to you, as it is very well, I was lately here in the end of a displeasing play, to pray your patience for it, and to promise you a better. I meant indeed to pay you with this; which, if like an ill venture it come unluckily home, I break, and you, my gentle creditors, lose. Here I promised you I 10 would be, and here I commit my body to your mercies. Bate me some, and I will pay you some, and (as most debtors do) promise you infinitely. And so I kneel down before you – but, indeed, to pray for the Queen.   [*He kneels*.

If my tongue cannot entreat you to acquit me, will you command me to use my legs? And yet that were but light payment, to dance out of your debt. But a good conscience will make any possible satisfaction, and so would I. All the gentlewomen here have forgiven me. If the gentlemen will not, then the gentlemen do not agree with the gentlewomen, which was never seen in such 20 an assembly.

One word more, I beseech you. If you be not too much cloyed with fat meat, our humble author will continue the story, with Sir John in it, and make you merry with fair Katherine of France; where (for anything I know) Falstaff shall die of a sweat, unless already a be killed with your hard opinions; for Oldcastle died a martyr, and this is not the man.[73] My tongue is weary; when my legs are too, I will bid you good night.   [*He dances*.

FINIS.

In these notes, the abbreviations include the following:

F1:   the First Folio (1623);
Fr.   French;
Holinshed: Raphael Holinshed and others: *Chronicles*, Vol. III
             (2nd edn.; London: 1587);
i.e.:   *id est* (Latin): that is;
Q: Quarto ;
Q1:   the First Quarto;
S.D.:   stage-direction.

Biblical quotations are from the Geneva Bible; I modernise the
spelling and punctuation.

In the case of a pun or an ambiguity, the meanings are distinguished
as (a) and (b), or as (a), (b) and (c).

HENRY IV, PART ONE

1 (1.1.38) *Mortimer*:   Shakespeare confused the Edmund Mortimer who was Hotspur's brother-in-law with the Edmund
   Mortimer (nephew of the former Edmund) who was the
   designated heir of Richard II.

2 (1.2.40–41) *As . . . durance?*:   Hybla Major in Sicily was famed
   for its honey. Next: 'old lad of the castle' puns on Oldcastle,
   Falstaff's original name in the play; and 'The Castle' was a
   London brothel. A 'buff jerkin' was a leather jacket worn by
   soldiers; and 'robe of durance' means (a) durable garment and
   (b) garment suitable for a convict.

3 (1.2.65–7) *For . . . wardrobe.*:   Here 'suits' means 'quests for
   advancement', 'lawsuits' and 'outfits of clothing'. The hangman could keep the clothing of his victims.

4 (1.2.82–3) *wisdom . . . it.*:   Hal conflates Proverbs 1:20 and 1:24.

5 (1.2.89–90) *and I do not,*:   'if I do not'. Here and at numerous subsequent places in the text, 'and' is not the customary connective but equals 'if'. In such cases, some editors change 'and' to 'an'; but I preserve 'and', as the context usually makes clear its local meaning.

6 (1.2.97–8) *'Tis . . . vocation.*:   He echoes 1 Corinthians 7:20 and Ephesians 4:1.

7 (1.2.146–7) *All-hallown summer*:   summer weather on All Hallows' Day (1 November): Falstaff, though ageing, behaves like a younger man.

8 (1.3.247–8) *Why, . . . me.*:   In her book, *Shakespeare's Imagery*, Caroline Spurgeon drew attention to the frequency with which Shakespeare associates melting sweets and treacherous dogs. A famous example appears in *Antony and Cleopatra*, 4.12.20–23 (Wordsworth edition): 'The hearts / That spanieled me at heels, to whom I gave / Their wishes, do discandy, melt their sweets / On blossoming Cæsar…'.

9 (2.1.58) *Saint Nicholas' clerks,*:   St Nicholas was the patron saint of (among others) clerks and travellers. The thieves have taken note, like clerks, of travellers who are their potential victims.

10 (2.1.71–2) *mad . . . maltworms,*:   'wild, moustached, purple-faced boozers,'

11 (2.1.73) *one-yers*:   individualists, singular people. Q1 has 'Oneyres'; F1 has 'Oneyers'. (In Thomas Hardy's *Jude the Obscure*, 1895, Arabella remarks that Sue Bridehead is 'a oneyer'.) I insert a hyphen to clarify the pronunciation. Some editors prefer to read '"oyez"-ers' or 'O-yeas', referring to the Old French for 'Hear ye' uttered by a court official or town crier. The *Oxford English Dictionary*, citing no uses of 'oneyer' before 1904, other than Shakespeare's, says that it 'perhaps' means 'sheriff'.

12 (2.1.83–4) *fern-seed,*:   This was said to confer invisibility.

13 (2.1.90) *Go to, 'homo' . . . men.*:   'Not at all: I may not be a true (honest) man, but I am truly (by definition) a man.' He echoes a definition in Lily's *Shorte Introduction of Grammar*.

14 (2.2.2) *frets . . . velvet.*:   Velvet treated with glue would 'fret' (be eroded) more quickly; Falstaff 'frets' – he is vexed.

15 (2.3. S.D.) They hide.:   As is the case elsewhere in this edition, various stage-directions in the scene are (like this one) editorial, the original stage-directions being relatively sparse.

16 (2.2.71) *happy . . . dole,*:   'May each man be allotted happiness' (proverbial).

17 (2.3.54–5) *palisadoes, . . . culverin,*:   'Palisadoes': defensive barriers of pointed stakes; 'frontiers': outworks, ramparts; 'basilisks': very large cannon; 'culverin': long cannon.

18 (2.3.73) *Esperance!*:   '*Esperance ma comforte*' (Fr.): 'Hope sustains me': the Percy family motto.

19 (2.4.22) *sugar,*:   used to sweeten wine.

20 (2.4.66–8) *not-pated, . . . pouch?*:   'close-cropped, wearing a signet ring with a carved agate, in dark stockings with garters made from caddis ribbon; he talks ingratiatingly, and carries a pouch made of Spanish leather'.

21 (2.4.70–72) *Why . . . much.*:   Hal, who sounds rather inebriated, intends to confuse Francis, and may well confuse *us* here. Perhaps he means: 'Brown bastard, a sweet wine sometimes further sweetened, should suit you if you stay here. If you desert your master, you will be sullied. Sugar may be worth something here; in North Africa, where it comes from, it is worth far less.' Implication: 'Keep your job.' See also: Sutherland and Watts: *Henry V, War Criminal? and Other Shakespeare Puzzles.*

22 (2.4.105) *'Rivo!' . . . drunkard.*:   The Latin verb 'rivo' can mean 'I draw off the liquid': loosely, 'I drink!'.

23 (2.4.117–18) *cup . . . lime in it.*:   Lime was sometimes added to wine to improve its appearance.

24 (2.4.124–5) *weaver . . . anything.*:   Weavers were noted for singing at work; some were Puritans.

25 (2.4.254) *the lion . . . prince*:   This was a traditional claim, propagated by (for example) the *Mirror for Magistrates.*

26 (2.4.259–60) *Watch . . . tomorrow!*:   Matthew 26:41 says 'Watch, and pray, that ye enter not into temptation.' Falstaff puns on 'watch', meaning not only 'keep vigil' but also 'carouse', and on 'pray', being a homophone of 'prey'.

27 (2.4.267–70) *nobleman . . . royal man,*:   A noble (coin) was worth six shillings and eightpence (one third of one pound) and a royal was worth ten shillings (half of one pound).

28 (2.4.304-5) *Choler . . . halter.*:   Bardolph means: 'A choleric (irascible) temperament, if rightly interpreted'. Hal puns on 'choler' and 'collar (halter, noose)', on 'rightly' (meaning 'correctly' and 'justly'), and on 'taken' (meaning 'interpreted' and 'arrested'). So Hal means: 'No, if you are justly arrested, you will eventually be hanged.'

29 (2.4.315-18) *gave . . . hook*:   'Amamon' is the name of a devil. The 'bastinado' is a beating on the soles of the feet. 'Made Lucifer cuckold' means 'gave Satan his horns' (as a cuckold traditionally wears horns). The bill-hook (cutting tool) has no cross.

30 (2.4.339-41) *if . . . hundreds.*:   'If June is hot, and the civil warfare continues, hundreds of virgins will sell themselves to us; it will be as easy for us as buying hob-nails.'

31 (2.4.362-3) *in King . . . vein.*:   i.e. in bombastic style, resembling that of Thomas Preston's *Lamentable Tragedie . . . of Cambises, King of Percia* (1569). Falstaff does not imitate the fourteeners (verse lines of fourteen syllables) which predominate in that play's speeches.

32 (2.4.369) *tristful Queen,*:   'sad Queen'. Here, 'tristful' is an emendation of 'trustful', found in the Quartos and F1.

33 (2.4.388-9) *pitch . . . defile,*:   Ecclesiasticus 13:1: 'He that toucheth pitch shall be defiled with it . . . ' In this speech, Falstaff parodies devices found in the works of John Lyly: notably, affected learning, rhetorical questions, verbal antitheses, parallelisms and alliteration.

34 (2.4.427-8) *Vice . . . Iniquity . . . Ruffian . . . Vanity . . .*:   These are all figures in Morality plays. 'Ruffian': (a) the devil; (b) a hooligan.

35 (2.4.447) *Pharaoh's . . . kine*:   Genesis 41:19-21: Pharaoh dreams of leans cows which portend years of famine.

36 (2.4.461) *the devil . . . fiddle-stick.*:   'a lot of fuss about nothing'.

37 (2.4.466-7) *thou . . . so.*:   This could mean: 'You yourself are essentially a true piece of gold, even if you appear false (a counterfeit).' Sonnet 79 originally spelt 'mad' as 'made', and some editors read 'mad' for 'made' here, so that a possible meaning, then, is: 'Without seeming so, you are essentially crazy – if you prefer political rectitude to our friendship.'

38 (2.4.476–7: S.D.) He hides . . . Exit Peto.:   The early texts do not make clear the movements of characters in this sequence, so these directions are editorial conjectures. Some editors prefer to send the hostess to admit the sheriff.

39 (3.1.48) *speaks . . . Welsh.*:   'To speak Welsh' could mean (a) to talk nonsense; (b) to boast.

40 (3.1.48, 58) *there is* [and] *I've*:   I emend the phrasing at these two points, to regularise the metre.

41 (3.1.181) *noble man*:   Some editors prefer F1's dactylic 'nobleman', but, here and elsewhere, Q1's 'noble man' improves the iambic metre.

42 (3.1.191) *my aunt Percy.*:   The Edmund Mortimer who was Glendower's son-in-law was Lady Percy's brother, not nephew. The Edmund Mortimer who was heir to the throne was her nephew, but not Glendower's son-in-law. Holinshed and Shakespeare muddled the two Mortimers together.

43 (3.1.254) *turn . . . teacher.*:   Tailors, like weavers, were noted for singing, as were (and are) robins.

44 (3.2.32) *Thy . . . lost,*:   because (according to various sources), Hal had struck the ear of the Lord Chief Justice.

45 (3.2.98–9) *He . . . succession.*:   'He, by his merit, has a better claim to the throne than you have by an insubstantial right of inheritance.'

46 (3.3.25–6) *the Knight . . . Lamp.*:   Amadis of Greece, 'the Knight of the Burning Sword', was the chivalric hero of *Amadis de Grecia* (1530) by Feliciano da Silva, a work admired by Don Quixote.

47 (3.3.30–32) *Dives . . . burning.*:   Luke 16:19–31 tells how a rich man went to fiery hell, while Lazarus, a beggar, went to 'Abraham's bosom' (heaven). 'Dives' is Latin for 'rich man'.

48 (3.3.109–10) *Maid . . . thee.*:   'Compared to you, Maid Marian is as respectable as the wife of a district magistrate's deputy.' Maid Marian was Robin Hood's legendary companion, but her name was also borne by a disreputable figure in games and dances.

49 (3.3.197) *I . . . drum!*:   (a) 'I wish I could take this tavern into battle with me!'; (b) 'I wish I could exchange martial drumbeats for the sounds of this tavern!'

50 (4.1.31) *sickness* -:   In the early texts, 'sickness' is followed by
a comma. The line, which apparently lacks a tenth syllable,
seems metrically and semantically incomplete ('stays him.'
could fill the gap). Perhaps Hotspur's hasty reading outstrips his
grammar. Nevertheless, line 31 could make sufficient sense, if
interpreted as 'His very writing, in this letter, transmits that
contagious moral disease -'; and the metre is partly mended
if 'here' be pronounced disyllabically ('*he*-er'). (In line 116,
'mailed' may be disyllabic: '*may*-ild'.)

51 (4.2.34-5) *prodigals . . . husks.*:   Luke 15:11-32 gives the
parable of the Prodigal Son, who was willing to eat the husks
that were swine-fodder. 'Draff' means 'pig-swill'.

52 (4.2.46-7) *they'll . . . hedge.*:   Laundered linen was sometimes
laid on hedges to dry.

53 (4.2.48) *blown . . . quilt?*:   'Blown' could mean (a) 'swollen',
and (b) 'short-winded'. 'Jack' was both the familiar form of
'John' and the name of a soldier's quilted jacket.

54 (4.2.72-3) *unless . . . bare.*:   A 'finger' was a measure of three-
fourths of an inch; so Falstaff, Hal alleges, has more than two
inches of fat over his ribs.

55 (4.4.1) *Hie . . . brief*:   Some editors attempt to regularise the
metre by adding a grave accent to 'sealed', thus: 'sealèd'; but this
line of pentameter is already regular if 'sealed' be pronounced
disyllabically: '*see*-uld'.

56 (5.3.11) *I . . . Scot,*:   Q1 has 'I was not borne a yeelder thou
proud Scot,'. F1 has 'I was not borne to yeeld, thou haughty
Scot,'. Take your pick.

57 (5.3.22) *A fool . . . goes!*:   'Wherever your soul goes, Blunt,
may a fool (yourself) accompany it!'.

58 (5.3.30-31) *Though . . . pate.*:   Falstaff's 'shot-free' means (a)
without paying the bill, and (b) unwounded; and his 'scoring'
means (a) adding to the bill, and (b) cutting.

59 (5.3.45) *Turk Gregory*:   Turks were reputedly fierce. Pope
Gregory XIII was said to have encouraged the St. Bartholomew's Day Massacre; and, in prints sold in London in 1579, he
was depicted with Nero and the Grand Turk as one of the
'Three Tyrants of the World'.

60 (5.4.24) *Hydra's heads.*:   The Hydra was a many-headed monster slain by Hercules. Where one of its heads was cut off, two new ones grew.

61 (5.4.136-7) *double man . . . Jack.*:   Falstaff, though bearing Hotspur, says that he is not two men in one, but, if he were not Jack Falstaff, he would resemble the Jack or Knave in a pack of cards, which is depicted as a double man, one head and torso being above, another (reversed) below.

HENRY IV, PART TWO

1 (Induction, 17) *of . . . stop*:   'so easily and simply fingered' (like a recorder).

2 (Induction, 29) *Harry Monmouth*:   Hal was born at Monmouth, in Wales.

3 (1.1.166-79) *You . . . be?*:   This passage is absent from Q but present in F1, as is a later passage in this scene, lines 189-209.

4 (1.2.33-4) *damned . . . glutton . . . Achitophel!*:   Luke 16:19-31 tells of the rich glutton (Dives) who was sent to hell, and begged Lazarus to cool his tongue. 2 Samuel 15 tells how Achitophel betrayed King David.

5 (1.2.44-7) *he hath . . . him.*:   The tailor has the horn of plenty, the cornucopia, being prosperous. He has a lanthorn, a lamp with sides made of transparent horn. His wife may be bright, resembling the light shining through the horn; but she is 'light' in the sense that she is promiscuous (in which case, he wears the cuckold's horn).

6 (1.2.52-3) *the nobleman . . . Bardolph.*:   The anonymous play *The Famous Victories of Henry V* dramatised this incident (although *1 Henry IV* did not): Hal boxes the ear of the Lord Chief Justice and is sent to prison. In that play, Hal is a thorough rogue, is impatient to take the throne, and promises that when he is King, his friend Ned will become Lord Chief Justice. Hal then undergoes a late conversion to virtue, shortly before becoming King. Afterwards, the Lord Chief Justice fears retribution, but is commended by Henry V, who makes him Lord Protector for the period when Henry is at war in France.

7 (1.2.111) *Galen;:*   Galen, an ancient Greek physician and an authority on physiology.

8 (1.2.120) *I am . . . patient.:*   The Book of Job tells how Job patiently endured many adversities, including poverty.

9 (1.2.162-3) *you . . . galls;:*   The liver was deemed the source of youthful passions; bile or gall was deemed to produce the melancholy and anger of old age.

10 (1.3.21-4) *Till . . . admitted.:*   These lines, absent from Q, appear in F1.

11 (1.3.36-62) *Yes, . . . tyranny.:*   These lines, absent from Q, appear in F1. Here, Lord Bardolph give a version of the parable of the builder: Luke 14:28-30.

12 (1.3.85-108) *Let . . . worst.:*   These lines, absent from Q, appear in F1.

13 (2.1.11-15) *he stabbed . . . child.:*   The hostess is fertile in malapropisms, as when, later, she says 'infinitive' instead of 'infinite'; and, unwittingly, she often utters bawdry. Here 'stab' could mean 'sexually penetrate', 'weapon' could be sword, dagger, or penis, and 'foin' ('thrust') is also ambiguous.

14 (2.1.23-32) *A comes . . . thought on.:*   She complains that Falstaff owes her money for numerous debts. Bawdy innuendoes abound. 'A saddle' could mean 'female genitalia' or 'whore'; 'my exion is entered' means 'my lawsuit has commenced', but hints at sexual entry; 'case' could mean 'vagina' as well as 'lawsuit'; and 'I have borne' (by which she means 'I have endured or suffered') could mean 'I have borne the weight of a man'.

15 (2.2.16-26):   *Or to . . . strengthened.:*   Hal suggests that Poins's lack of shirts prevents Poins from playing tennis. The money that he might have spent on fine shirt-linen ('holland') has been spent on 'low countries' (meaning not only 'The Netherlands' but also 'female sexual organs' and 'brothels'); what linen he has supplies his children. (Lines 22-6, from 'And God' to 'strengthened.', were present in Q but absent from F1.)

16 (2.2.83-4) *Althaea . . . dream.:*   Hecuba, Queen of Troy, when pregnant with Paris, dreamt that she would give birth to a firebrand which would set the city ablaze. Althaea was told that her son, Meleager, would live only until a brand in the fire was

consumed, so she snatched it from the hearth. The Page confuses the two Greek legends.

17 (2.2.141) *Ephesians . . . church.*: 'long-term carousers.' St Paul's Epistle to the Ephesians (5:18) warned them against drunkenness.

18 (2.2.163-4) *It . . . case.*: Jove (Jupiter) transformed himself into a bull to carry Europa away.

19 (2.3.23-45) *He had . . . grave.*: These lines are absent from Q but present in F1.

20 (2.4.43-50) *we catch . . . bravely.*: Falstaff says that men catch venereal diseases from Doll's 'sect' (prostitutes). Doll says that men catch (steal) the women's chains and jewels. Falstaff refers to 'brooches, pearls and ouches', meaning the pimples, carbuncles and sores which are symptoms of the diseases. Just as to fight bravely entails a limping return, to fornicate vigorously entails suffering. A soldier returns from a contested gap (the breach) with his pike handsomely bent, and a man returns from a prostitute with his penis clearly damaged: both men proceed courageously to the surgeon. A 'charged chamber' may be (a) a loaded gun, (b) aroused female genitalia, and (c) a diseased vagina.

21 (2.4.53-60) *You . . . hogshead?*: The hostess offers two malapropisms: 'rheumatic' should be 'choleric' (hot and dry), and 'confirmities' should be 'infirmities'. 'What the goodyear!' means 'What the devil!'. The woman must 'bear', meaning (a) suffer, (b) bear children, and (c) bear the weight of a man. 1 Peter 3:7 (Geneva Bible) says that 'woman [is] the weaker vessel'. The hostess recalls the proverb which *Henry V* will render as 'The empty vessel makes the greatest sound'. Doll complains that it is hard for a 'weak empty vessel' to bear the weight of (and receive sexually) such a vast heavy cask as Falstaff is.

22 (2.4.103-6) *Here, . . . bullets.*: Sexual innuendoes abound here and in subsequent lines. 'Sack' is wine; 'charge you' means (a) drink a toast to you; (b) load you with ammunition (punning on the name 'Pistol'); and (c) arouse you sexually; and 'discharge' means (a) return the toast; (b) empty the cup; (c) shoot; and (c) ejaculate sexually. The 'two bullets' imply 'both testicles'. Doll swiftly understands the innuendoes, though the hostess is slow

to do so. Doll is 'pistol-proof' (line 107), as (a) she will not succumb to Pistol, and (b) she is past child-bearing ('pistol' implying 'pizzle', penis).

23 (2.4.115-23) *Away, . . . Pistol.*: 'Bung' means (a) thief of purses and (b) penis; 'chops': cheeks; 'and you': if you. 'Play the saucy cuttle' may mean 'try your impudent thieving tricks', as a 'cuttle' was a knife used by cutpurses. 'Bottle-ale' may mean 'frothy, effusive'. A 'basket-hilt stale juggler' could be a worn-out, cheating amateur; basket-work hilts (to protect the hand) were often found on swords for practice. 'Since when . . . ?' probably means 'Since when have you been a real soldier . . . ?'. The 'points' would be laces to secure armour. 'Discharge yourself of' means 'Depart from'. (Lines 122-3 are in Q but not in F1.)

24 (2.4.131-5) *he lives . . . to't.*: 'Mouldy stewed prunes and dried cakes' would be rotten brothel-fare and bakers' stale fare. Stewed prunes were served in brothels as a supposed pre-caution against venereal disease. 'Occupy' ('move into') could mean 'copulate with'; F1 omits this allusion.

25 (2.4.141-53) *To Pluto's . . . toys?*: Pistol delights in uttering quotations from, or allusions to, stage-dramas. Some of his classical learning derives from John Eliot's *Ortho-epia Gallica* (1593). Pluto is a ruler of Hades, the underworld. Erebus is the son of Chaos and Night, and his name often serves as that of the underworld. 'Faitours' (cheats) became 'Fates' in F1. 'Hiren' combines 'iron' (his sword) with 'Hyrin' (Irene), the name of a dramatic heroine, which could also mean 'whore'. The hostess's 'aggravate' is a malapropism for 'moderate'. Lines 148-9 parody two lines from Christopher Marlowe's *Tamburlaine*, Part Two. 'Cannibals' is unlikely to be a malapropism for 'Hannibals', since John Eliot refers to 'Tartarians, Cannibals, Indians, and Muscovites' as formidable foes. Cerberus was a three-headed dog which guarded the underworld. 'The welkin': the heavens. 'Fall foul for toys': quarrel over trifles.

26 (2.4.161-6) *Then . . . nothings?*: Line 161 parodies part of Peele's *Battle of Alcazar*, in which Muly Mahomet offers meat (on his sword) to his starving mother. The tag beginning '*Si fortune*' means 'If fortune torments me, hope contents me'. Line 166 means 'Have we come to a stop? Is there no further

satisfaction in the remainder?'. (Both 'etceteras' and 'nothings' can mean 'female genitalia'.)

27 (2.4.200-202) *Thou . . . Worthies.*:   Hector was the bravest of the Trojan warriors; Agamemnon was the eminent Greek leader; and the 'Nine Worthies' varied in membership, but a popular list was: Hector, Alexander and Julius Cæsar; Joshua, David and Judas Maccabeus; and Arthur, Charlemagne and Godfrey of Bouillon.

28 (2.4.245-7) *And look . . . counsel-keeper.*:   The zodiac's signs were divided into four groups of three (trigons). Aries, Leo and Sagittarius (constituting one of the trigons) were regarded as fiery signs, and thus are apt for red-faced Bardolph. Allegedly, Bardolph is wooing the hostess, Falstaff's confidante and keeper of secrets.

29 (2.4.319-26) *Marry, . . . against.*:   Falstaff alleges that the hostess has broken the law by selling meat during Lent; and 'suffering flesh to be eaten' hints at 'allowing women to be enjoyed'. 'His Grace says that which his flesh rebels against' means 'Although the Prince has referred to Doll as a lady (a "gentlewoman"), his manhood knows her to be no lady but a whore whom he now finds repugnant'.

30 (3.1.52-5) *O, if . . . die.*:   These lines, present in Q (second issue, QB), are absent from F1.

31 (3.1.64-78) *But which . . . amity.*:   The King here recalls the speech represented in *Richard II*, 5.1.55-9 (Wordsworth edn.), though neither Bullingbrooke nor Warwick was present then.

32 (3.1.101-2) *I have . . . dead.*:   'Instance' means 'proof'. In fact, Glendower outlived Henry IV by two or three years. Henry died in 1413, Glendower in 1415-16.

33 (3.2.35-7) *Death . . . fair?*:   Shallow probably recalls Psalm 89:48: 'What man liveth, and shall not see death? Shall he deliver his soul from the hand of the grave? Selah.' 'How a good yoke . . . ?' means 'What is the price of a good pair . . . ?'.

34 (3.2.44-6) *A would . . . half,*:   'He would hit the target from 240 yards, and could shoot an arrow straight (instead of in a curving trajectory) for a distance of 280 or 290 yards,'.

35 (3.2.110-12) *I was . . . drudgery.*:   'To "prick me" (mark my name) was unnecessary, because I was amply pricked (vexed, and provided with a penis) already. My wife will be downcast

now, because she will have nobody to perform the sexual duties of a husband or to undertake the hard farm-work.'

36 (3.2.127-30) *Thy mother's . . . substance!*:   'Yes, it is very likely that you are your mother's son, and named "Shadow" after your father. So the son does have a resemblance to the father; but often, the resemblance is only "shadowy" (nominal), like that, and not substantial.' (In other words, the father is often cuckolded by his wife, and therefore is not the biological father of the son.)

37 (3.2.132-3) *Prick . . . muster-book.*:   'Mark Shadow's name for recruitment, because the book of recruits contains numerous "shadows".' (Such 'shadows' were fictitious names, so that pay could be falsely claimed.)

38 (3.2.141-2) *It were . . . pins.*:   'There is no need to prick (or pin) him, because his ragged clothing is joined together on his back, and the whole structure depends on "pins" (pegs) – and stands on his "pins" (legs).'

39 (3.2.160-61) *I cannot . . . thousands.*:   'I cannot make him a private in the army (or offer him sexually to a private), when he is the leader of so many thousands (of warts, or of lice).'

40 (3.2.177-9) *We will . . . thee.*:   'We will get rid of your cold (by letting you die on a battlefield), and I will arrange matters so that your friends will ring the bells instead of you (and *for* you – at your funeral).'

41 (3.2.246-8) *A shall . . . bucket.*:   'He will load and fire for you as quickly as a pewterer hammers the pewter into shape; he will retreat and advance (or raise and lower his gun) more swiftly than a man hangs a bucket on the wooden yoke (gibbet) borne by the brewer.'

42 (3.2.256) *Hold, . . . Thas!*:   Either (a): 'Hold the gun, Wart; march to and fro, thus, thus, thus!'; or (b): 'Hold the gun, Wart; aim it thus, thus, thus!'.

43 (3.2.263) *Sir . . . show*:   Sir Dagonet was King Arthur's fool, and 'Arthur's show' was an archery pageant (at Mile-End Green) celebrating King Arthur and the knights of his Round Table.

44 (3.2.287-8) *duer . . . tribute.*:   'rendered more predictably to the hearer than taxes are paid to the Turkish Sultan.'

45 (3.2.294-9) *yet lecherous . . . good-nights.*:   This passage appears in Q but not in F1.

46 (3.2.309) *I'll make . . . me.*: 'I'll make him as valuable to me as possession of the philosopher's two stones would be.' One 'philosopher's stone' was a method or talisman for transmuting base metals into gold; another was the *elixir vitæ*, a medicine for perpetuating youth and health.

47 (4.1.55-79) *And with . . . wrong.*: These lines, in which an Archbishop advocates rebellion against his monarch, are absent from Q but present in F1.

48 (4.1.93-6) *And . . . particular.*: Lines 93 and 95 appear in QA, the uncorrected text of the 1600 quarto, but not in the corrected version (QB) or in F1. Lines 94-6 may mean: 'The grievances of my brothers at large, the populace, together with the cruelty particularly experienced by my blood-brother, have made me forward this dispute personally.' (Shakespeare assumes that the Archbishop's brother, Sir Stephen Scroope, was executed by Bullingbrooke; but it was the Archbishop's cousin, Sir William Scroope, who was executed by him.)

49 (4.1.103-39) *O, my good . . . King.*: These lines are absent from Q but present in F1.

50 (4.1.173-7) *Acquitted . . . peace.*: 'granted a reliably effective formal pardon and the prompt fulfilment of our demands concerning ourselves and our causes, we withdraw respectfully within our boundaries, and devote our strength to the cause of peace.'

51 (4.2.38-40) *Hydra . . . desires,*: The Hydra was a many-headed monster (slain by Hercules): if one head was cut off, two heads grew in its place. Juno's hundred-eyed watchman, Argus, was charmed to sleep by Mercury's music. (The Archbishop blends both allusions.)

52 (4.3.40-42) *I may . . . overcame.'*: Plutarch says that after defeating King Pharnaces of Pontus, Julius Cæsar wrote '*veni, vidi, vici*': 'I came, I saw, I overcame'.

53 (4.3.49-53) *if you . . . noble.*: The silver twopence coin was the same size as the gold half-crown, and therefore it was sometimes gilded so as to be fraudulently passed as the much more valuable coin. Falstaff says that John and his associates will look like mere frauds compared with himself: he, among the famous, will resemble the bright moon, while John and the others will resemble the little stars.

54 (4.4.79–80) *'Tis . . . carrion.*: 'That is unlikely, for the bee seldom abandons the honeycomb in the rotting carcass.' (Judges14:8 says that Samson saw honey made by a swarm of bees in the carcass of a lion.)

55 (4.5.77–9) *like . . . father.*: The drones, not the workers, are lethally evicted from the hive by other bees when swarming ends. The sentence from 'This bitter taste' to 'father' means 'His amassed treasure is therefore bitter to the dying father.' (The King thus comments ironically on the proverb 'The bee sucks honey out of the bitterest flowers'.)

56 (4.5.92–137) *Thy wish . . . inhabitants!*: The King's reproaches apply more aptly to the Hal of *The Famous Victories of Henry V* than to Shakespeare's Hal.

57 (4.5.161–2) *Other . . . potable;*: He refers to *aurum potabile*, a liquid medicine containing gold, believed to conserve youth and health.

58 (5.1.28–31) *they are . . . Davy.*: Shallow says that the men will 'backbite' (complain slanderously); but Davy observes that, as the men wear dirty linen, their backs are bitten by lice or fleas. 'Well conceited': 'very witty'.

59 (5.1.71–2) *four . . . intervallums.*: 'the four terms of the legal year, or the duration of two lawsuits, and he will laugh without intervals.'

60 (5.2.6–13) *I would . . . fantasy.*: Recalling the incident (dramatised in *The Famous Victories of Henry V*) when Hal had boxed his ears and been jailed, the Lord Chief Justice fears retribution now that Hal is King.

61 (5.2.48) *Not Amurath . . . succeeds,*: On becoming the Turkish Sultan in 1574, Murad III had his brothers killed; his successor did the same in 1596.

62 (5.2.140–41) *we will . . . state;*: 'we will summon, as I mentioned previously, all our noblemen;'.

63 (5.3.94–101) *A foutre . . . lap.*: 'A *foutre* for' (citing the French noun and verb) means 'Fuck'. Africa was deemed to hold great wealth. Assyria was associated with pillaging. Cophetua was a legendary African king who married a beggar. Justice Silence is prompted to sing part of a ballad about Robin Hood (who robbed the rich). Line 99 means 'Shall dirty dogs oppose true poets (such as Pistol)?' Mount Helicon was a haunt of the

Muses, the nine goddesses of the arts. The Furies were the goddesses of revenge.

64 (5.3.113-14) *fig . . . Spaniard.*:   The *fico* (Italian for 'fig'; the Spanish is *higo*) was an obscene gesture in which the thumb was thrust between the two adjacent fingers to represent a penis between legs.

65 (5.4.7) *Nut-hook, . . . lie!*:   A beadle is an arresting officer, and this one is thin. He is therefore likened to a nut-hook, a hook-ended pole for pulling nuts from trees.

66 (5.4.8-15) *and . . . now.*:   The hostess and Doll suggest that if Doll miscarries, the beadle may be charged with murder; but the beadle says that Doll has merely used a cushion so as to appear pregnant.

67 (5.4.18-28) *you thin . . . thou!*:   The phrase 'thin man in a censer' refers to figures depicted on incense-burning pots; 'bluebottle' is prompted by the beadle's blue uniform; he is a 'correctioner' because he comes from the 'House of Correction', Bridewell Prison; 'swinged': beaten; 'half-kirtles': skirts; a 'she-knight-errant' is a female roaming knight, but also (punning on 'night-errant') a female nocturnal sinner; 'right should thus overcome might' garbles the proverb 'Might overcomes right'; and 'atomy' means 'anatomy' – skeleton.

68 (5.5.26) *semper . . . est;*:   Pistol's Latin phrases mean 'Always the same' and 'Apart from this, there is nothing'.

69 (5.5.31-6) *Helen . . . truth.*:   Helen of Troy was beautiful (but unfaithful); 'durance': confinement; 'contagious': disease-ridden; 'haled': hauled; 'ebon den': black dwelling': hell; 'fell Alecto' (cruel Alecto) was one of the Furies (who had serpents twined in their hair); and 'Doll is in' means 'Doll has been jailed'.

70 (5.5.84-6) *but a colour . . . colours.*:   Falstaff says that the King was offering 'a colour', a concealment of his real intent; but Shallow responds that Falstaff may die of such a 'colour', punning on 'collar', the hangman's noose. Falstaff's 'Fear no colours' is proverbial, meaning 'Fear no enemy'.

71 (5.5.94) *'Si . . . contenta.'*:   He cites again 'If fortune torments me, hope contents me'.

72 (Epilogue) *EPILOGUE.*:   This Epilogue, as printed in Q and F1, combines two different epilogues. The original one,

represented by the first paragraph (lines 1–14), was evidently intended to be spoken by Shakespeare, who expresses his hopes that this play has made amends for a previous one which was 'displeasing'. (In F1, his cheeky final words, from 'and so I kneel' to 'the Queen.', are moved to the end of the double epilogue, and the 'I' is omitted from 'I kneel'.) The second epilogue, represented by the second and third paragraphs (lines 15–28), was evidently meant to be uttered by Will Kemp (or Kempe), the comic actor with Shakespeare's company, who was also a celebrated dancer. (He left the company in 1599, and in 1600 danced from London to Norwich.)

73 (Epilogue, 22–7) *If you . . . man.*:   *Henry V* will indeed portray Katherine of France in a 'merry' light. Falstaff will indeed die, though off-stage, and his death will not appear to be caused by 'a sweat' (the 'sweating sickness' resulting from the plague or venereal disease). 'Oldcastle died a martyr, and this is not the man' is a form of apology to Oldcastle's descendants, as the Falstaff character had originally been named 'Sir John Oldcastle'.

GLOSSARY

Where a pun, a metaphor or an ambiguity occurs, the meanings are distinguished as (a) and (b), or (a), (b) and (c), etc. Otherwise, alternative meanings are distinguished as (i) and (ii), or as (i), (ii) and (iii), etc. Abbreviations include the following: adj., adjective; adv., adverb; e.g., for example; etc., and so on; fig., figuratively; It., Italian; mal., malapropism; n., noun; perh., perhaps; vb., verb.

Line references to *Henry IV, Part 2* are preceded by T (for 'Two').

a: (sometimes) he (e.g. at T: 1.2.41); (sometimes) on (e.g. at 2.4.63); **a God's name**: in God's name; **John a Gaunt**: John of Gaunt.

accents: 1.1.3: accounts.

accite: induce.

aconitum: aconite: poison.

acquitted: T: 4.1.173: pardoned.

action: T: 2.1.1: lawsuit.

admiral: flagship.

advertisement: (i: 3.2.172:) news; (ii: 4.1.36:) advice.

affect: desire.

agate: jewel often carved to display an image.

ague: fever.

alarum: battle-noises.

amaze: (a) bewilder; (b) alarm.

anatomize: dissect.

ancient: (n.; i: 4.2.23:) standard-bearer; (ii: 4.2.31:) flag; **Ancient** (T: 2.4.65:) Ensign, standard-bearer.

and (sometimes): if (e.g. at 1.2.89).

angel: coin worth about half one pound; **ill angel**: (T: 1.2.151–3: a) evil spirit; (b) bad coin.

anon: at once; I'm coming.

Antic: Clown.

apes of idleness: layabouts.

apoplexy: paralysis.

apple-john: long-keeping apple, eaten when shrivelled.

approve: (i: 4.1.9:) prove, test; (ii: T: 1.2.147, 177:) confirm.

argument: topic.

arras: 2.4.473: curtain across recess.

assemblance: (T: 3.2.244: a:) structure; (b) appearance.

attempt (n.): 3.2.13: exploit.

attend: await.

avoirdupois: weight.

back-sword man: fencer who practises by using a stick with a basket-work guard.

balked: 1.1.69: heaped.

bare: 3.2.13: wretched.

Bartholomew boar-pig: young boar fit to be roasted at Bartholomew Fair.

bastard: 2.4.26: wine mixed with honey.

bate: (i: 3.3.2:) shrink; (ii: 4.1.99: a) ruffle; (b) beat wings; (iii: 4.3.26:) weary; (iv: T: 2.4.229:) discord.

battle: 4.1.129; T: 3.2.152: army.

bavin: kindling (soon gone).

beard (vb.): defy.

bear in hand: lead on.

beaver: visor.

become: 2.4.470: adorn.

beetle: T: 1.2.214: sledge-hammer.

beldam: grandmother.

besonian: ignoramus.

betimes: early.

bide the touch: be put to the test.

biggen: coarse nightcap.

birlady, by'r Lady: by our Lady (the Virgin Mary).

blue-caps: Scots in blue head-gear.

bolter: sieve.

bolting-hutch: sifting-bin.

bombard: big leather wine-container.

bombast: 2.4.307: (a) padding; (b) arrogant oratory.

bona-roba: courtesan; showy whore.

boot: to boot: as well;

bootless: (i: 1.1.29:) pointless; (ii: 3.1.64-5: a) with no gain; (b) without boots.

bots: worms.

bottom: (i: 3.1.102:) valley; (ii: 4.1.50:) basis.

'Bounce!': 'Bang!'.

brach: bitch.

brave: (i: 1.2.60: a) admirable; (b) well-dressed; (ii: 5.2.42:) proud.

brawn: fattened boar.

breathe: rest; pause to recover.

bringing up: 2.4.471: (a) upbringing; (b) being arrested.

Bristow: Bristol.

brook (vb.): bear, tolerate.

bruited: reported.

buckler: shield.

buckram: coarse fabric stiffened with size.

buss: kiss.

by-drinkings: drinks between meals.

cabileros: roistering lads.

caddis: coloured tape for garters.

Cain: first person to be born on earth; slayer of his brother.

caliver: light musket.

cankered: corrupted.

canstick: candlestick.

cantle: segment.

canvass (vb.): trap.

capitulate: 3.2.120: (a) head together; (b) enter an agreement.

capon: castrated cockerel.

caraways: T: 5.3.3: (i) caraway seeds; (ii) kind of apple.

carbonado: grilled slashed meat.

carded his state: 3.2.62: (a) adulterated his dignity; (b) reduced his majesty to that of a playing-card king.

carman: carter.

case: (i: T: 2.1.27: a:) law-suit; (b) vagina; (ii: T: 2.2.164:) situation.

case ye: disguise yourselves.

cast: T: 5.1.17: added up; **cast th'event**: assessed the outcome.

catastrophe (fig.): rear end.

catechism: question-and-answer sequence.

cess: **out of all cess**: excessively.

chamber-lye: bedroom urine.

channel: gutter.

charge: (n.: i: 2.1.43:) cargo; (ii: 3.2.161:) a command; **charge of foot**: infantry company.

Charles's Wain: the Ursa Major constellation.

chewet: 5.1.29: (a) jackdaw: chatterer; (b) minced-meat pie.

choler: anger.

chops: (fat) cheeks.

chuff : 2.2.82: (a) spoilt rich man; (b) bumpkin; (c) miser.

cital: account.

cloak-bag: portmanteau.

close: (n.: 1.1.13:) clash; (adv.: 2.2.3, 2.4.513:) concealed, secret.

cloud of dignity: aura of greatness.

coat: 4.1.100: (a) coat of chain-mail; (b) coat of arms.

cock: **by cock and pie**: by God and the rule-book.

Cofill: Coldfield.

coif: night-cap.

Colossus: statue of Helios, said to bestride Rhodes' harbour.

colour: (i: 3.2.100:) pretext; (ii: 5.4.26:) royal insignia.

colted: (2.2.36: a) tricked; (b) given a young horse.

comfit-maker: confectioner.

commit: (i: T: 5.2.111:) send to prison; (ii: T: 5.2.112:) submit.

commodity: (i) supply; (ii) profit.

community: 3.2.77: familiarity.

comparative (n.): mocker; (adj.): mocking.

compass: **in good compass**: within bounds.

competence of life: adequate living-allowance.

concealments: secret arts.

conceit: imagination, wit.

confines: **neighbour confines**: bordering regions.

consigning to: endorsing.

continent: 3.1.107: bank.

conversations: T: 5.5.99: conduct.

coped: T: 4.2.95: fought.

Corinthian: rich hedonist.

corrival: worthy associate.

corse: corpse.

Cotsole: Cotswold.

couching (couchant): recumbent.

countenance: (i: 1.2.28: a) face; (b) protection; (ii: 1.2.144–5, 3.2.65; T: 5.1.37:) protection; (iii: 5.1.69:) manner, conduct. 2.4.368: **holds . . . countenance**: keeps . . . straight face.

course: T: 4.4.90: stage.
cousin, coz: kinsman.
cozen (vb.): cheat.
crack (n.): young rascal.
cranking: winding.
cresset: fire-basket.
crest: (i: 5.4.71:) plume or
  ornament on helmet;
  (ii: 5.5.29:) helmet.
crib: hovel.
crisp: rippled.
cross (n.): affliction; **bear
  crosses**: (a) endure afflictions;
  (b) carry coins marked with a
  cross.
crown: 2.3.95: (a) head; (b) coin.
curry with: flatter.
cushes (cuisses): thigh-armour.

daff: toss aside.
dear: (i: 3.1.177:) noble; (ii: T:
  4.5.140: a) dire; (b) heartfelt.
defend: **God defend**: God
  forbid.
denier: tenth of a penny.
determined: ended.
Diana: chaste goddess of the
  moon and hunting.
disdained: disdainful.
distemperature: (i: 3.1.32:) disorder: (ii: 5.1.3:) unhealthy hue.
Dives: rich man who went to
  Hell.
division: 3.1.205: embellishment.
doom: judgement.
doublet: short jacket.
dowlas: coarse linen.
draff: pig-swill.
drawer: waiter.
drawn fox: hunted fox.
drench: dose of medicine.

dropsy: excess bodily fluid.
dull: T: 3.1.15: drowsy.
durance: 1.2.41: (a) durability;
  (b) imprisonment.

Ebrew Jew: Hebrew Jew: Jew
  indeed.
ecce signum (Latin): Behold the
  proof.
ell: 45 inches.
embossed: 3.3.150: (a) swollen;
  (b) slavering.
embowelled: 5.4.108-10:
  (i:) disembowelled (for
  embalming); (ii:) gutted, for
  dogs to eat the guts.
enfeoffed: surrendered.
engaged: held as hostage.
Esperance (French): Hope.
estridge: ostrich.
exeunt (Latin): they go out.
exit (Latin): he or she goes out.

face-royal: T: 1.2.21-4: (a)
  royal face; (b) first-rate face;
  (c) coin worth ten shillings.
factor: agent.
fall off: 1.3.93: change sides.
fancy: T: 3.2.298:
  improvisation.
fattest soil: richest earth.
favours: (i: 3.2.136:) features;
  (ii: 5.4.95:) ornaments.
fazed: tattered.
fie: shame.
fillip: strike.
finger: **three fingers**: 2.25 inches.
finis (Latin): the end.
flap-dragons: burning food-
  items floating on liquor.
fledge: covered with down.

Fleet: the Fleet: a jail in London.

flocks: wool for padding.

floods: state of floods: flowing grandeur.

foil (n.): contrasting setting.

foin: thrust.

fond: foolish.

force: of force: necessarily.

foutre (French): T: 5.3.94: fuck.

frame: T: 4.1.180: bring to pass.

frank (n.): pig-sty.

franklin: free-born land-owner.

fretful: 3.3.11: (a) anxious; (b) fretted, worn.

fronting: impending, confronting.

fub: thwart.

furniture: equipment.

fustian (adj.): ranting.

fustilarian: (perh.) slut.

gage: pledge.

gall: rub to soreness; vex.

gelding: cutting.

gentle: 5.2.54: noble.

gib cat: tom-cat.

gird: mock.

God's me: God save me.

good-night: T: 3.2.298-9: serenade.

goodyear: devil.

gorbellied: pot-bellied.

gormandizing: gluttony.

gossip: female friend.

gravy: grease, sweat.

green-sickness: anaemia of adolescent girls.

gripe (vb.): seize.

groat: coin worth fourpence.

gull: 5.1.60: nestling.

gyves: fetters.

habit: clothing.

hackneyed: vulgarised.

hade land: field-edges.

hair: 4.1.61: character.

hallowing: shouting to hounds.

hands: proper fellow of my hands: doughty and valorous person.

haply: perhaps.

harlotry (adj.): vagabond; 2.4.37i: naughty; (n.: 3.1.193): hussy; naughty person.

harness: 3.2.101: (a) armour; (b) soldiers.

haunch: T: 4.4.92: end.

hazard: nice hazard: risky gamble.

head: 1.3.278, 3.2.167, etc.: army; **set off his head**: not counted.

heady: headlong.

heaviness: (i: 3.1.212:) sleepiness; (ii: T: 4.5.8:) grief.

heavy: (i: 2.3.65:) grave; (ii: 5.4.104:) a) sad; (b) weighty.

heels: by the heels: in the stocks.

'Hem, boys!': 'Drink up, lads!'.

Hercules: strong hero of Greek legend.

hest: command.

hilding (adj.): worthless.

hind: peasant.

hogshead: cask.

holiday and lady terms: dainty and effeminate expressions.

holland: fine linen.

hollow (vb.): yell.

Holmedon: Humbleton.

Holy-Rood Day: Holy Cross Day (Sept. 14).

home: pay us home: repay us fully.

homo (Latin): man.

honeyseed, honeysuckle (mal.): homicide, homicidal.

hose: breeches.

housewives: T: 3.2.297: hussies, whores.

humorous: 3.1.226: whimsical, capricious.

humour: (i: 1.2.182:) character; (ii: 2.4.88, 3.1.167:) temperament; (iii: 2.4.423:) bodily fluid; (iv: 3.1.229: a) mood; (b) whim; (v: T:2.1.142:) mood..

hunt: you hunt counter: you are quite wrong.

hurly: tumult.

husbanded: T: 4.3.116: cultivated.

Hydra: monster that grew two heads when one was cut off.

ignis fatuus: marsh-light.

ignomy: ignominy.

images: effigies.

imbrue: shed blood.

imp: offspring.

impressèd: conscripted.

incomprehensible: boundless.

innovation: rebellion.

instance: T: 3.1.102: proof.

intelligence: (i: 4.3.98:) spying; (ii: 5.5.10:) information.

intemperance: wild behaviour.

intestine (adj): internal.

investments: robes.

it: (sometimes) its.

Jack: 5.4.137: (a) knave, rogue; (b) Knave in card-pack.

jade: worn-out horse.

Japhet: Noah's third son; ancestor of all Europeans.

jordan: chamber-pot.

Jove: the supreme god.

jump with: agree with.

justling: turbulent.

juvenal: youth.

ken: T: 4.1.151: field of vision.

Kendal green: green cloth for the clothing of rural folk and Robin Hood's robber-band.

kickshaws: fancy dishes.

kirtle: skirt with bodice.

land-service: military duty.

leaping-house: brothel.

leather-coats: russet apples.

leman: sweetheart.

Lethe: underworld river of oblivion.

lewd: 3.2.13: (a) low; (b) crude.

lief: gladly.

liegeman: follower, ally.

liggens: (perh.) eyelids.

link: taper; small torch.

livery: uniform; **sue . . . livery**: seek . . . inheritance.

loggerhead: blockhead.

Lucifer's privy-kitchen: Satan's private kitchen.

lugged bear: tormented bear.

maid . . . of war: Bellona.

main: 4.1.47: (a) betting stake; (b) army.

major: 2.4.469: (a) main premise; (b) mayor.

make up: 5.4.4: go forward.

malmsey-nose: with red nose from drinking red wine.

malt-worm: drunkard.

mammet: doll.

manage (n.): *manège* (French): horsemanship.

mandrake: plant with divided root, said to resemble a man; deemed aphrodisiac.

manner: **with the manner**: in the act.

Manningtree: Essex market town where a fair was held.

mare: T: 2.1.71–2 (a) nightmare; (b) woman.

mark: **save the mark**: avert evil.

marry (as mild oath, e.g. at 2.4.108): (a) by the Virgin Mary; (b) indeed.

Mars: Roman war-god.

Martlemas: the feast of St Martin (Nov. 11).

meer: sheer, utter.

meet (adj.): appropriate.

Mercury: Roman messenger-god.

Merlin: legendary wizard.

mercy: **cry you mercy**: beg your pardon.

mete: assess.

micher: truant.

mincing: with affected gait.

minion: darling; favourite.

misprision: mistake.

moiety: portion.

moldwarp: mole.

Moorditch: open sewer in London.

mure: wall.

name: 3.2.65: reputation.

neaf: fist.

near: **come near me**: probe me shrewdly.

neat: ox.

nether-stocks: stockings.

nice: T: 1.1.145: (a) foolish; (b) unmanly.

noble: gold coin worth about a third of one pound.

nonce: **for the nonce**: for the occasion.

ob: *obolus* (Latin): halfpenny.

odds: **take the odds**: have the advantage.

one-yer: singular person.

orb: 5.1.17: orbit.

other: T: 4.4.77: others.

overscutched: (T: 3.2.297: i:) well beaten; (ii:) worn out.

owe: T: 1.2.3: own.

paid: 2.4.179, 5.3.46: killed.

pallet: simple low bed.

pantler: pantry-man.

paraquito: parrot.

parcel: part.

parmacity: spermaceti: sperm-whale grease.

part (n.): 5.4.118: (a) portion; (b) rôle.

Partlet: (a) hen; (b, fig.) fussy or nagging woman.

passing (adv.): extremely.

Paul's: St Paul's Cathedral.

pay (vb.): 5.3.46: put paid to: kill.

peach (vb.): impeach.

Pegasus: mythical winged horse.

peppered: mortally wounded.

perfect: proficient.

pickthanks: flatterers.

pippin: apple kept for a long time before eating.

pismire: ant.

pizzle: **bull's-pizzle**: bull's penis.

point: (n: i: 2.1.6:) saddle-bow; (ii: 2.4.201–202: a) sword-point; (b) hose-fastening; (iii: T: 1.1.53, 2.4.119:) lace for tying; (iv: T: 4.1.52:) signal.

politician: schemer.

Pomfret: Pontefract.

Pomgarnet: Pomegranate (room).

popinjay: (a) parrot; (b) dandy.

ports: T: 4.5.23: gates: eyes.

post: (n.: i: 1.1.37:) rapid messenger; (ii: T: 4.3.36:) post-horses; (vb.:) ride swiftly; (adv.:) post-haste.

post-horse: hired horse.

pottle-pot: four-pint tankard.

pouncet: perfume.

powder me: pickle me in salt.

pregnancy: mental agility.

Priam: king of Troy when it was burnt by the Greeks.

prick: (vb.: i: 5.1.129:) spur, urge; (ii: 5.1.130:) mark; **prick him** (T: 3.2.109): tick his name; select him.

prithee: pray thee: ask you.

Prodigal: **the Prodigal**: the Prodigal Son: Luke 15:11–32.

Proface!: Welcome to it!

profited: proficient.

proof: **come to any proof**: turn out well.

prune (vb.): preen.

pudding: 2.4.426: stuffing.

puissance: strength.

quean: whore.

quiddities: word-play.

quit: 3.2.19: acquit myself of.

quiver (adj.): nimble.

rabbit sucker: unweaned rabbit.

rack: torture-machine to stretch victim.

rampallion: ruffian.

rampant: rearing.

rank: gross.

rascal: 3.3.151: (a) rogue; (b) hunted deer.

rash: (i: 3.2.61:) volatile; (ii: T: 4.4.48: a) violent; (b) volatile.

rate (vb.): (i: 4.3.99:) expel angrily; (ii: T: 3.1.67:) berate.

ratsbane: poison.

raze: 2.1.21: root.

reason: 2.4.224: (a) explanation; (b) raisin.

remission: **ragged and fore-stalled remission**: (perh.) tawdry and compromised pardon.

reversion: inheritance ahead.

rigol: circle.

'Rivo!': perh. from It. *riviva*: 'Another toast!'.

road (fig.; T: 2.2.156): whore.

roan: (horse) of mixed colour.

roundly: (i: 1.2.21:) plainly; to the point; (ii: T: 3.2.17:) directly.

rout: **abject routs**: degenerate riotous mobs.

rude: 1.1.41. 3.2.14: uncivilised.

sack (n): white wine.

salamander: lizard said to live in fire.

Samingo: Sir Mingo (Latin *mingo* means 'I urinate').

sarcenet: thin silk.

Saturn and Venus: the planets of old age and love.

scab: rascal.

scape: escape.

score: 5.3.31: (a) record a debt; (b) cut.

scot and lot: in full.

scruple: T: 1.2.125: (a) small weight; (b) fine doubt.

scutcheon: funeral hatchment.

sealed up . . . expectation: confirmed . . . fears.

sense: in common sense: as all can see.

sensible of: aware of.

set off: T: 4.1.145: forgotten.

several: separate.

shadow: T: 3.2.133: fictitious name.

sherris-sack: Spanish sherry.

shot-free: scot-free: without paying.

shotten herring: herring after its roe has discharged.

Shrieve: sheriff.

Shrovetide: season of festivities preceding Lent.

sign of the leg: boot-maker's shop-sign.

Sisters Three: the Fates: Clotho, Lachesis and Atropos.

skimble-skamble: nonsensical.

slops: baggy britches.

smug: smooth.

sneak-up: cowardly rascal.

sneap: reproof.

snuff: in snuff: 1.3.40: (a) as inhalation; (b) angrily.

soft: 1.3.153, 5.4.129: wait.

soil: T: 4.5.189: dirt.

sooth: truth.

soused gurnet: pickled gurnard (fish).

spleen: 2.3.80, 3.2.125, 5.2.19: (a) anger; (b) impatience.

stand to me: T: 2.1.57-8: (a) support me; (b) be erect for me.

staves: armèd staves: lances.

stew: brothel.

still (adv.): constantly.

stock-fish: dried cod.

stout: 5.4.92: valiant.

strands: shores: lands.

strappado: rig to torture by hoisting.

strike sail: submit.

successively: by right of succession.

suffer: permit.

superfluous: excessive.

supplies: T: 1.3.12: reinforcements.

surfeit-swelled: bloated by excess.

surprised: captured.

swagger (vb.): be aggressively boisterous.

swinge-buckler: swashbuckler.

tall: 1.3.61: brave.

tane: (i: 3.2.114:) captured; (ii: 3.1.68:) made; (iii: 2.4.148:) taken.

tasking: challenge.

tempering: T: 4.3.126: softening.

termagant: quarrelsome.

tester: sixpence.

therefor: for that.

thick: speaking thick: speaking rapidly.

thrill (vb.): chill.

tickle-brain (slang): strong liquor.

tilt (vb.): duel.

tirrits: (perh.) terrors and fits.

Titan: 2.4.112–14: the sun.

tithe: tenth.

touch: **bide the touch**: submit to the test.

trace (vb.): follow.

tristful (adj.): sad.

Trojan (slang): roisterer.

tuck: **standing tuck**: 2.4.232: (a) erect rapier; (b) inflexible rapier.

underskinker: assistant tapster (barman).

unhappy: unfortunate.

utis: **old utis**: (perh.) noisy festivity.

vail . . . stomach: lose . . . courage.

vaward: vanguard.

velvet-guards: folk dressed with velvet trimmings.

venom of suggestion: dire instigation.

wag (n.): mischievous lad.

wanton: (i: 3.1.208:) profuse; (ii: T: 1.1.148:) effeminate.

ward (n.): parry.

wassail candle: large candle for festivals.

watch: (n. i: 2.4.463:) group of constables; (ii: T: 4.5.27:) period of duty.

wax: T: 1.2.147: (a) beeswax; (b) growth.

wen: T: 2.2.99: (i) wart; (ii) tumour, swelling.

wherefore: why.

whoreson: whore's son.

wildfire: blazing gunpowder.

wind: **break . . . wind** 2.2.12: (a) be breathless; (b) fart.

winking: with eyes shut.

withal: with.

womb: T: 4.3.22: belly.

wonted: customary.

woosel: ousel: blackbird.

wot thou?: will you?

wrung in the withers: hurt between the shoulder-blades.

yard: **tailor's yard**: tailor's one-yard measuring-stick.

younker: naïve lad.

Zounds: By Christ's wounds.